OFFICE
SYSTEMS
INTEGRATION

OFFICE SYSTEMS INTEGRATION

A DECISION-MAKER'S GUIDE TO SYSTEMS PLANNING AND IMPLEMENTATION

Barbara S. Fischer

Q

QUORUM BOOKS

NEW YORK
WESTPORT, CONNECTICUT
LONDON

Library of Congress Cataloging-in-Publication Data

Fischer, Barbara S.
  Office systems integration.

  Includes index.
  1. Office practice—Automation.   2. Business—
Data processing.   3. Business—Communication
systems.   I. Title.
  HF5547.5.F56   1987   651.8   87-2498
  ISBN 0-89930-109-6 (lib. bdg. : alk. paper)

British Library Cataloguing in Publication Data is available.

Library of Congress Catalog Card Number: 87-2498
ISBN: 0-89930-109-6

First published in 1987 by Quorum Books

Greenwood Press, Inc.
88 Post Road West, Westport, Connecticut 06881

Printed in the United States of America

The paper used in this book complies with the
Permanent Paper Standard issued by the National
Information Standards Organization (Z39.48-1984).

10 9 8 7 6 5 4 3 2 1

Copyright Acknowledgments

Exhibits are reprinted courtesy of Butler Cox Inc., excluding the
following:

Information for Exhibit 2.2 is provided courtesy of the Cores Corporation.

Exhibit 3.2 is reprinted courtesy of Marc A. Butlein, the Garther Group.

Exhibit 4.4 is reprinted courtesy of Lance R. Brilliantine.

This book is for Ray and Adam and Bill.

Contents

Exhibits

Acknowledgments

The author wishes to thank George Cox and Randy Goldfield of Butler Cox Inc. for their invaluable information and support. Also to Janet Allen, and Coleen Sullivan of Butler Cox. In addition, valuable information was obtained from Lance Brilliantine of Consulting Support Systems Inc., New York management consultants, and Betsey Schneider of Cores Corporation, a New York market research firm.

Introduction

by Randy Goldfield

During the past 25 years, virtually every large organization has built up extensive computer-based information systems. The pace of development, propelled by staggering technological advances, has never slowed, and it has brought continuous enhancements in computing capability. Despite this, most corporate systems currently in use are based on yesterday's ideas and yesterday's technology. The extensive base of installed systems, with its attendant equipment, software, procedures, and design philosophy creates a massive barrier to exploiting tomorrow's—and even much of today's—technology.

Whether they fully recognize it or not, many organizations face a major problem in escaping from yesterday's systems.

Information systems managers have grown used to living with constant change in their information systems, and there is a temptation to think that the subject of change is now well understood. After all, most of those concerned with developing or managing information systems have spent the majority, perhaps all, of their working lives in this environment.

As a consequence, change is taken for granted; it is perceived as a way of life. Regular advances in technological capability and ever-improving price performance are accepted as the norm. Information systems managers—accustomed to instability and uncertainty—expect tomorrow to be different from today.

The danger comes from failing to realize that change on this scale does not apply to other areas of business life in industry, commerce, or government. It applies to no other function of the business. Even in other high-technology areas, nothing changes with such pace or so relentlessly. The mind-boggling advances in computer technology make it difficult both to see the changes in perspective and to evaluate their future effects.

The progress has been stunning. In not much more than half a generation, technology will have advanced computers from being impossibly complex devices nearly the size of a major city to equivalent practical devices whose size is measured in inches. The implications of this progress are all the more dramatic when Clive Sinclair's projection of the associated cost is considered as well. Those of us expecting to be working at the turn of the next century can take comfort from the fact that, although the artificial brain may be no more than the size of our own, it will cost around $10 million. That should make us still a pretty good value to our employers.

But Sinclair also predicts that by 2020 the cost of the artificial brain will have dropped to $10,000. Moreover, because it will transmit internal messages electronically rather than physically, it will operate about six million times faster than the human brain. Now that is an integrated system!

The point I want to emphasize is that there have been tremendous advances in our information systems over the past 25 years, but all the capability made available still has not been exploited. Moreover, the capability is increasing year by year; there is far more technical innovation and vast new capability yet to come.

These developments will open tremendous new opportunities, but careful thought and organization are needed to exploit it. However, unlike most product manufacturing industries, the information systems industry is different. Computers do not rust, and we are not too concerned about their physical appearance. An organization like IBM therefore must keep innovating simply to protect its revenue. The computer suppliers are on a giant treadmill, which requires a lot of effort to keep it turning because each round of innovation improves the price/performance ratio of the product. The net result is that a supplier needs to ship substantially more units of basic computer power just to maintain its revenue.

Technical innovation, at a sustained high pace, is therefore an assured part of the future of information systems. However, the results of the changes do not flow directly, continuously, or smoothly into corporate information systems. There is a time lag; systems move forward in uneven surges; occasionally they go up blind alleys.

With the benefit of hindsight, it is tempting to rationalize the historical development of corporate systems, seeing it as evolutionary, a series of natural, progressive steps. But that is not the way it is in practice.

The last decade has seen some major developments that affect the office users of information technology, including

- the personal computer
- the expanded scope of "systems"
- advances in telecommunications and the telecommunications environment
- user pull replacing MIS push
- the extension of computing into everyday life and everyone's awareness
- recognition of the systems development problem and the demise of the hand-crafted system
- adjustment to a permanently tough economic environment and
- changing goals: from efficiency to effectiveness to competitive edge.

During this period, the scope of systems, and the application of advanced technology, has spread out from the traditional areas of data processing. The focus used to be entirely on information that consisted of codes and quantities and that could be tabulated either on paper or on a screen. Today, information systems are perceived in a wider context, encompassing voice, data, text, graphics, and video. In other words, technology now has the potential to handle all forms of information. Still lacking is the wide recognition of this fact and the skills to exploit it.

Originally, most computer systems were aimed at improving efficiency because they helped to carry out the administration of the business faster and cheaper. That is still an important use. More recently they have become concerned with improving effectiveness by providing better controls, new ways of doing things, and better decision support. We are now beginning to see systems deployed for a more important advantage—that of providing a competitive edge for the business.

This last point is extremely significant. There is a growing list of firms exploiting their systems in this manner; they include banks, insurance companies, retail firms, airlines, and others. There are striking examples of where systems have been used either to change the company's services or to lock in customers.

The implication of all these developments is that systems need to be viewed a different way. A new perspective is required. Throughout the early years of computer use, computers were perceived as a tool. This was reassuring, but inaccurate in retrospect. The computer is not like any other tool at all. The computer provides a different kind of capability altogether. Competitive edge comes not from acquiring computer equipment, but from using it in an imaginative way, coupled with the ability to apply change quickly.

What are the policies and skills required to exploit the future opportunities? What are the problems that will have to be faced?

The question of policies is an important one. Given the changing technology, the changing nature of systems, and the changing role of information systems departments, an organization needs to set a clear framework within which systems can be developed, operated, and exploited.

I believe there are five problems that those concerned with developing corporate systems will have to face. The first is to keep the initiative: to stay ahead of forces pushing and pulling corporate systems forward. I believe this is the greatest challenge facing systems departments and their managers today.

The second problem is to identify and establish the right role for the systems function, recognizing that most companies do not even know what yesterday's role should have been. For the systems function to be effective, its role has to be understood and accepted by the rest of the organization, not just by the department itself.

Third, reorganizing to take advantage of systems is an important and somewhat unpalatable point for most companies to accept. In the past, systems have been eased into firms with as little disruption as possible. However, it is becoming increasingly clear that to take full, often strategic, advantage of new systems, the company has to be redesigned to suit the systems. This is not an example of the tail wagging the dog. The fact is that organization structures are built, inevitably, around the old way of doing things. While earlier computer systems simply did the old things quicker or at less cost, they could be exploited properly within the existing structures. Today, technology provides the capability to do things differently, or even to do altogether new things. The business can be controlled differently; its administration can be grouped more effectively; communication can be faster and more complete; information can be shared more widely; and markets and customers can often be reached in entirely new ways. But to take advantage of this capability, the structure of the firm has to be viewed as part of the overall system design.

The fourth problem, or perhaps challenge, is to redirect the skills within the systems function. The information systems department is not there just to program and operate computers. Its role is to help the organization recognize and exploit the ways of handling information in its many different forms. Often this information is the lifeblood of the business.

The fifth challenge effectively sums up the basic problem: We have to break free from yesterday's systems and that means yesterday's thinking, skills, and concepts. I am not advocating a sudden or dramatic escape—many of today's systems will still be around for some time. Today's skills will still be needed while we develop the new environment. But if today's and tomorrow's technology is to be fully exploited, then we really do have to break free from yesterday's systems.

OFFICE SYSTEMS INTEGRATION

1

The Office of the 1980s

1.1 DEVELOPING INTEREST IN "THE ELECTRONIC OFFICE"

For most of the decade, office systems and, in particular, the concept of "the electronic office" have been pursued both by information technology suppliers and by pioneering user organizations. Some products have indeed changed the way people work, such as word processors, personal computers, spreadsheet software, and local area networks. The emphasis now is on "the electronic office," or the automated office or the office of the future—all different names for the concept of tying together all the information technology tools we have gotten used to over the last decade. In most organizations, however, the electronic office has been viewed with a combination of interest, concern, and caution.

When the electronic office emerged as a fashionable idea, several arguments were advanced for implementing the concept:

- The significant increases in productivity that had been achieved through automation on the factory floor had not been matched by improvements in office productivity. This was particularly important because a large, and growing, percentage of staff worked in offices.
- The need to improve office productivity had been heightened by a sharp increase in labor costs and by increasing competitive pressures.

- The quality and timeliness of management information was highly variable, leading to doubts about the quality of decision-making. Better office systems were seen as a means of overcoming these limitations.
- The concept of automating the office had been made feasible by the convergence of office, computer, and communications technologies, and by the ever-decreasing costs of electronic components.

In the early enthusiasm for the electronic office, however, the practical problems involved in creating such an environment were often overlooked. In particular, the immaturity of the available products and the benefits that could be achieved from an integrated system were not clearly understood.

This uncertainty made it difficult to plan the electronic office. In this confused environment, it was also difficult to guide the introduction of office systems in a farsighted, strategic way. Suppliers claimed to have produced "integrated" office systems, but these products usually provided only a limited range of applications, such as word processing, electronic mail, spreadsheets, and basic information storage and retrieval facilities. The vision of a highly flexible electronic office, with multifunction terminals providing access to both specific and general-purpose systems in a dynamic and responsive way, has proven to be elusive.

Managers are now demanding more sophisticated document processing to allow them to create, revise, distribute, store, and present quality documents across the firm and across the nation. New products offer more integrated and compatible tools that help produce high-quality documents and images faster and more efficiently. The task is no longer creation and editing but also producing, communicating, and storing.

Users now want to produce not only text documents, but documents with charts, spreadsheets, mathematical equations, and illustrations. And these documents must be created by teams integrating information from other resources, who then transfer data electronically into their document. In creating the document, the office worker today needs access to tools that help in correcting spelling and grammatical errors and to advanced editing features such as automatic footnoting, indexing, table of contents creation, and paragraph numbering. Specific professions, such as the legal profession, also need specialized tools such as red-lining or legal dictionaries, not to mention cost accounting systems.

Once created, the document must pass through an approval and re-editing cycle, or go directly to the ultimate recipient via electronic mail or another electronic transfer method. And hard copy is not dead yet: Publication quality output is an ever-increasing demand. Forrester Research predicted that the U.S. expenditure for publication services would reach $1 billion in 1986.[1] And the documents must be stored in an easily accessed manner that allows users to search for documents by key word, author, title, date, or file name. Finally, there has to be an array of file management tools to allow for re-filing or disposal.

If integrated and flexible office system products have been slow to materialize, a clear understanding of how to install and benefit from office systems has been even slower to appear. Early predictions of significant increases in managerial and professional productivity, of reductions in the numbers of middle managers, of increases in the span of management control, and of the elimination of the secretary have all proven to be premature, if not erroneous. Certainly the electronic office has a long way to go. Computer makers with models of so many shapes, sizes, and technologies have generated as much confusion in the office as order. The paperless office is not in sight. However, most people who are involved with office systems are reluctant to dismiss completely the electronic office concept. They have a very real feeling that integrated systems are possible, "somehow."

1.2 THE GROWING IMPORTANCE OF OFFICES

The office is becoming the focus of our so-called service economy. Following World War II, the United States became the world's first service economy—that is, the first nation in which more than half of the employed population was not involved in the production of food, clothing, houses, automobiles, or other tangible goods. The United States has since been joined in this trend by most of the developed countries.

As the service economy has grown, so has the proportion of white-collar workers. Most of these workers are office workers, and a continuing growth in the office population can confidently be predicted over the next ten years. The number of office workers today is large indeed. In the United States there are about 12 million secretarial and clerical workers and about 40 million managerial workers (Exhibit 1.1). Slightly over 50 percent of these work in companies that employ fewer than 100 workers in all, so many of the offices will be quite small.

The growing importance of the office to the economies of the Western world has made it a natural target for computer manufacturers eager to exploit this potentially huge and largely untapped market. The growth in the use of office systems has, however, been slower than many overly optimistic observers foresaw when the technology first began to take shape during the 1970s. Yet there are indications that this is now changing.

1.3 THE CURRENT STATUS OF "THE ELECTRONIC OFFICE"

One reason why office systems were slower to develop than some forecasters expected is the problem of achieving critical mass. Some important developments were, it was argued, feasible only when a high

Exhibit 1.1
Growth and Composition of the U.S. Office Work Force

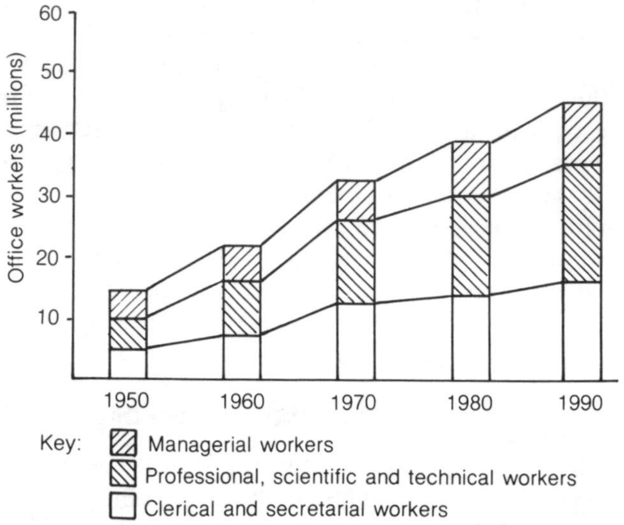

Key: ▨ Managerial workers
      ▧ Professional, scientific and technical workers
      ☐ Clerical and secretarial workers

proportion of users had access to a workstation. One crucial finding of recent research is that the penetration of workstations in the United States market is so deep that in certain markets the suppliers may soon have to consider the possibility of saturation. Butler Cox Inc. estimates that one workstation exists for every four workers, excluding computer terminals linked to mainframe computers for data processing or dumb terminals used to access data bases. The figures do include dedicated word-processing workstations and personal computers.

The growth in the use of office systems in both the United States and Europe over the last decade had been slower than expected until the arrival of the personal computer. That, in turn, created a mild form of back-office chaos with individuals buying whichever equipment seemed best to them, regardless of interface capacity. Systems integration has been slowed because of several main factors:

1. The difficulty in quantifying the benefits of using office systems to improve the productivity of managerial and professional staff. (Secretarial and typing productivity gains are very small in terms of the overall financial performance of large organizations.)

2. The inadequacy of many office system products for tackling the variety of tasks required by many, but not all, managers and professional staff. The high cost of many office systems has also been a deterrent to their widespread use. Managers have to balance the cost of the investment with the expected ben-

efits, even if on paper those benefits appear to bear the potential for total office integration.

3. A great deal of confusion about the future of office system products and, particularly, their compatibility both with existing and future computers and with other office systems. Vendors do not even agree on the definition of compatible: PCs claiming to be "IBM-compatible" are only 80 percent compatible in many cases. Speculation about the likely integration of data, text, voice, and image media has added to this confusion.

Nonetheless, office systems are increasingly becoming an integral part of the office of the 1980s. Microcomputers particularly are leading the way. Where once word processors were the dominant form of screen-based office system used by secretaries and typists, the trend is now to using multi-function personal computers with word-processing software packages. Studies by The Omni Group indicate that personal computers are, and will continue to be, the secretarial workstation of choice in small companies, and in the Fortune 1000 firms, personal computers have shown the strongest growth during 1984 and 1985, up to a mean of 26 percent of support staff who regularly use them (Exhibit 1.2). And a study made by the National Computing Centre confirms that most companies feel that the implementation of office systems has been successful.

Not only is the level of use of office systems increasing, but so is the variety of applications for which office systems are used (Exhibit 1.3). In the largest organizations that Omni researched, most of the office system applications used by managers and professionals are associated with data analysis, such as budgeting, statistical analysis, modeling, and other spreadsheet applications. The prime application area for clerical and secretarial staff is, by contrast, associated with text processing. The figures clearly indicate that most office workers are using an increasingly wide range of applications. In smaller organizations, there is still room for increasing the level of word processing use by clerical staff, but in many companies the emphasis, in terms of growth areas, is shifting from word processing and other individual applications such as spreadsheets to a wider range of applications and to managerial and professional tasks.

Omni estimated in 1983 that about one in ten managers and professionals would be using some form of screen-based terminal, mostly personal computers, by the end of 1984. Their 1985 survey indicated that 24 percent of professionals and managers in the Fortune 1000 companies use personal computers, and that mean expenditure per person for software in Fortune 1000 firms is over $1,000. Not surprisingly, most of the office system applications used by managers and professionals are associated with data analysis (budgeting, statistical manipulation, modeling, and other spreadsheet applications). And now these managers and

Exhibit 1.2

Secretarial Workstation Status and Trends: Fortune 1000 Companies

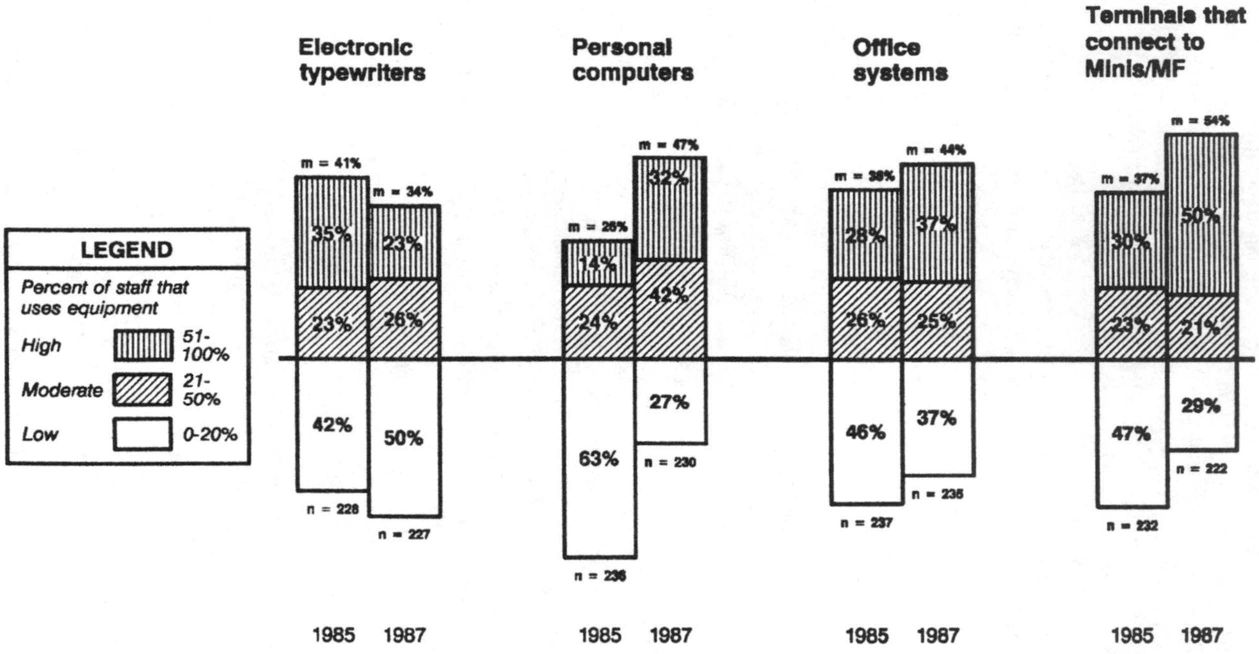

Electronic typewriters

1987: m = 34%, 23%, 26%, 50%, n = 227
1985: m = 41%, 35%, 23%, 42%, n = 228

Personal computers

1987: m = 47%, 32%, 42%, 27%, n = 230
1985: m = 26%, 14%, 24%, 63%, n = 236

Office systems

1987: m = 44%, 37%, 25%, 37%, n = 226
1985: m = 39%, 28%, 26%, 46%, n = 237

Terminals that connect to Minis/MF

1987: m = 54%, 50%, 31%, 29%, n = 222
1985: m = 37%, 30%, 23%, 47%, n = 232

LEGEND

Percent of staff that uses equipment

High — 51-100%
Moderate — 21-50%
Low — 0-20%

6

Exhibit 1.3
Use of Office System Applications by Clerical Staff in the United States (present and expected)

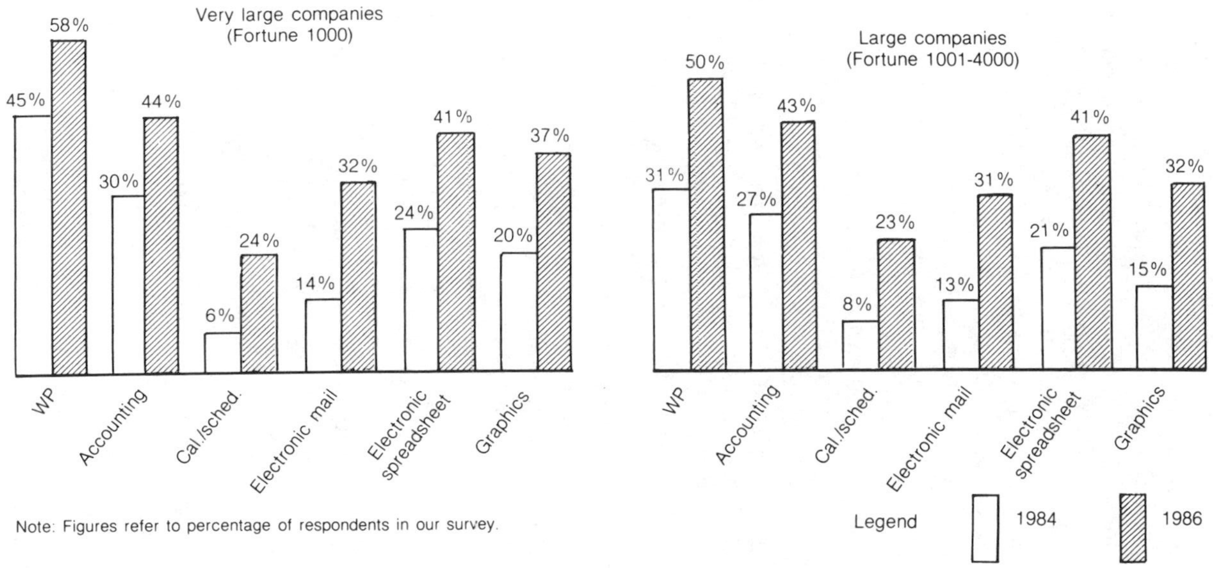

Large companies
(Fortune 1001-4000)

Application	1984	1986
WP	31%	50%
Accounting	27%	43%
Cal./sched.	8%	23%
Electronic mail	13%	31%
Electronic spreadsheet	21%	41%
Graphics	15%	32%

Very large companies
(Fortune 1000)

Application	1984	1986
WP	45%	58%
Accounting	30%	44%
Cal./sched.	6%	24%
Electronic mail	14%	32%
Electronic spreadsheet	24%	41%
Graphics	20%	37%

Legend

1984 ☐

1986 ▨

Note: Figures refer to percentage of respondents in our survey.

professionals want to be able to communicate with the company's data-processing systems, as well as use integrated office applications such as electronic mail and word processing (Exhibit 1.4).

As proposed by Butler Cox Inc., there are four phases in the evolution of office systems use (Exhibit 1.5). In Phase 1, office systems provide one or two isolated applications, frequently word processing or spreadsheets. Phase 2 sees more and more complex applications such as integrated packages, but these are still aimed at the individual user. In Phase 3, group applications appear, designed to support an office or department or to permit a horizontal stratum of managers to undertake a specialized job such as budgeting. Finally, Phase 4 sees a large base of terminal and workstation users provided with companywide office systems that depend on achievement of a critical mass of users—for example, an electronic mail interface for users who already have a workstation or terminal and access to data-processing systems.

Of course, not all organizations necessarily move forward through these phases in the exact order listed. And any one company could be in more than one phase at a time. Nevertheless, Butler Cox feels that over the next five years we will see a general move from Phase 1 to Phases 2, 3, and 4.

Given this widening base of installed personal computers and word processors, the installation of local area networks is a phenomenon within departments of personal computer users. Indeed, the Omni 1985 survey indicated that of the 76 percent of respondents who had plans for a personal computer communications project, almost one-third intended to connect personal computers to each other, particularly using a local area network (Exhibit 1.6). These are the result of strategies and plans formulated at a variety of corporate levels. The National Computing Centre study revealed that the correlation between the attempt to formally cost-justify investments and successful implementation is significant. Firms who undertook this business practice had a 33 percent better chance of success than those who did not.

1.4 POLICIES, PLANS, AND PEOPLE

As organizations move from individual office systems toward group applications, the questions of who is responsible for office systems becomes an increasingly pressing issue. A major concern is that, as individual systems and applications proliferate, they may leave the organization with a legacy of equipment and software that is not appropriate in terms of future requirements for either technical or functional reasons, or both. Two main issues may cause concern: the introduction of office system policies, and the role of the management information systems (MIS) or data-processing (DP) department.

Exhibit 1.4
Relative Importance of Office Computer Applications for Professionals and Managers (1984 and 1986)

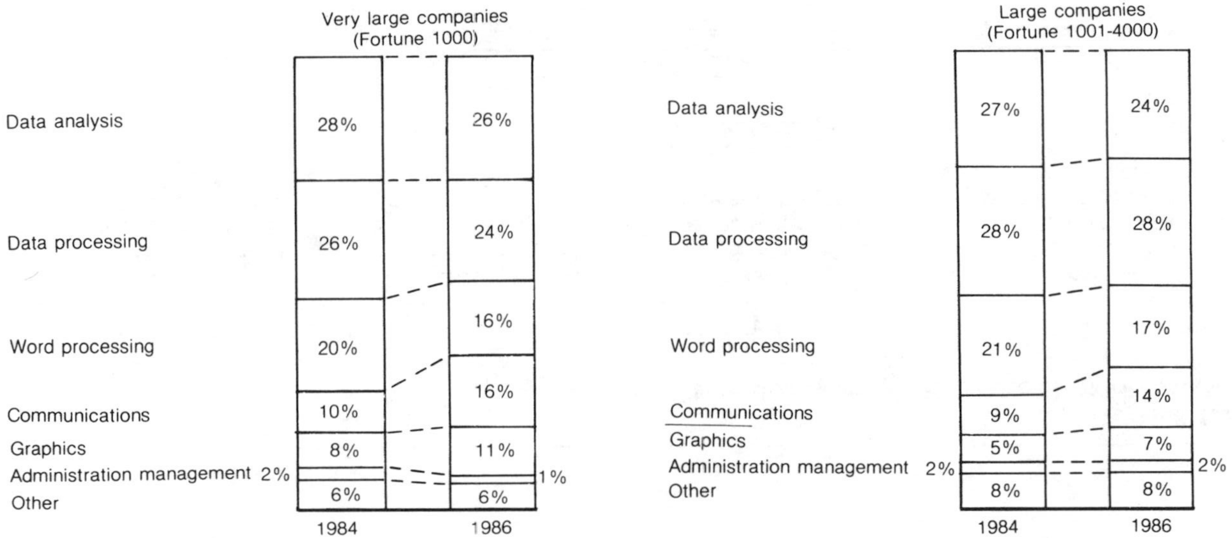

Large companies
(Fortune 1001-4000)

	1984	1986
Data analysis	27%	24%
Data processing	28%	28%
Word processing	21%	17%
Communications	9%	14%
Graphics	5%	7%
Administration management	2%	2%
Other	8%	8%

Very large companies
(Fortune 1000)

	1984	1986
Data analysis	28%	26%
Data processing	26%	24%
Word processing	20%	16%
Communications	10%	16%
Graphics	8%	11%
Administration management	2%	1%
Other	6%	6%

Note: Figures refer to percentage of respondents in our survey.

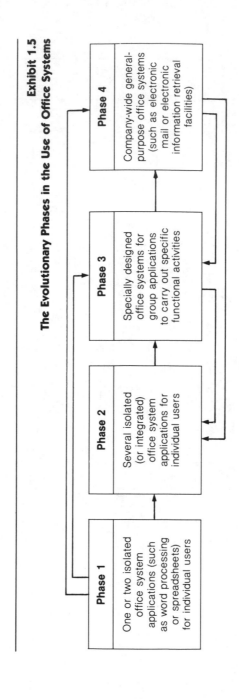

Exhibit 1.5

The Evolutionary Phases in the Use of Office Systems

Phase 1

One or two isolated office system applications (such as word processing or spreadsheets) for individual users

Phase 2

Several isolated (or integrated) office system applications for individual users

Phase 3

Specially designed office systems for group applications to carry out specific functional activities

Phase 4

Company-wide general-purpose office systems (such as electronic mail or electronic information retrieval facilities)

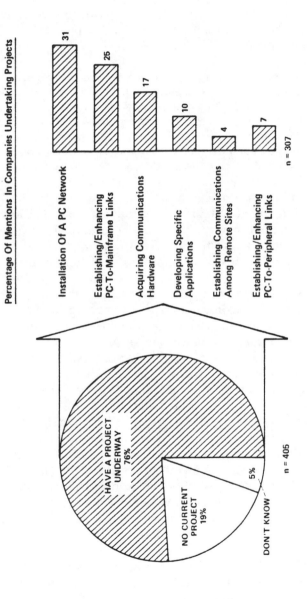

Exhibit 1.6
Most Important PC Communications Projects

Percentage Of Mentions In Companies Undertaking Projects

Installation Of A PC Network — 31

Establishing/Enhancing PC-To-Mainframe Links — 25

Acquiring Communications Hardware — 17

Developing Specific Applications — 10

Establishing Communications Among Remote Sites — 4

Establishing/Enhancing PC-To-Peripheral Links — 7

n = 307

HAVE A PROJECT UNDERWAY 76%

NO CURRENT PROJECT 19%

DON'T KNOW 5%

n = 405

11

The issues are complex, emotional, and linked. One MIS executive interviewed by Butler Cox Inc. for their research stated, "As usual, our end users have tried to go it alone, have succeeded in spending a fortune for little tangible benefit, and now look to us to pull their chestnuts out of the fire. It will take years to put it right. In the meanwhile, MIS will prove convenient scapegoats." Yet in the same company, a senior executive in marketing said,

For three years we made undeniable progress, led by people who understand the need because they work in marketing. Several experiments were launched and valuable experience gained. Then our MIS director became involved. He used his contacts with our mainframe computer supplier (who was missing out in office system sales) to convince the CEO we were on the wrong path. End of progress. The MIS department has imposed rules, procedures, approvals . . . Do it our way or not at all is the message. Bureaucracy triumphs again.

Having the technology in place does not automatically imply proper usage. Integrated systems must be managed just like any resources. The skills needed to manage information technology systems are often not part of the more technical background of MIS, word-processing, or telecommunications managers. End-user computing and training and evaluation skills are also vital. People skills are necessary to handle the ultimately diverse population of users of the integrated system. The manager must not only understand technology and office systems, he or she must also understand the user. The manager must be creative, sensitive to user resistance, aware of environmental conditions, and understanding of the system being managed.[2]

Large organizations are more likely to have a coherent office systems policy than smaller organizations. Corporations have formed policy committees, even formalized departments, to help create and implement policies for corporate office systems. Where once the data-processing and word-processing managers spoke different languages and reported to different corporate groups, now the management information manager has emerged as the dominant corporate planner and implementer for all forms of office systems, often including telecommunications. The Omni study found in 1985 that in Fortune 1000 companies, the MIS/DP manager was named as the most powerful office system decision-maker by 63 percent of the respondents (Exhibit 1.7). The office automation functions performed by the MIS manager include selection of approved vendors for personal computers and software, integrated office systems, even vendors for dedicated word-processing equipment. In addition, the MIS manager now often approves purchases of all this equipment and provides support and frequently maintenance (Exhibit 1.8).

Systems policy generally falls into two categories: guidelines and pilot

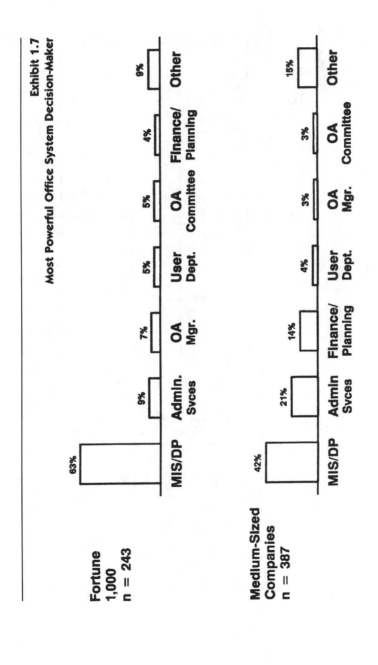

Exhibit 1.7
Most Powerful Office System Decision-Maker

**Fortune
1,000
n = 243**

63%	9%	7%	5%	5%	4%	9%
MIS/DP	Admin. Svces	OA Mgr.	User Dept.	OA Committee	Finance/ Planning	Other

**Medium-Sized
Companies
n = 387**

42%	21%	14%	4%	3%	3%	15%
MIS/DP	Admin Svces	Finance/ Planning	User Dept.	OA Mgr.	OA Committee	Other

Exhibit 1.8

Office Automation Functions Performed by MIS (Percentage of Companies)

	TOTAL	TIER I	TIER II(A)	TIER II(B)
Selection of approved vendors for PCs	90	91	88	91
Selection of approved vendors for IOS	83	88	84	68
Selection of approved PC software	78	83	73	76
Software support for OA equipment (including PCs)	78	79	77	79
Hardware maintenance	76	75	75	81
Approval of end-user PC purchase	74	76	74	72
Selection of approved vendors of dedicated WP equipment	72	81	64	66
End-user OA education and training	72	77	66	70
Approval of end-user purchase of IOS	69	73	71	55
Approval of end-user PC software purchase	64	66	68	53
Approval of end-user purchase of WP equipment	59	64	55	53

n = 293 n = 137 n = 103 n = 53

projects. Groups can be found in the majority of the Fortune 500 corporations to establish policies on approved vendors for all office equipment, particularly for the once chaotically purchased personal computer and guidelines for supporting the use of the system within the corporate setting. For instance, systems support may be provided only for the preferred products; access to mainstream systems may be limited to those products and systems that fall within the guidelines; and justification procedures may be enforced more rigorously if office systems products do not conform. Most large organizations that have an office systems policy have introduced guidelines to control the purchase of office systems.

The second type of policy is based on the active promotion of office systems through the creation of office system plans, pilot trials, and large-scale implementations. Many large corporations have established special support groups to be responsible for the implementation of office systems and the support of office system users. Increasingly, these support groups form part of the management information group and are not necessarily mutually exclusive of the approved-vendor committee.

This management control and guidance in the policy and practice of implementing office systems has had some effect on the organizational structure of corporations. Generally, the trend is to decentralize secretarial and typing staff, with more emphasis on local departmental productivity rather than on totally centralized document production.

Along with this trend has been a shift in the responsibility for office systems away from the traditional administrative departments that used to select typewriters and photocopiers, and toward computer departments who are more technically competent to deal with the newer systems-based equipment. As word processors were usually the first kind of office system to appear in many companies, the office manager or purchasing department often took charge of the equipment. This was especially so for standalone, as opposed to shared logic, word-processing equipment. However, the proliferation of personal computers and the increasingly complex and sophisticated requirements of users meant that the typical office or purchasing manager was usually ill-equipped to handle the new office tools. In particular, he or she often lacked both the technical experience and the organizational stature required.

At the same time, most MIS departments began to regard the new pieces of technology as being in "their" domain, and, as a consequence, the MIS department usually took over. Thus while the word-processing center remains a viable and integral part of the corporate support system, the chances are that today the word-processing manager reports into the management information group rather than into corporate support services.

The rationale frequently espoused for this takeover is that office systems are, at the end of the day, nothing but data processing for the office workers. Subscribing to this idea can, however, be dangerous as it ignores fundamental differences between an office system and a data-processing environment. In particular,

- Office systems are a tool for the office workers. Using an office system is not the purpose of his or her work; whereas, for data-processing staff, using the equipment is.
- Office workers often have considerable discretion over whether and how they use an office system.
- Usage of office systems is relatively low and irregular compared with data-processing staff operations.
- Office systems can directly affect the content of the work of office workers, which may lead to new job descriptions and even loss of status.
- Office systems users are more numerous and tend to be organizationally and often geographically dispersed.

For these reasons, the organizational and human aspects of office systems should not be underestimated by MIS and DP managers. Conceptually, office systems may be merely an extension of data-processing facilities into the office, but for organizational, functional, and human reasons, they are not.

The importance of user involvement in office systems planning and management (see Chapter 6) has to some extent counterbalanced the increased authority and spending power of the MIS department. Thus, centralized control of the MIS department is loosening in response to growing pressure from key user groups, and organizational changes are being introduced to improve and increase user input into MIS planning. The most successful office system installations are almost invariably those in which significant user involvement is present from the early stages.

1.5 USING OFFICE SYSTEMS

Recently, organizations have begun to use office systems as a key element in their business strategies. Financial institutions, such as banks and brokerages, are discovering strategic applications to improve customer sales and relationships. Examples include providing customers with personal computers on attractive terms (or free) in order to facilitate electronic ordering, thereby making it less attractive for the customers to change to another supplier, or preparing quotations by personal computer that facilitate the ordering process by creating electronic links with the sales force through portable terminals or voice-response systems.

In some industries, simple office system applications have had dis-

proportionate impact on business performance. For instance, a pharmaceuticals company that used word-processing systems over a period
of years to document its research and development results may be in a
position to produce very quickly the regulatory documents that must be
approved by the relevant governmental bodies before a new drug is
launched onto the market. By saving several months of document production time, an office system could speed the introduction of a new
drug ahead of the competition's product, thus generating additional
income to the firm.

A Big Eight accounting firm uses portable computers to link into their
corporate mainframe to benefit their clients, who gain not only in timeliness of information vital to their business but also share with other clients
the customized software developed by the Big Eight firm to improve their
competitive edge in the highly competitive public accounting field.

Yet managers continually encounter resistance to these valuable,
work-enhancing products and tools. Often an integrated system, even a
small departmental one, changes the work and authority relationships
users have grown accustomed to. And the informal lines of communication tend to change with the advent of integrated systems. Most people
in all areas of their lives find change difficult and stressful. Routines are
disrupted, equipment changed, and furniture altered. Many staff feel
that information technology in itself is change, rather than a useful tool.

People show their resistance in a variety of manners. Some reduce
their productivity in spite of the new workstation or personal computer.
Some accidentally-on-purpose withhold information. Some people get
sick. The office technocrats too often inflict equipment on end users with
little preparation and virtually no support. The tale of the self-taught
personal computer user is all too familiar. When planning for entire
integrated systems, it is far too easy to simply install the systems technically and then give the staff little time to adjust to the new hardware
and software.

Proper and sensitive planning can go a long way to alleviating some of
the user resistance naturally encountered when dealing with new technologies (see Chapter 6). User involvement, while it may seem annoying
to the technically sophisticated manager, is vital in understanding the
requirements of the job being automated. No one benefits from an idle
personal computer.

Support in the form of instruction, hands-on experience, quality documentation, and back-up support is vital to a successful implementation.
Implementations, to succeed, need to be sensitive to the peaks and
valleys of work flow, and managers should not expect too much of
employees suddenly confronted with new systems. Preparation, user
involvement, and close work with the end user during and after installation all play an integral role in office system success.

1.6 THE IMPACT AND BENEFIT OF OFFICE SYSTEMS

Studies to identify and quantify the theoretical benefits of general-purpose office systems have been carried out by a number of respected consultancies. These studies were based on an analysis of work patterns for different types of office staff in a limited sample of companies. Assumptions were then made about the likely increases in productivity that would result from the applications of office systems to each type of activity. From a knowledge of how office staff spend their time and an estimate of how office systems would increase the productivity of each activity, the likely productivity increases for different types of office staff was estimated.

As an example, suppose that a typical manager spends 12 percent of his or her time on the telephone. If this time can be reduced by 20 percent by using electronic mail or voice-messaging facilities, then 2.4 percent of the typical manager's time will be saved by introducing these systems. Generally, the results of studies of this kind predict theoretical productivity improvements of between 10 percent and 20 percent for managers and professional staff, and improvements of between 20 percent and 30 percent for clerical and secretarial staff.

The cumulative cost-benefits of general-purpose office systems tend to follow a cyclical pattern, with early net cost-benefits from applications such as word processing in centralized production groups and inter-site electronic mail being followed by an extended period during which substantial costs are incurred. In this period of substantial expenditure, the use of terminals would be built up, and infrastructure investments such as local area networks, electronic information storage and retrieval, and other needs would be added. Finally, as organizations adapt to the new electronic systems environment, significant organizational changes are made in order to realize the full theoretical productivity benefits of general-purpose office systems. To be significant, these reorganizations would primarily have to affect managers and professional staff (Exhibit 1.9).

The theory is fine, but in practice many organizations have failed to achieve real benefits from general-purpose office system implementation because they have held back from the challenge of managerial and professional reorganization. Although clerical and secretarial reorganization is commonplace, most firms have avoided the much more difficult and fundamental managerial and professional changes that would be needed if the theoretical benefits described are to be realized.

As a result, the cost-benefits experienced by too many organizations have been disappointing. The widespread use of personal computers, only recently being controlled, has contributed to a continuing increase

Exhibit 1.9
Cost-Benefits of General-Purpose Office Systems

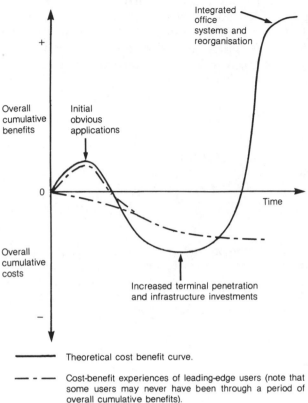

——————— Theoretical cost benefit curve.

— · — Cost-benefit experiences of leading-edge users (note that some users may never have been through a period of overall cumulative benefits).

in the overall cumulative costs of general-purpose office systems without the measurable savings expected.

Despite all of these complications and difficulties, the potential benefits to be gained by fundamentally reorganizing a corporation so that it employs the optimum number of managers and professionals in an efficient organizational structure using integrated systems can be significant indeed. Not only may integrated office systems result directly in a 10 percent or 15 percent reduction in the number of managers and professionals employed, but the reorganization planning exercise may well identify many existing inefficiencies. Experiences of fundamental reorganizations, usually necessitated by business crises, suggest that a stringent analysis of essential staff requirements can lead to a reduction of 20 percent or more in the number of middle managers, supervisors, and professional staff.

Thus a significant "reward" awaits many of the organizations with the courage to use modern office systems as the key to a carefully planned reorganization of managerial and professional staff. Indeed, organizations that adopt this approach may be able to avoid many of the traumas associated with forced reorganizations carried out in the short time scales dictated by a sudden business crisis.

NOTES

1. Jackie Kahle, "Managers Increase Office Productivity Through Document Processing," *Words* (April-May 1986): 41–42.
2. Bridget O'Connor, "Office Systems: New Managers for New Technologies," *Administrative Management* (May 1986): 13.

REFERENCES

Butler Cox Foundation Reports, "Office Systems: Applications and Organizational Impact," and "New Opportunities in Office Systems."
The Omni Group Ltd., Catalysis '84 and '85 Reports, including "Office Workstations: Status and Trends," "Software," "Marketing Opportunities for Office Technologies," "Office Communications."

2

Hardware and Software Components of the Integrated System

When considering the impact of office systems on the corporate structure, today's manager needs to know what technology is available, how it is used, how it could be used, what new technological developments are likely to occur, and what impact these developments might have. This chapter will outline the technological developments that have been the cause of major changes in computer-based products over recent years. Products and services that have sprung up around new developments in computer technology and communications will also be discussed. While other volumes in this series focus greater attention on telecommunications, record and micrographics, and other office automation products, this overview is meant to be a guide to understanding the components of the integrated office system of today and, we hope, of tomorrow.

2.1 PROCESSING TECHNOLOGY

The computer industry and microelectronics have advanced hand in hand since the mid–1960s. The achievements of each have led to greatly increased demand for the other. The cost reductions in computers were due in large part to the ever-improving techniques for producing integrated circuits. This device fabricated, separated, and interconnected the transistors and all the other circuit elements electrically instead of physically as had been done prior to 1959. This meant that an entire electronic circuit—not merely one element—could be produced at one time, including all the interconnections among the elements.

The application of integrated circuits to digital computers was ideal. Digital logic required very large numbers of active circuit elements compared with devices that employed analog amplification, such as radios. Computers could make use of large quantities of identical components, because the basic circuits were replicated many times in the architecture of a computer. Finally, the computer's use of transistors as binary switches, which had only two operation states (on/off), overcame the practical difficulty of producing integrated circuits with small tolerances and precise electrical characteristics. The production techniques were encouraged because of the growing market for integrated circuits created by the increasing number of less expensive computers being sold.

In 1971, the Intel Corporation produced the first microprocessor for use in a new, small desk calculator to be made by a Japanese company. Although it was possible to build the calculator from custom integrated circuits, designing several complex custom circuits would be expensive, and the resulting integrated circuits would serve only the one purpose for which they had been designed. And being complex digital devices, they could contain errors in their design that might not be detected until many integrated circuits had already been produced. Intel's novel idea—and it seems obvious today—was to make the circuits simpler but more general and to allow them to be programmed in an easy way. Such an approach would circumvent the custom-design errors and, at the same time, would permit the circuits to be employed elsewhere in a different role. This idea resulted in a tiny general-purpose programmable processor, the Intel 4004, which could become a special-purpose device through specific programming rather than through custom manufacturing. In 1972, Intel followed the 4004 with the 8008, an 8-bit (as opposed to a 4-bit) version of the microprocessor, which became widely used and was soon imitated by other semiconductor manufacturers.

Microprocessor designs now range beyond the 32-bit micros. However, most microprocessor chips contain the following function units on a single chip:

• A decoding and control unit to interpret stored program instructions
• An arithmetic/logic unit to perform basic operations
• General-purpose registers
• An accumulator

- Address buffers to supply the address of the next instruction
- Input/output buffers to hold data flowing to or from the microprocessor

Newer models of some microprocessors might contain both the clock circuits and the main memory as well as the central processor function on a single chip, thus comprising a complete programmable computer in a space that is less than a quarter of an inch square. And the microprocessor manufacturers have yet to reach the fundamental limits of size or speed imposed by the laws of physics.

The most significant effect of these dramatic improvements is a fall in the cost of main computer memory. Memory is now more compact, uses less electricity for each bit stored, and has become more reliable. These trends have also had a dramatic effect on the cost of computers. First, they make it economically feasible to computerize functions for which automation would not previously have been justified, such as word processing and optical character recognition. Second, falling costs and the reduced physical size of processors make it possible to incorporate processing power in consumer goods, office machines, system components (such as washing machines, calculators, microwaves, and photocopiers), and intelligent terminals and printers. The falling cost of processors also means that all systems will tend to become distributed, at least internally. Mainframe computers have been communities of specialized processors for some time, and the same trend has now reached as far as personal computers.

In addition to changes in basic technology, suppliers of microprocessors are increasingly incorporating software into chips. This firmware, as it is called, is a very efficient and fast way to run software in a computer. It is used for many frequently accessed software routines in computers and also in peripherals such as disks and printers. This approach speeds system response time.

2.2 STORAGE AND RETRIEVAL TECHNOLOGY

2.2.1 Semiconductor Memories

In its simplest form, the semiconductor read-write memory cell consists of one transistor and one capacitor. The value of the capacitor is extremely small but is adequate to store a small electrical charge indicating a binary one, while the absence of this charge represents a binary zero. The transistor is used as a switch to connect the storage capacitor to a data line when the cell is selected for reading or writing.

This type of storage cell, however, loses its stored information each time it is read, and also loses it by leakage of the capacitor's charge.

Leakage can take place in as little as a few milliseconds. This kind of memory cell, known as a *dynamic RAM* (random access memory), therefore requires its stored charge to be refreshed about once every two milliseconds, as well as after every read operation. Other designs, called *static RAMs*, do not require refreshing, but they incur the penalty of requiring additional transistors, which correspondingly take up more chip area and result in a higher cost per bit. Today, single-chip random access memories of 256K are commonplace. As they fall in price, they offer the manager an attractive means of upgrading the large numbers of personal computers now working with less memory in offices of all sizes.

Some applications require random access memories containing permanently stored information, such as control program instructions or constant data values. A practical example is a pocket calculator's control program, which is never changed. This type of storage is provided by the *read-only memory* (or ROM). In its simplest form, the storage capacitor of the RAM may be replaced either by an open circuit or by a direct connection to earth, representing a binary zero or one, respectively. The desired data pattern is fabricated on the chip itself and incurs a high initial production cost.

An alternative is to manufacture a blank memory which contains tiny fusible wires in all bit positions. By applying a suitable high voltage in an appropriate pattern, the undesirable links may be "blown," leaving an arrangement of intact wires representing the required data bit pattern. This type of memory is known as *programmable read-only memory* (or PROM). Obviously, the program is permanent because the fusible links cannot be reformed. It has the compensating advantage that its information is always retained when external power is removed, which is not generally true of semiconductor RAMs.

Other applications require a memory that can be altered, but for which read operations are much more frequent than write operations. A solution provided by microelectronics is the read-mostly memory, of which there are two principal variants. Most commonly, a store of charges on pairs of electrodes may be built up to form the desired pattern of information. This charge will remain reliably in place for years. To alter the pattern, however, the contents of the entire memory must be erased by exposing the chip to ultraviolet radiation, which allows the charges to lead away rapidly. After this erasure, a new pattern of information may be imposed. These devices are called *UV-erasable PROMs*.

The alternative device is called the *electrically alterable read-only memory* (EAROM), which can be altered selectively without the need to erase the entire array of data. This device employs special materials during its fabrication to build small circuits that may be selectively charged and discharged. Each cell will hold a charge until it is erased by a strong pulse of current, after which a new charge may be electrically imposed on the cell while leaving other cells uncharged.

2.2.2 Bubble Memory

Although magnetic bubble memory has little in common with semiconductor technology, it is an important component of microcomputer systems. The magnetic bubble memory is a serial device which cannot be randomly accessed. It exploits a rather obscure physical phenomenon: the local variations created in uniform magnetic materials, such as garnet. Both the materials and the physical principles employed are thus very different from those of transistor-based semiconductor integrated circuits. However, the device can be fabricated on chips of a sort, and it is, therefore, *microelectronic* in the broad sense of the word.

Data in a bubble memory may be thought of as circulating around and around a closed loop within the device. The data pass a single "window" at regular intervals, at which time they may be read or written. It is necessary to wait for the desired item to pass by the window before accessing it. The device is thus inherently serial in operation and so is very slow compared with semiconductor memory, having an access time of tens of milliseconds instead of a fraction of a microsecond. However, bubble memory has the great advantage in that it is nonvolatile.

The most attractive application of the bubble memory is to replace small disk and tape memories with a capacity of up to 10 to the seventh power bits or so. When produced in quantity, it has a price advantage over small disks of comparable capacity. It has similar performance characteristics, as well as being much smaller and more reliable.

2.2.3 Hard Disk

A hard magnetic disk is a round metal plate about the size of a 33 rpm record coated with a thin layer of ferromagnetic material used for recording electronic information. A number of disks are mounted on a common shaft to form a disk pack. Disk packs may either be permanently fixed inside an electronic read-write disk drive, or they may be removable. Rigid disks rotate at high speed, usually twelve to fifteen times faster than floppies, and allow for high-performance data storage. Basically, the read-write head is a fraction above the disk on an air cushion created by the spinning surface, so its lack of friction allows for speedier data retrieval.

The Winchester hard disk drive, which has one or more disks in a hermetically sealed and nonremovable unit, has become a viable alternative to the floppy disk in some devices (Exhibit 2.1). Since the disks are

Exhibit 2.1
The Winchester Hard Disk Drive

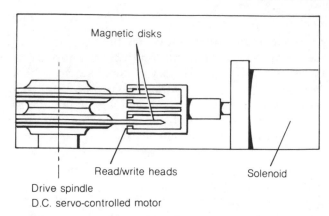

Magnetic disks

Read/write heads   Solenoid

Drive spindle
D.C. servo-controlled motor

not subjected to the stresses of insertion and removal, and since they are protected from environmental pollution, the read-write heads can be smaller, lighter, and closer to the recording surface, thus providing higher recording densities. These Winchester drives are the leading storage devices for the 10-to-60 megabyte (Mb) range. The time it takes to access information held on Winchester disks, however, tends to be longer than for more conventional, removable hard disk drives. Problems such as an interruption of power, dust between the head and the disk, or a sudden vibration can cause the head to crash onto the disk surface, destroying data stored there. This could be potentially disastrous for some small firms. In addition, security is difficult to maintain because anyone can access the data stored on a fixed Winchester disk unless software protected. Nevertheless, response times for Winchester disks are usually more than adequate for most business applications. Recently, removable Winchester drives, with capacities mirroring non-removable drives, have come on the market. While they have the convenience of removability, they are difficult to transport and susceptible to the same problems of the fixed disk drives. Duplication of data is a wise idea.

Another popular 10M or 20M removable hard disk is the Bernouli box made by Iomega. A stationary plate is placed parallel to a rotating disk, channeling air tightly between the two which prevents the usual air turbulence found in floppies. Flexible media spinning over a stationary plate can be drawn toward the plate and will stabilize and float on an air cushion. Again, the read-write head sits within a tiny distance of the recording surface that is "floating" on the air cushion. By using the flexible recording media, the Bernouli box is less susceptible to head crashes, as the magnetic media, suspended by air, drop away from the recording head. The media are in removable cartridges which are more easily stored and transported. This removability allows the box to be used by several people with greater security of data.

The cost of hard disk systems has fallen while the storage capacity has risen, a trend that can be expected to continue in the near future. Hard disks will remain a primary method of online storage, and prices will continue to fall.

2.2.4 Floppy Disk

Floppy disks are thin, flexible plastic disks used to store information in an electronic form, with technological principles similar to those for hard disks. They are coated on a sheet of mylar 3.5 mils thick. In flexible drives, the disk wavers when it spins. So to control the media at the read-write point, the disk is "pinched" between the read-write head and a pressure pad. Friction between this pad and the disk wears down the media and keeps the spin rate lower than optimal. The most common sizes are 8 inches, 5.25 inches, and 3.5 inches. Floppy disks are capable of storing up to 1.2MB on double density 5¼" disks.

Floppy disks are used for word processors and personal computers where their low weight and small size are important advantages. The volume of data that can be held on a single floppy has been increased substantially since the introduction of floppy disks in the late 1970s, but the improvement in access speed and transfer rate has been more modest. Double-sided, double density disks can store up to approximately 1.2M of data. Drive manufacturers continue to increase the amount of data storage on the 5.25-inch disk by putting more bits per inch of track and more tracks on the disk. Experts believe that storage of 3MB of data on this format is possible.

The continuing improvement in hard disk and memory technology is progressively displacing floppies for many business applications, although floppies give the user data security, transportability, and expandability, all at an affordable price.

The trend will be to smaller disks, the 3.5-inch sealed disks, which hold more data than the 5.25-inch floppy disks. A recent study by the Cores Corporation estimated that the growth rate of the smaller format will double from 1986 to 1988, while the older 8-inch disks will basically be discontinued. The 5.25-inch disk will remain popular because of the installed base of equipment using this size. With the advent of newer disk drives and software that can easily convert between 5.25-inch and 3.5-inch formats, the sturdier, greater capacity 3.5-inch format will come to dominate the floppy disk market (Exhibit 2.2).

Floppy disks are relatively inexpensive and flexible but require some

Exhibit 2.2
U.S. Floppy Disk Market 1986

3.5 reg (8.3%)   8 inch (9.1%)

3.5 HD (1.3%)

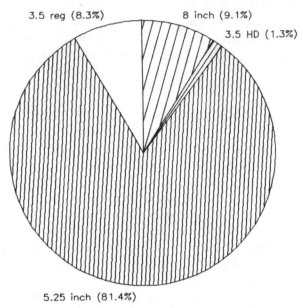

5.25 inch (81.4%)

Estimated 1988 Floppy Disk Market

8 inch (2.2%)   3.5 reg (5.8%)

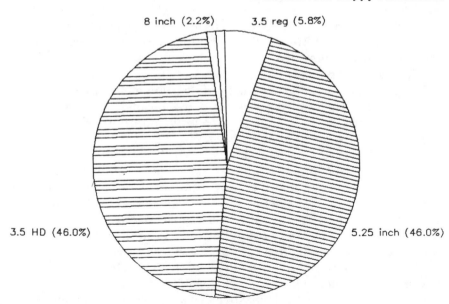

3.5 HD (46.0%)   5.25 inch (46.0%)

Exhibit 2.3
Optical Disk Storage

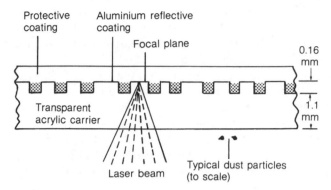

sensitivity in handling. They are exposed at three openings through which information is read and recorded, and any contact with these areas could cause data loss. Touching disks leaves a film of skin oil that confuses the magnetic head. Dust is a particular problem, causing the read-write head to jump over data. Given the investment that firms make in these disks, it is surprising how poorly they are treated. (One secretary stapled carbons to the disk and filed the set away!) Durability testing by manufacturers can be obviated with one spilled cup of coffee. Data compiled over days can be wiped out or distorted by devices with electric motors such as typewriters, printers, air conditioners, or even magnets. Never store the disks near these devices, and always, always make back-up copies.

2.2.5 Optical Disk

Current optical disks have high-capacity, low-cost, digital coding systems and the inability to amend recorded data, although data may be added. A single-sided 12-inch optical disk can store 1 gigabyte (GM) of information, equivalent to about 50,000 pages of typing. The time to access data, however, is about 135 milliseconds, compared with 35 milliseconds or better for hard disk drives. Optical disks, therefore, are sometimes unsuitable for applications that require frequent disk access.

The optical disk drive is so called because data are written to and read from the disk surface by means of an optical laser beam (Exhibit 2.3). This eliminates many of the mechanical and physical problems associated with magnetic disks. More than three dozen companies now have optical digital recording systems available or under development for use with computer-based systems.

The optical disk itself consists of a thin sheet of clear acrylic backed by a reflective surface. Information is recorded on the disk by burning small pits into the top of the disk. Once the pits have been burned into this top acrylic layer, they are covered with a thin coating of a reflective aluminum material, and the whole thing is then sealed in a protective coating. To read the information back from the disk, a low-powered laser is focused onto the pits. These pits, and the absence of pits, represent the information stored in binary form.

While many firms are working on erasable optical disks with capacities up to 400MB, current devices can be written on once and cannot be erased or written over, and have capacities up to 1 gigabyte per side. Thus they are useful for archival storage or such applications as service manuals where instructions could be combined with video demonstrations. Pre-recorded compact read-only disks (CD-ROM) are becoming more popular due to the low cost of CD players and the commercial success of musical CDs.

Although the capacity of a single optical disk is impressive compared to hard disks, a steadily increasing requirement for large-scale information storage has led to the development of multidisk optical systems. These systems either allow several disks to turn on a single spindle or adopt a "jukebox" approach. Disk selection time obviously increases the time needed to access information, so most multiple disk systems also employ magnetic disks as buffer storage to improve the speed of operation.

2.2.6 Multimedia Storage

The rising capacity and falling cost of auxiliary storage makes it increasingly attractive to store images and speech digitally. Continuous improvements in compression techniques are also making this approach much more attractive for routine business use.

This trend toward improved compression techniques has already made it possible to hold very large facsimile image files on-line for special purposes, and systems using the digital storage of speech have become commercially available in recent years.

Integration of data, image, and voice, however, poses more problems than just the cost of storage, notably in the management of the storage and in retrieval. An integrated filing system must be able to handle records of any length—from a few bytes to a hundred thousand bytes. It is difficult to maintain optimum efficiency under these circumstances, and most existing data-processing filing systems cannot accept such large records at all.

The integration of text and data storage is a relatively simple matter and has been achieved in many data-processing systems in order, for instance, to hold postal addresses. This integration is increasingly being supported by standard information management and retrieval systems.

The integration of text and facsimile images has already been achieved in the most sophisticated office systems, such as the Wang and IBM image systems. Text, data, and structured graphics have been integrated in computer-aided design systems.

2.2.7 Information Retrieval

In data-processing applications, records are normally broken down into a number of sections or "fields" of information, and some or all fields can be defined as keys for indexing, selection, and file searching. Text-based systems may have different characteristics in that at the time of assembling a file or text records, it is frequently not known what criteria will determine the need to access particular items of information.

Two main approaches to solving this problem have been adopted. In the first, key words are identified at the time of origination, and these are stored in an index, which also contains a reference to the location of the document. Searching is thus a matter of defining combinations of key words to retrieve all documents that contain them. Practical problems arise in that different people will specify key words in different ways. Compiling index entries as well as the original document requires considerable effort; therefore, key word retrieval systems are expensive to set up.

An extension to this approach is the so-called self-indexing system in which every word in a document is treated as a possible key word for retrieval. The index thus becomes as large as the original document. This approach, although demanding in storage capacity, does eliminate indexing effort. As the cost of electronic storage falls, this type of retrieval system will become increasingly cost-effective compared to the alternative.

Another promising approach is the use of a specialized hardware "search engine," which provides fast parallel searching of data bases and can also provide some intelligent "fuzzy matching" for searches in which the keys are not always known in advance and cannot therefore be precisely defined.

For the integration of facsimile images or voice with data and text, the current practice is to have separate files linked by software pointers. In some cases, these are arranged to give the user the impression of dealing with an integrated file store.

2.3 DATA CAPTURE TECHNOLOGY

2.3.1 Optical Character Recognition

Transference from paper documents can be a major cost regardless of the storage media. Until the advent of the optical character reader (OCR), it meant extensive copy typing. Services such as in-house publication departments, data publishing, and data-entry bureaus all faced the formidable task of keyboarding data. In the 1960s, expensive machines were recognizing a few characters per second, but with difficulty.

An optical character recognition device optically scans data and text, converting the information into electronic pulses. OCR devices are designed to read handwritten or printed characters as well as special characters from checks, orders, cash register rolls, stock tickets, and so on. Generally, once a document is in position within the reader, it is scanned with a beam of light. As the beam moves back and forth across the page, images on the document reflect different amounts of light which are then decoded into computer-readable forms. The recognized characters are sometimes displayed on a terminal, and the terminal operator may make any necessary corrections using a keyboard. In recent years, the flexibility and accuracy of OCR devices has improved considerably. The more sophisticated readers can recognize a variety of different fonts and can tolerate a limited degree of document misalignment. They can also be "taught" to recognize new fonts if that is required.

The simplest approach is template matching and is used in less versatile machines such as the Dest Corporation's line of products. OCR devices under $3,000 now work specifically with IBM personal computers and the clones. Most readers look at a very thin horizontal line which shifts down the page as the paper or reading head moves. An image of the line is focused on a long horizontal array of many light-sensing devices that electrically register the black-to-white transitions across the page width. As the line shifts, it examines the height of a line of type. Each tiny element in electronic form can then be compared with all the similarly constructed electronic templates of the alphabet which are stored in the OCR's memory. Each identified character emerges from the reader in computer code and can then be stored on disk for later retrieval and use. These OCR devices are 10 to 20 times faster than a typist, and much more accurate, but they are limited to typewriterlike characters of identical width. Some devices are preprogrammed to deal with proportionally spaced type.

More sophisticated devices have been developed by firms such as Kurzweil. These are much more computer-dependent and work more like a brain than the template devices. They look for generalized letter shapes rather than a particular typeface, and the software then determines the letter found. Legal and publishing houses particularly invest in these OCR devices because of their flexibility, even though the price is usually $35,000.

Handwriting, however, has proven particularly difficult to translate into a form suitable for electronic systems. Current handwriting input devices can only accept hand-printed characters rather than normal script, although research continues, and experimental models are being tried.

2.3.2 Voice Recognition

The potential for using the telephone as a device for gathering and retrieving information is enormous, but to unlock this potential requires that speech can be recognized and constructed automatically to provide recognizable responses. Most researchers in the field of voice recognition technology agree that systems must be at least 96 percent accurate before they can become usable. Despite the uniformly high levels of accuracy that suppliers set for themselves, the prices of the least expensive and the most expensive voice recognition devices available today differ by a factor of 50. This price difference stems largely from the sensitivity of the device to the environment in which it is designed to operate. For example, the price will be higher if a device has to operate successfully against background noise from typewriters, from printers, from doors banging, and so forth.

Another major problem that has yet to be solved is that of making voice recognition devices easy to use. Most systems available today work best if the operator speaks in a somewhat flat and monotonous manner. Although operators can be trained to speak in such a fashion, it hardly enhances the working environment. The chosen vocabulary for a voice recognition system also affects the overall system performance. If the vocabulary is too large, then the accuracy will decrease. System performance will also be impaired if the vocabulary contains similar-sounding words.

Voice recognition systems can be designed either to recognize isolated words where the speaker is required to pause for about one-tenth of a second after each word, or to recognize continuous speech. Devices of the latter type have to determine the word boundaries from a stream of continuous speech. Another distinction among voice recognition systems concerns their sensitivity to individual voices. The simpler systems have to be speaker trained, which means that each user has to go through a laborious process of teaching the system to recognize the way in which he or she pronounces all the words in the vocabulary. At present, the only systems that are truly speaker-independent are those that have a small vocabulary.

The problems associated with continuous speech recognition are complex enough, but the problem of trying to comprehend automatically the speech that has been captured introduces a still higher level of complexity. Speech comprehension poses problems in the fields of syntax, semantics, and linguistics that are still at the stage of theoretical research.

Voice recognition technology is used mainly for information entry applications where the information takes the form of commands, data, or queries. The commands are usually single words, such as *start*, *stop*, *left*, *right*, *scroll*, and *next*. Data are usually numeric but may also include information related to the applications, such as color or size. Queries may sometimes trigger off very complex recognition processes that require complex searches and analyses to determine the true significance of the question asked. To date, few information entry applications have successfully used voice recognition. Other applications, such as security checks, where the user's claimed identity is checked against a voice-print are as yet too expensive and too unreliable for general use.

2.3.3 Hand-held Terminals

A number of different types of hand-held keying devices with a small data viewing window are available. Generally, these devices have a display and store keyed information in digital form on a magnetic medium for transmission to a computer at a later time. These devices are frequently linked to bar code readers.

2.4 WORKSTATION TECHNOLOGY

2.4.1 Data Terminals

Data terminals are unintelligent (dumb) or semi-intelligent terminals that are connected to a computer which carries out all or most of the processing of the data. They may be either desktop or portable devices.

Data terminals have been evolving in two distinct directions. The prices of ASCII, character-mode, terminals have fallen despite some increase in facilities. The prices of screen-mode terminals with synchronous communications have, by contrast, tended to rise as extra features, such as color, have been added. Graphics terminals, with their intelligence and high-resolution screens and high data rates have remained a separate field until recently.

Some of the features now becoming available on data terminals are touch sensitive screens, voice output, multiple windows, and dynamically labeled function keys. The falling cost of electronics makes it increasingly attractive to include processing power in the terminal, and this has been used so far mainly for screen management and the communications protocol. The most recent stage has been to use the power of the on-board microcomputer to complement that of the host computer. As the price of personal computers has fallen, they have become a real alternative to traditional data terminals. Many corporations now purchase data terminals only for specific, limited function applications, preferring the flexibility of the more intelligent personal computer.

2.4.2 Text Terminals

Current text terminals include typewriters (yes, people still use them), telex machines, word processors, video terminals, and data terminals used to access word-processing systems on shared computers. Typewriters and telex machines are both evolving into intelligent typewriters with single line displays and a communications feature. The cheapest intelligent typewriters are currently about the same price as the more traditional electric typewriters. The new telex machines offer businesses a means of transmitting messages using well-established national and international networks. Modern telex machines have screens, editing features, and sometimes word-processing facilities. Telex services are coming under pressure from electronic mail services and, in some countries, from the new teletex services.

Word processors are currently coming under severe competitive pressure from business microcomputers with word-processing packages. Where once word processors used to have a better screen and keyboard than personal computers, the personal computers have improved and fallen in price to such an extent as to depress the market for dedicated word-processing equipment.

Word-processing suppliers must now learn to adapt or perish. They have sought to meet this competition by adding extra editing features, like dictionaries, but even more by adding data-processing capabilities. The distinction between personal computers and professional word processors is soon to disappear. Indeed the distinction between standalone and shared-logic word processors is undergoing a similar transformation. Shared-logic systems share the cost of the processor and storage among a number of users, often at the expense of slow and variable response. The falling cost of electronics has greatly reduced the economies of scale in processing power, though they remain significant for disk storage. Word processors can also file and retrieve documents faster with hard disks than with the floppies that are still offered with many standalone systems.

It is possible to obtain the advantages of both approaches by dedicating a processor to each user but sharing the storage among all users. A local area network may be used for this, in which case the sharing of printers and communications gateways can also be arranged in a modular fashion.

Most existing stand-alone word processors are tied to printers which can display only one typeface and can print in only one size depending on the wheel or thimble in use. Typefaces on the printer are generally changed by changing this wheel, which is convenient enough for whole documents but unacceptable for the inclusion of italicized words in an otherwise standard presentation. Also, word processors are usually unable to handle even simple graphics. As the quality of business system displays improves and as high-quality nonimpact printers become more commonplace, these problems will be alleviated.

2.4.3 Teletex and Videotex Terminals

European countries are ahead of the United States in the use of these two types of workstations. Teletex is an intercompany text communication service that is gradually becoming available through the different PTTs (national telephone companies) in Europe. It is intended to replace the intercompany communication traditionally carried by telex.

Videotex has been designed to use cheap adapted domestic televisions as terminals, but this does not preclude the use of other types of terminals. Adapting a television for use as a videotex terminal requires the addition of three main components: a keypad or keyboard, a device for interfacing with the telephone line, and a decoder. In its simplest form, the keypad is like a remote TV channel changer with a few function keys. The keyboard is more extensive (and expensive) with alphabetic and numeric keys and function keys. The telephone line interface consists of a modem, a line isolator, and usually an autodial and auto-identification unit. The decoder converts the incoming signals from the telephone line interface to text for display on the screen and also generates return signals from the keypad or keyboard. Although inferior to many computer graphics workstations, videotex systems are adequate for the majority of business graphics applications, and the costs of most terminals are substantially lower.

Particularly popular in France, trial programs have been established in the United States with little success to date.

2.4.4 Image Terminals

In a facsimile system, any form of image—text, graphics, signatures, and so forth—can be communicated. Facsimile transmission has been used for decades in specialized fields such as newspapers. To establish technological similarity between fax machines, the CCITT (International Telegraph and Telephone Consultative Committee) has developed and adopted standards that must be adhered to by equipment manufacturers, who were quick to realize that compatibility would be vital to the marketplace. The CCITT in 1981 established groups of standards relating to machine protocol and transmission techniques for particular types of equipment. Transmission speeds have accelerated in recent years so that Group 3 standards provide a resolution of about one page in one minute or less using digital techniques. Group 4 devices (a standard as yet unadopted) are high-speed digital and high-resolution machines which connect directly to digital circuits and may even have satellite compatibility. Group 4 machines may eventually have store-and-forward capabilities for electronic mail and other communications features for computer interface.

Services that permit incompatible machines to communicate with one another are provided by a number of vendors. They provide store-and-forward facilities, with buffer storage either electronically or on paper.

Certain office system suppliers, such as Wang and IBM, have introduced products that scan images, store the images on magnetic disk, and enable the images to be viewed on high-resolution visual displays. In this way, facsimile images have been integrated into office systems that traditionally have handled only text and data. The market penetration of these products has been modest because of the cost of the scanners and particularly the cost of the extra disk space required to store the images, but demand for "desk top publishing" will increase the use of scanners.

2.4.5 Personal Computers

Undoubtedly the major event in computing over the last decade has been the widespread use of the personal computer. In recent years, the personal computer has become cheaper for the given level of facilities, lighter and physically smaller, as well as more reliable, more powerful, with larger memories and better visual displays. Software, now a major industry, continually enhances the utility of these machines. When used as a standalone personal computer, the microcomputer offers unparalleled responsiveness for appropriate applications but lacks the storage, power, and sophisticated software found on minicomputers and mainframes. These hardware limitations can be ameliorated by interconnecting a number of personal computers in a local area network, allowing expensive resources, such as hard disks and printers, to be shared and potentially allowing personal computers to work cooperatively on a single task. The power obtained in this way will then enable a group of networked microcomputers to run more sophisticated software.

Additionally, an increasing number of organizations now regard the personal computer in its various forms as the terminal of choice for connection to the corporate mainframe computer, since it provides much more flexibility than the traditional dumb terminal. As the price/performance of the personal computer continues to fall, this trend will become even more pronounced.

Portable personal computers weighing over 15 pounds tend to be called transportable. Laptop models often weigh less than 10 pounds. Increasingly sophisticated, the limitations of size in terms of memory capacity are quickly being addressed by the extremely competitive suppliers.

2.4.6 Office Workstations

The office workstation often combines the personal computer, screen, keyboard, and telecommunications features in desktop format. Executive workstations, designed for data manipulation more than text entry, are increasingly popular and can combine graphics creation and display, even slide projection, in one device. Some experts are predicting the integrated voice/data terminal replacing the telephone, the PC, terminal, modem, electronic mail software, and calculators by the year 2000. Leading office system suppliers all have available workstations that combine data, text, image, and digitized voice features, as well as advanced telephone features, although the market has been slow to take off.

The combination of personal computer and telephone into the integrated voice/data terminal evolved as the cost of processing power dropped and advances in telecommunications technology and the divestiture of AT&T opened the way for vendors to market new products. In 1982, Northern Telecom introduced its Displayphone, which had only one outside line attached to a dumb terminal for $1,300. It was not a success. Attempts to market these executive workstations were also not a success, as CEOs had little use for electronic gadgets, had no desire to learn, and had secretaries readily available to perform all the functions of the executive workstation and more. Executives await a product that saves time and makes their firms more competitive, while convincing them that it is worth their while to press buttons.

Experts predict, nevertheless, that the more terminal-oriented managers and professionals will soon be turning to these integrated voice/data terminals. The time savings of having all of the devices integrated into one workstation can be substantial in spite of the relatively high cost. In addition, most executive workstations are fairly compact and readily upgradable. They can provide personal computer functions, access to a host computer, single-button access to data bases both internal and external, as well as the full range of telecommunications facilities. Because most have two outside phone lines, users can carry on verbal communication while working on the terminal or receiving electronic mail. (Access to the host computer is possible only if the phone system has that capacity, otherwise additional hardware and software are necessary.) Some executive workstations even offer teleconferencing, video conferencing, and modes that allow users to share files on the screen simultaneously. For example, the Centerpoint 1000 by Santa Barbara Laboratories allows for voice notations on typed dictation on the screen.

Integrated voice/data terminals can be used in a multi-user, multi-tasking environment. Used in place of personal computers such as the higher-priced IBM PC-AT, these workstations offer savings while offering convenience with built-in modems and ties to the phone system. Executive workstations can be set up as a local area network or to access data from the mainframe. Some have local area network capability built into the workstations.

Because of the relatively high cost of the integrated voice/data workstation, vendors are targeting specific markets that allow for more readily cost-justified acquisition. For example, with customization, some models can specialize in legal timekeeping and expense reporting as well as legal document annotation. Others interface to high-density electronic mail for access to stock quotations and data bases for financial traders. Customer service, credit and collections, real estate, and other markets that need instant access to data bases are finding these useful tools. And some experts feel that once the major personal computer vendors enter the marketplace, acceptance will grow.

2.5 PRINTER TECHNOLOGY

2.5.1 Current Printer Types

The traditional line printer, using revolving drum or chain, or reciprocating train technology, is still responsible for much of the output from large computer systems, but is far from letter quality.

The earliest electrical impact printer was the IBM Selectric golfball. Until 1982, when Diablo Systems invented the daisy wheel, the Selectric was the only letter-quality printer available. The daisy wheel was recognized as more reliable, less noisy, and faster than the golfball.

Matrix printers, like the golfball and the daisy wheel, are single-character printers. But unlike the others, the matrix printer forms each character from a dot matrix. Print speeds of over 600 characters per second are now attainable. Near-letter-quality matrix printers produce documents acceptable to most internal business communications at speeds above 70cps.

Nonimpact printing technologies include ink-jet, thermal, dielectric, ion deposition, magnetic, and electrostatic printing. All nonimpact printers have the limitation that they are unable to produce multiple simultaneous copies, and thermal printers also require special and costlier paper. However, they frequently allow for mixing of fonts as well as graphics printing, are much faster than daisy-wheel printers, offer two-sided printing, are quiet, and offer convenience copying as an application on some models.

The electrostatic process is much like a traditional office copier except that the light source used to expose the document is a laser, a CRT, or an array of light emitting diodes (LEDs) rather than reflected light. The electrostatic process is popular as it offers high character resolution, generates copies on plain paper, and can mix fonts with graphics. It performs at speeds ranging from 10 to 100 pages per minute, although costs are relatively high and service is required to replenish supplies and maintain performance.

Thermal transfer printing is a Japanese process wherein an electrode transmits heat to the thermal ribbon, causing the ink to melt, and it is then transferred to plain paper by contact. It is fairly low cost and reliable. Dielectric printing uses specially coated paper which is charge-sensitive. It passes over an array of electrodes which are activated by incoming signals and apply voltage to the surface of the paper. These too operate at speeds ranging from 10 to 200 pages per minute and reproduce text and graphics. They are quite reliable and are frequently used with digital facsimile machines.

Ink-jet printers squirt ink selectively from a multi-nozzle print-head at over 200 characters per second. They are quiet and produce high-quality print, although image quality can degenerate at high speeds, and the jet nozzles frequently become clogged with ink. They do not perform well with 100 percent rag paper, as the ink tends to blot. Ion deposition printing uses an array of electrodes activated by incoming digital signals, much like office copiers. The toner image is transferred and fused to plain paper. This technology shows promise as an alternative to laser printing.

2.5.2 Laser Printers

The laser printer is a development of photocopier technology. In practice, a laser is only used as a light source in some models, but the term *laser printer* is the usual one. The original laser printers were intended for use as high-volume line printers with a capacity of 100 pages per minute and, as such, were usually found in mainframe computer sites in companies with large output requirements. The laser printer, suitably equipped, has the unique advantage that it can be used for graphics and can approximate typeset material. Earlier models cost hundreds of thousands of dollars—for example, the Xerox 9700 was introduced in 1977 at a cost of $390,000 and produced 115 pages per minute. Even so, it was sold to Fortune 500 data centers, insurance firms, banks, and other large companies. By 1983, Xerox was selling over a thousand Xerox 2700 laser printers, which produced 12 pages per minute at a cost of about $20,000. The Hewlett-Packard Laser-Jet produced 40 pages per minute, and with its removable toner, service was less of a problem. Recent developments have included a low-cost, 150 cps laser printer under $500 suitable for office use. Although laser print speed is quite high (27 pages a minute) the volume is limited by the printer mechanism to about 30,000 sheets per month in a typical model.

These printers will undoubtedly be enhanced over the next few years, and likely improvements will be higher-volume throughput and increased dot densities, with print speeds of 10 to 20 pages per minute. Dataquest predicts that more than 30 percent of the total computer printer market will be laser printers by 1988.

Managers selecting laser printers need to evaluate the monthly and daily output requirements in addition to print quality desired. Low-end machines are priced below $2,000 and produce quality text documents at 6 to 12 pages per minute. The duty cycle, or recommended monthly volume, should match your needs. In addition, supplies such as replaceable drums and toner should be considered. Users needing quality graphics will need a full bit map memory, available in laser printers in the $4,000 price range. However, word processing may or may not be available depending on the emulation mode of the printer. For in-house publishing or mainframe support, you need a machine capable of producing hundreds of thousands of copies at between 12 and 60 pages per minute. Should you wish to network the laser, you must have a serial—not parallel—interface.

In their simplest form, quiet laser printers will undoubtedly displace the standard printer to some extent, although higher costs and the need for more frequent servicing will be a limiting factor. Particularly promising to end users will be developments to enhance the laser printer's graphics capabilities, to include forms, illustrations, and other graphics. And the widespread use of color displays will probably lead to developments in color laser printing. Industry experts also predict a drop in price.

2.5.3 Typesetting and Composition

The complex activities usually undertaken by graphics-trained professionals are, to some extent, now being done in-house with desktop publishing equipment. For the more standard layouts, it is already quite feasible to have a predetermined batch stream set up to be run on a data-processing system and output on a laser printer with the requisite font library. This removes the burden of inserting complex coding into the text by the office worker but does not solve the problem of unique documents or of graphics, forms, and illustrations.

To some extent, certain products today go part way to solving this problem, through the display of the full-page layout. By using a scanner to load the required illustrations, these can be combined with the text. Some training in graphics and layout will be essential, nevertheless, for the best results to be achieved.

Undoubtedly, packaged systems will emerge over the next five years that will allow straightforward word-processor output to be output on a laser printer, with some graphics inserted. The font library will be limited, and pagination, indexing, and layout will follow some simple rules. For more complex work, the present practice of interfacing with typesetting and printing services will continue, and the complexities of interfacing word processors and typesetters, page layout, illustrations, and so on should not be underestimated.

2.6 SOFTWARE TECHNOLOGY

The United States holds 70 percent of the world software market, and that is expected to rise in the next few years. The growth rate may slow but is still expected to grow at 22 percent per year, according to the Computing Services Association. Single-user products should represent nearly a quarter of the market, and users can expect to see the vendors of hardware getting into this lucrative business.

2.6.1 Applications Software

Word processing is the most developed of office systems applications. Essentially, it provides a facility to input text, to rearrange, delete, and add to the text, and to print it in the desired format. While word processors are installed in almost all businesses today, their penetration of the potential secretarial and typing market is still quite modest. Even so, they are the dominant form of screen-based office systems used by office workers, and their use is expected to continue to grow somewhat. Developments in word processing are at present focused on the incorporation of spreadsheet output and graphics into textual material, the production of final documentation to print-quality levels, and the transmission of completed output via electronic mail to the intended recipients.

Spreadsheet packages allow the use of a screen-based workstation to work directly with a matrix of figures. Original spreadsheet packages have more recently become integrated packages allowing data to be passed from data bases to the spreadsheet and on to software that will produce graphics, for example. The spreadsheet package is probably the main application for the personal computers on the desks of professionals and managers. A recent survey (Omni Catalysis '84) indicated that over 85 percent of managers and professionals in the largest U.S. corporations use personal computers for data analysis. Future developments in spreadsheet packages can be expected in two directions: further integration with other, more complex analysis and graphics facilities, and the application of spreadsheet techniques to micro-mainframe links. (See Exhibit 1.4.)

Data management refers to records processing systems, a type of internal information storage and retrieval facility offered by most office systems suppliers. The software provides a simple set of screens that allows the user to define records, enter data, and retrieve data based on different selection criteria. Future trends for these packages are toward making them easier for the unsophisticated user. This ease of use can be achieved by three features: (1) relational data bases, where the data are viewed as a collection of simple tables, making it very easy for the user to define data relationships and to retrieve data from the data base; (2) high-level query languages, allowing the user to carry out complex retrievals using nonprogramming procedures; (3) and data dictionaries, essentially documenting the organization of the data base.

Electronic mail systems (see Chapter 3 for more detail) have the potential to become convenient communications media for many types of messages, including messages that might otherwise be carried by the public mail or telex systems. Internal systems for basic document transfer can run on most mainframes, and minicomputers enable users at terminals and personal computers to send and receive messages. An alternative to computer-based messaging is facsimile, especially for requirements involving graphics, forms, and other complex documents. Standard electronic mail and facsimile are unsuitable for revisable document transfer where both the sender and the receiver want to be able to revise the document. Users of incompatible equipment find this a particular problem.

Electronic mail services are generally based on in-house computer systems or on value-added network services (VANS) operated by private services. The VANS provide support for document interchange between relatively incompatible systems. Most in-house electronic mail systems are being constructed on a base of existing terminal and microcomputer users, which leads to ready acceptance of the application both because of the familiarity of the users with their equipment and because of the relatively low marginal costs involved.

In addition to the most popular management applications, there is a range of other generic applications available on office systems. Typical examples include diary management for appointments and meetings, action checklists, a desk calculator, access to telex, and booking meeting rooms. By knowing your application before you buy, you should be able to find the program most closely suited to your particular needs.

2.6.2 User Interface Software

Workstation interfaces must provide for functionality, ease of learning, ease of use, and documentation and explanations of what is going on, what should be done about it, records of what has been done so far so that the user can retrace the steps, and so on. To meet these goals, several features are popular today.

Windows are an extension of the operating system that allows simultaneous viewing of different outputs and processes. They make it easier for the user to keep track of where he or she is and what is going on in the system.

Integrated applications provide the convenience of similar command structures and data formats and reduce the requirement for disk loading and unloading. Redundant data entry can be reduced or eliminated with integrated software through sharing data files or a data base. Recent introductions allow the user to work with an original document in all modes (word processing, spreadsheet, data management, graphics) without transferring the document between the modes.

Icons—visual representations of features or functions—greatly speed up certain types of interaction, especially when used with a mouse or pointer. This represents a move away from the traditional user interface that is simply a higher level of programming using command codes but that avoids the tediousness of menu-based interfaces. Further advances are likely in image handling, particularly for illustrations, video, and photographs, over the next few years.

A natural language system allows a person to interact with a computer by using the same language he or she uses to interact with another person. Such a system needs to cope with the richness of the language as people use it, along with its ambiguities, and overcome the typical ungrammatical language that most people use in everyday communication. The most obvious advantage of a natural language system is that people do not have to be trained in a programming language before they can program a computer. In addition, it is often much easier to express a request in natural language than in a formal programming language.

As most large companies purchase a number of different application tools and packages from different vendors, a benefit of natural language query systems would be their ability to perform the function of organizer and integrator of these different systems. Thus users would only have the natural language interface to issue a single request to have data selected, analyzed, and displayed, irrespective of the command structures and intricacies of the software systems that may be used. The obvious advantage of a natural language interface is that users need less training and may not quickly forget the nuances as they might in a more structured, traditional type of interface. Furthermore, the natural language inquiry is often shorter and more comprehensible. Slow progress is being made in this intriguing software area, and the greatest improvement is likely in dialogue design for specialized systems.

Integration of the telephone and the user workstation enhances the user interface by using the capabilities of the workstation to improve the telephone facilities (see Chapter 4). Integrated voice and data worksta-tions usually provide telephone directory facilities and the ability to use short codes to dial the desired number, as well as various facilities nor-mally associated with smart or feature telephones. A side benefit is the smaller "footprint" or desk space taken up by the combined telephone and workstation.

2.6.3 Systems Software

For a while, the introduction of competing microcomputer operating systems caused confusion to corporate purchasers. Having an operating system that could vary from machine to machine within the office with considerable variation in the range of software available and the com-plexities of user interface encouraged most major corporations to develop corporate standards and approved-vendor purchasing policies. Today, the overwhelming majority of personal computers in the office operate on MS-DOS (PC-DOS), with proprietary systems or the earlier CP/M operating system by far in the minority. This standardization allows for portability of programs and software, uniformity of use across the var-ious systems within a firm, and the ability of the operating system to make the hardware and network capabilities readily available to more users.

The UNIX operating system, developed by Bell Laboratories, is based on a program that runs input/output devices, supervises switching and scheduling, and allocates memory among other functions. Around this is a shell program that allows the user to address the operating system directly to read and write files, to direct input and output, and to build new programs for various jobs. UNIX utility programs layered on top of this shell include programs for editing text, setting mathematical equa-tions, using interactive graphics and electronic mail, and updating data bases, among the many programs available. UNIX is a general-purpose, interactive, time-sharing operating system on which it is relatively easy to create files. Although UNIX is not as popular as the MS-DOS operating system, many personal computers and other workstations now have UNIX compatibility. Users interested in a general-purpose system that has good file structure, although it is somewhat cumbersome to learn, may find this operating system worth investigating.

Network architectures provide a structured environment for computer system interconnection, as explained in the next chapter. They incorpo-rate rules for interconnect and specify how the software must perform to carry this out. Network architectures are becoming an increasingly im-portant issue for the office systems user with the emergence of requirements for links to the data-processing systems and for links among office systems.

REFERENCES

Black, George. "IDC Forecasts Growth for Euro Market." *Computer Weekly* (Nov. 7, 1985).

Butler Cox & Partners Inc. "New Opportunities in Office Systems: A Practical Guide" (Oct. 1985).

Butler Cox Foundation. "Information Technology: Its Impact on Marketing and Selling" (Dec. 1984).

Charlish, Geoffrey. "Text Transfer: How Lower Costs Can Be Put on the Line." *Financial Times* (April 22, 1986).

Datapro Research Corp. "Minicomputer Winchester Disk Drives" (Oct. 1985).

Datapro Research Corp. "Nonimpact Printers" (May 1986).

Datapro Research Corp. "Perspective: UNIX: An Operating System that Means Business" (Nov. 1983).

Ellis, Raff. "Integrated Voice/Data Workstations." *Words* (Feb.-March 1986): 31–34.

Fischer, Barbara S. "Word Processing into Print." *Words* (Oct.-Nov. 1983).

Fischer, Barbara S., Lance Brilliantine, and Chris Rankin. "W.P. Hardware: Vendors Must 'Adapt or Perish'," *Office Administration & Automation* (June 1985).

McVay, Scott D. "Bernouli Box—The Best of Both Worlds?" *Words* (Dec.-Jan. 1986): 16–18.

Meth, Clifford. "Write with Light!" *Administrative Management* (March 1986): 39–43.

The Omni Group Ltd. Catalysis '85, "Work Group Computing."

Reed, Charles Jr. "How Magnetic Media Works." *Words* (April-May 1985): 31–33.

Siragusa, Gail. "The Executive Workstation—Fancy Phone or Productivity Tool?" *Administrative Management* (Feb. 1986): 31–35.

3

Distributed Information

The technology of office systems is advancing rapidly, along with other computer-based technologies, and does not appear to be slowing down for the foreseeable future. These advances lead to new ways of doing things, as well as to continuing improvements in the cost-performance of existing systems.

There is a well-established trend for the underlying cost of computer hardware to fall by about a factor of 10 every eight years. The familiar microcomputer is as powerful as many substantial minicomputers of only 15 to 20 years ago, and this at a cost of perhaps one-tenth or less. Long before 1995, desktop personal computers are expected to be as compact and portable as a good-sized hardcover book and to cost only a few hundred dollars.

The idea of technological convergence first became prominent in the late 1970s. In its original form, it identified three then noncooperating industries—telephones, computers, and office machines—and suggested that these were coming to depend on a single technology and, therefore, would become for all practical purposes three branches of a single industry. We are less concerned today with whom the supplier is and more with the practicalities of making the office system, the computer, and the telecommunications work together in a meaningful way.

Exhibit 3.1
Importance of Data-Base Access Applications, 1985–1987

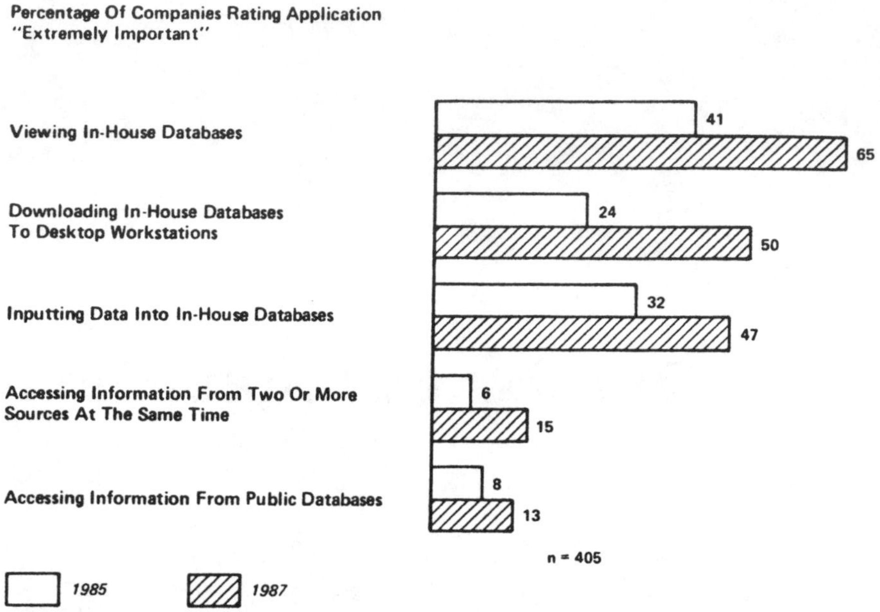

Percentage Of Companies Rating Application
"Extremely Important"

Viewing In-House Databases — 41 / 65

Downloading In-House Databases To Desktop Workstations — 24 / 50

Inputting Data Into In-House Databases — 32 / 47

Accessing Information From Two Or More Sources At The Same Time — 6 / 15

Accessing Information From Public Databases — 8 / 13

n = 405

☐ 1985   ▨ 1987

Ultimately, it is the organization's information systems that are converging, not the suppliers' systems.

The personal computer proliferation has spurred the demand for information directly from the corporate mainframe. Fortune 1000 decision-makers have begun to place greater emphasis on integrated applications, with communication to the corporate data-processing system as the most highly desired workstation feature for managers and professionals (Exhibit 3.1).

Many vendors of integrated office systems market their products to enable users to access data-processing applications found on minicomputers or mainframes.

3.1 MAINFRAMES, MINICOMPUTERS, AND SUPERMICROCOMPUTERS

In the 1950 movie *Desk Set*, Spencer Tracy battles librarian Katharine Hepburn over the room-size installation of a computer which, according to Spencer, would answer all questions faster and more cost-effectively than Kate and her staff. Needless to say, he was wrong, yet in the end Kate agrees that the computer could indeed be useful. Today, no large office is without its mainframe computer, and in three-quarters of all firms, that computer is an IBM model. The primary use of these impressive machines is for corporate accounting and data storage, and as the source of all corporate data, the computer is an attractive source of information for users far removed from the host environment.

Where once this computer was off limits to the end user, there is increasing demand for access. According to a Gartner Group report,[1] a typical mainframe in 1988 will be idle about 39 percent of the time. The balance of the time will be spent on environmental software, batch processing, on-line transactions, and development. And end-user time, which was nil in 1979, will be about 4 percent. Gartner attributes much of this idleness to a sharp increase in the amount of mainframe time spent in on-line transactions, which by 1988 should account for 20 percent of the mainframe time (Exhibit 3.2).

This increased demand for systems integration has great appeal to the vendors of mainframe products. IBM's strategy of announcing products months before release frequently stymies competitors while IBM customers wait for the promised products. Many companies prefer to buy some technology and equipment from outside the IBM fold, for reasons not only of price but also of quality and state-of-the-art technology. Some are even predicting that the term *mainframe* will go the way of *dedicated word processor*, although, given the ever-increasing power and speed of the mainframe, that is doubtful.

While the hardware vendors are trying to decide what to do, the mainframe software vendors are having a difficult time too after the early flush days. Many customers are now purchasing sophisticated interre-

---

Exhibit 3.2
How Mainframe Machine Time Is Used in a 168-hour Week

	1979	1983	1988
	%	%	%
Environmental software (operating systems etc.)	18	20	22
Batch processing	42	25	7
Online transactions	10	17	20
End-users	—	1	4
Development	15	13	8
Idle time	15	25	39

Source: Gartner Group.

lated products that combine data-base management and applications programs that can cost upwards of $1 million. This implies a slower purchase process, more decision levels, and a greater demand on the software houses. As with the mercurial PC market for hardware and software, these mainframe software vendors are experiencing a difficult time, and many experts expect the numbers of firms to dwindle in the future as the hardware manufacturers start to take over the mainframe software marketplace. This could be good news for the end user, but it is too soon to say.

When mainframes are tied into the integrated system, companies may have to buy 50 percent more computer power just to operate it, according to an Arthur Andersen and Co. study. Yet, on average, only about 20 percent of any information needs to be accessible beyond its original department.

Although increasingly pressured by the ever-more-powerful personal computer, a minicomputer offers several advantages over the smaller machine, particularly in expandability. Main memory of 1 gigabyte or more (as compared to a PC's 30M memory), plus the ability to handle large numbers of printers, terminals, or disk drives, keep the minicomputer market alive. Easily upgraded, minicomputers allow purchasers to reuse their existing equipment thus saving the costs and headaches of conversion or junking. Upgrading memory or disk space is much easier with a mini than with a PC, and most vendors offer larger systems that are readily installed.

In addition, minicomputers are becoming office information centers through the use of local area networks (see Chapter 4). Thus the capabilities of one mini can be enhanced to connect with several other devices within the office allowing for shared resources and information, as well as peripherals such as high-speed printers. Using a minicomputer as a departmental "host" is becoming increasingly popular, and vendors are frequently offering personal computers in addition to terminals for the system. The vendor competition in the area of superminicomputers is intense, and new products to enhance existing lines such as the DEC VAX or the All-in-1 office automation line are carving out markets often at the expense of industry giant IBM. In addition, many vendors of these superminis have gained tremendous market share by focusing on such specific industries as the scientific or engineering fields. This heated competition is a boon to the end consumer for ultimately prices will fall while quality increases.

The vast availability of minicomputer software further enhances the value of this system in the office. Although vendors offer a large array of packages on their own, the trend in recent years has been to third-party software developed for particular applications, such as payroll systems, accounts receivable, medical billing, and so forth. Some vendors of minicomputers have indeed specialized in particular markets, such as scientific calculation, to the extent that personal computers are rarely found. The minicomputer market is dominated by Digital Equipment Corporation and IBM.

The line between minicomputers and supermicrocomputers is a fine one. High-powered PCs can support several users, multi-tasking, and multi-user operating systems. These supermicros use faster microprocessors and offer memory management, which allows the CPU to access data stored. Virtual memory, included on some chips, keeps track of where the programs are stored and automatically transfers the programs from the disk to the main memory. Many of these supermicros use operating systems such as UNIX, to allow for multiple users to work at the same time by assigning part of the computer's RAM to each user.

Once supermicrocomputers are installed, the basic concept of "personal" computing becomes irrelevant, as more than one user accesses the information stored. Shared systems are usually less expensive to set up initially, but if demand grows for memory capacity, the user could be better off with a minicomputer, which initially might appear to be overkill.

Many supermicros support protocols that allow for communications to host computers or other networks. It is important when planning for the systems integration that the specific protocols supported by the vendor be appropriate to the mainframe the user seeks to access.

3.2 NETWORK ARCHITECTURES

One way to allow access to mainframe data is to connect directly to the central computer system. Network architectures provide a structured environment for computer system interconnection. They incorporate rules for interconnection and specify how the software must perform to carry this out. Network architectures are becoming an increasingly important issue for the office systems user with the emergence of requirements for links to the data-processing systems, and for links between office systems. There are two main network architecture approaches to interconnection: integrated communications and multistandard communications.

Integrated communications use an integrated set of standards, while multistandard communications require equipment to be interconnected where necessary by using either commercially available products or custom-built solutions. In corporations where there are strong pressures for business units to work together, data-processing systems are largely being built around the integrated communication approach. The role of an overall architecture is to set up corporate policies and rules which can lead to the ultimate network desired.[2]

The implication of this direction is that the choice of office system technology will be constrained because of the need to be part of the integrated communications, or be able to connect with the integrated communications. While some corporations have developed their own high-level communications software, most use a proprietary network architecture supplied by vendors such as IBM (SNA) or Digital Equipment (DECnet), among others. These architectures represent an established framework which offers a solution to the interconnection problem provided that equipment and software purchased have this architecture in mind.

3.3 DISTRIBUTED DATA PROCESSING

The idea of distributed data processing is based on communications between devices using some logic. It can refer to micros as well as terminals, minis, and other products communicating among themselves or the host mainframe. The amount of interaction can vary from once a week to intensive daily transactions. Alternatives for users include alternative protocols, media, network architectures, topologies, and communications software.[3] Unfortunately, standards are sorely lacking, and there is little immediate hope that standards will emerge.

There have been nearly as many definitions of distributed data processing as there are data-processing managers. A survey performed in 1981 by *Fortune* magazine limited the definition to, "Minicomputers or intelligent terminals operating in locations remote from the central MIS department operating interactively, maintaining local data bases and generating reports locally."[4] The ultimate aim was to put the function of power access in the hands of the end users.

That aim is still of major importance to users. The Omni survey showed a strong increase in the need to view in-house data bases by surveyed management personnel (see Exhibit 3.1). But getting there can still be bewildering to the end user, and each network alternative has its good and bad points, as previously noted. The International Organization for Standardization (ISO) is completing high-level protocol specifications in conjunction with its ongoing open systems interconnection (OSI) project. There is still a ways to go, however, and while vendors state that they will support the ISO protocols, they may not favor them over their own existing sets of protocols.

3.4 DOCUMENT TRANSFER

Document transfer provides the capability of formatting documents at the receiving end and allows for revision by the recipient. In this way, several workers can edit the same document or make a series of alterations or amendments to the document.

The document transfer software, therefore, must be able to separate out the format control parameters, to cope with revisions, and to format the output of the final document according to the control parameters. There are five basic approaches to transferring documents between systems:

1. Disk converters, which take disks and translate not only the media formats but also the document coding so that the document is fully revisable on the target system. Many independent businesses exist today to convert disks from one system to another.
2. Communicating black boxes, which are essentially on-line disk converters.
3. Dedicated document interchange systems, perhaps based on personal computers.
4. Value-added network services externally offering electronic mail with revisable form document transfer.
5. IBM's host-based document interchange system, DISOSS, which several suppliers have now adopted as a de facto standard.

IBM's DISOSS (Distributed Office Support System) provides a basis for revisable document interchange between systems using IBM's Systems Network Architecture (SNA). It handles filing, retrieval, and internal mailing of text and image documents in a mainframe environment. IBM supports DISOSS on its now-defunct Displaywriter, the PC line, the 5520 Administrative System, the 8100 Distributed Office System, and the Systems /36 and /38.

A key aspect of IBM's system is the Document Content Architecture (DCA). The revisable-form DCA provides for the interchange of editable documents, and it permits formatting parameters, text-processing control, and revisable text to form part of the data stream.

At a different level, the Document Interchange Architecture (DIA) specifies how devices are to interchange intentions and data. It specifies the rules and a data structure that establish the discipline for predictable information exchange between devices, meaning that documents can be transferred from one device or system to another without change in form or coherence.

Another IBM mainframe system, PROFS (Professional Office System) does not use DCA and DIA and is essentially an electronic mail system that runs under IBM's VM operating system and supports users of IBM's 3270 terminals—the standard computer terminal used on IBM systems. It has the advantage of providing electronic mail to the installed computer user base and also provides time management through a calendar facility, a meeting scheduler, and a reminder facility. It does not offer the full range of document transfer capabilities provided by DISOSS. At the moment, there exists no DISOSS/PROFS software bridge, so no fully integrated system is possible.

Despite all the attention they have received, DISOSS and PROFS are not widely installed products, according to Omni's 1985 survey (Exhibit 3.3). And even in those firms who have purchased them, these systems are not widely used right now, although most plan to connect the majority of their PC users within the next year or two using the system they purchased. Nevertheless, the strength of the IBM name will continue to pressure vendors to offer compatible products and services while IBM users wait for the firm to make things easier all around.

3.5 MICRO-TO-MAINFRAME LINKS

When personal computers were first becoming popular, it was not uncommon to find managers requesting computer printouts from the central data-processing department and then re-keyboarding the appropriate data from the printout onto their personal computer. The personal computer explosion has quickly made this an obsolete, although still used, system. With over 35,000 mainframes and 2.5 million personal computers in the top 2,500 U.S. corporations,[5] there is a great potential market for a variety of linkage methods.

There are a number of ways to link personal computers to internal or external mainframes. Terminal emulation software, integrated software links, mainframe software, protocol converters, hardware enhancements, and specialized microcomputers all serve to allow varying degrees of linkage with internal or external host mainframes. It should be remembered, however, that this ability to link up is a developing field, and many products still need testing and improving before mainframe guardians will allow them to access the corporate data bases. Security remains an important issue, and as the products evolve, they will become easier to use, less costly, and provide deeper levels of security. At the moment, however, the field is still muddled, and managers wishing to link their PCs to the corporate mainframe should tread cautiously and seek MIS assistance.

The most common method of accessing mainframe data for use on a personal computer involves terminal emulation, using either asynchronous communications or terminal emulation boards that convert the personal computer to a 3270-type terminal. The terminal emulation card lets the PC emulate both a control unit and a display station from the 327x family, communicating with the mainframe over dial-up or leased lines through internal or external modems. The 327x terminals use either bisynch (BSC) or SDLC (synchronous data link control). Because

Exhibit 3.3
Market Status of PROFS Today

Percentage Of Companies

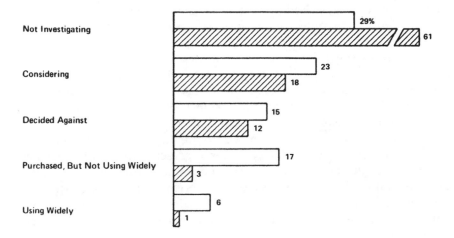

Market Status of DISOSS Today

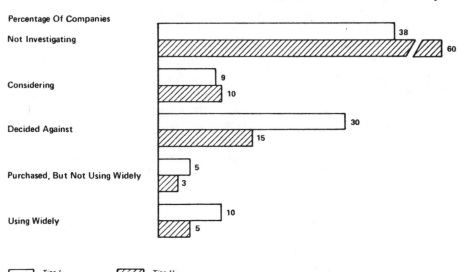

BSC has been around for over 20 years, most older mainframes have the BSC interface standard. However data go only in one direction at a time, which is known as "half-duplex" protocol. The sending computer must wait for an acknowledgment to each data block it sends before it can send more.

The SDLC protocol is newer, and because it is full duplex, the transmitter can send a certain number of data blocks before getting an acknowledgment. And because both BSC and SDLC are synchronous protocols, only modems with synchronous, not asynchronous, communications can be used.

Access from the PC to external data bases such as The Source or CompuServe is accomplished using asynchronous communication software programs, such as Crosstalk or PCTalk. These software packages are relatively inexpensive (under $1,000 including a modem) and allow users to receive, send, store, and print data in a basic manner.

File transfer between the PC and corporate mainframe using terminal emulation is usually accomplished either by screen dumps or file transfer using the mainframe's operating system program editor. While a screen dump is simple, the user has to save to disk one screen at a time including extraneous mainframe data. While the results for textual material are fairly uncomplicated, numeric data retrieval can be somewhat cumbersome.[6]

Many micro-mainframe links that go beyond simple terminal emulation are designed to give a personal computer user access to the mainframe data bases via the vendor's mainframe computer software. Integrated software link products, such as McCormack and Dodge's Interactive Personal Computer Link, have the ability to move files into such familiar application software packages as Lotus 1–2–3. For example, downloading data from the general ledger package into a standard spreadsheet package could be used for modeling and comparisons when preparing the annual budget.

Several mainframe software package suppliers already provide a downloading feature to personal computer spreadsheet or database software packages on personal computers. This presupposes that the requisite combination of software is in use on the mainframe computer. There are software products which provide powerful computer programs based on mainframe database manager software, an example being Cullinet's Information Database. Another approach that has been adopted in several firms is to install a database package with downloading capability in parallel with existing systems. The corporate data can then be transferred in the mainframe environment from the main corporate files to the parallel "shadow" files.

Some software tries to make the mainframe in essence a peripheral with virtual disk software installed on both ends of the link. These programs require terminal emulation software and a pre-established hardware link—either a 3278 emulation board or a protocol converter that uses the asynchronous RS–232C interface. Some programming is also necessary to set up the mainframe end. The PC user receives the data in what appears to be DOS mode but is actually a translation from the mainframe system. For example, if the user enters DIR D:, the PC software must translate the command that both the DOS of the PC and the file management utility of the mainframe can understand. The command is transmitted to the mainframe, where the mainframe virtual disk software executes the mainframe equipment of DIR D:, which is then re-translated into DOS and sent back to the PC. Depending on the number of users, it can take several seconds to obtain a virtual disk directory, and a file transfer from the mainframe to the personal computer can take upwards of half an hour. However, these software packages, such as Free-Link from On-Line Software, or Tempus-Link from Micro Tempus, are convenient pathways for micro-mainframe data exchange and more importantly, between PCs. Users gain access to a single virtual disk library, which enables them to swap disks from one library to another offering virtually endless possibilities for data exchange.

Some vendors today are marketing both the personal computer and mainframe software to allow for "invisible" connection to the mainframe for data retrieval. This is a complex problem to solve and is not an efficient use of the mainframe, aside from being expensive.

There are several thorny problems in allowing personal computer connectivity to mainframes. Aside from cost involved in acquiring special-purpose database software with downloading capabilities, this type of solution inevitably takes time to implement and will still require extensive effort to identify the data to be made available and to anticipate what data the user is likely to ask for. Finally, the problem of data security and integrity is an increasingly important issue.

Ultimately, it will be possible for a personal computer user to access any data base he or she is allowed without considering where the data is, what kind of computer, and so forth. An all-encompassing data base such as this must also include access to data provided by outside services as well.

When linking personal computers to a mainframe, the technology of the mainframe, telecommunications, and the software must be carefully chosen. The mainframe system should allow for relational database access so that personal computer users can most easily understand what they are asking for and retrieving. In addition, the speed of that access cannot be so slow as to discourage the use for which it was set up in the first place. Casual data retrieval may be fine over a slower modem link, while daily access would be better going over dedicated lines on a 3270-emulation terminal (see Chapter 4). Ideally, work should be done primarily on the more cost-effective personal computer rather than tying up the mainframe.

Connecting personal computers to minicomputers is slightly easier than connecting them to mainframes. Several vendors have developed hardware, software, and other peripheral devices that link relatively easily. For example, the IBM System/36 computer combines the IBM processor and a directly attached personal computer. This allows up to four users to share data and programs from both the System/36 and the PC computer groups. The PC connects to the processor by cable and also runs a program that allows its processor and part of its main memory to be used for System/36 diagnostics, maintenance, communications, and other functions. Switching between the PC and the System/36 is done by a "hot key" sequence: When the end user has keyed into the PC mode, the System/36 screens are not displayed although the applications remain active and continue processing. Then, when the user keys into the System/36 mode, the PC job is temporarily suspended.

Several firms are offering hardware and software to access IBM systems from the personal computer line, and some mainframe vendors such as Prime also have products enabling linkage to the personal computer from their superminicomputers.[7]

3.6 ELECTRONIC FUNDS TRANSFER AND CASH MANAGEMENT SERVICES

Changes in the banking world are not merely of academic interest to businesses outside the banking sector. They have very real effects on other companies, whether in the form of new types of banking services, new tariffs or tariff structures for services, or changes in the banking relationship.

New services are being developed and launched, many in electronic form, and among the most important of these are electronic funds transfer and cash management services.

Companies will not be able to ignore some of these services. The decisions about whether to implement them and, if they are to be implemented, whether to lead or to follow others can have a considerable impact on business. Electronic funds transfer at the point of sale (EFTPOS) for retailers is one example. As it is introduced, some existing services may be withdrawn or the basis of charging for them changed, causing difficulties for those who see no benefit in joining the new services.

For convenience, electronic funds transfer services may be categorized under three headings:

1. Bank networks. Networks have been and are being developed for handling money transfers and a range of other messages between banks, both within and between countries (see Chapter 4).

2. Payment services. In addition to interbank payments, there are services to handle large volumes of payment instructions input by banks and corporate customers, and to clear high-value payments rapidly. A somewhat different type of service, electronic funds transfer at the point of sale (EFTPOS), allows payments made by private individuals to retailers to be handled electronically. Services exist for specialized payment instruments such as bills of exchange. Finally, customers can withdraw cash from cash dispensers (CDs) or automated teller machines (ATMs).

3. Cash management services. Whether the customer who is offered such services is the largest multinational corporation or an individual managing the family budget, the basic principles are the same. The services provide electronic means of managing cash more efficiently—in particular, by providing up-to-date information about balances in one or more accounts, statements of recent activity in an account, and funds transfer services to enable money to be moved between accounts. Payment facilities may be provided. Some services also offer analysis or modeling capabilities to support decision-making.

These services can be described in terms of the kinds of facilities they make available to different types of customers: banks, other financial institutions, retailers, large and small businesses, and private individuals.

Services for banks are of two main types, payment clearing services and bank networks. Traditionally, the clearinghouse for banks was a central exchange where banks brought checks paid in to claim cash from the originators' banks. Instead of each transaction being settled separately, net settlements between banks could be calculated. The modern clearinghouse receives payment instructions, debit or credit, from banks or other large organizations, distributes them to their recipient banks, and arranges net settlements between banks. In some countries, clearing is now done electronically.

Bank networks provide a secure medium for a wide variety of messages for exchanges between large numbers of banks. Instructions for funds transfer constitute a significant element of the traffic, but the networks also carry account statements, foreign exchange deal confirmations, and query and administrative messages. BankWire and Fed-Wire in the United States are major examples of such networks, and the Society for World Interbank Financial Telecommunications (SWIFT) provides an international bank network.

SWIFT operates four computer centers around the world that are connected by leased telecommunications circuits. Banks access the centers from standalone terminals or through interface devices located on their own premises via regional processing centers which service a country or their regional division (Exhibit 3.4). SWIFT offers a variety of messaging and transaction services, including customer funds transfers, bank transfers, credit/debit advices, statements, foreign exchange and money market confirmations, collections, documentary credits, interbank securities trading, balance reporting, and payment systems. It defines standard message formats for each type of service and transaction.

The main benefits of SWIFT that banks can pass on to their customers are fast and accurate transmission of messages and execution of transactions, and low cost compared with other telecommunications media. To international treasury managers, who need to quickly ascertain their balances around the world and reliably adjust them by funds transfers, these facilities could be particularly useful. The bankers of the world frequently complain about the cost of SWIFT, but many of them have used it as a valuable tool for securing profitable business.

A new SWIFT2 program is scheduled for 1986 introduction. It will be a distributed system capable of faster message delivery, greater traffic-carrying capacity, and modular expansion. It will have additional and improved capabilities, for example, better message retrieval services, and is designed to enable transmission costs to be reduced. The growth of message traffic is expected to arise through further automation of back-office procedures by existing members, rather than through a significant increase in the number of member banks.

The electronic funds transfer requirements of other financial sector companies are broadly similar to those of the banks, insofar as they are concerned with collecting and distributing payment instructions. Credit card companies have a particular interest in the electronic capture and distribution of transaction data, and computer bureaus now provide services which sort onto magnetic tapes such data that have been input by retailers on-line. Similar services are also provided as an additional facility by automated clearinghouses.

Retailers and their customers are the potential users of EFTPOS. These services enable the customer to pay the retailer for goods or services using a plastic card which is inserted in or passed through a terminal at the point of sale. Data identifying the customer and specifying the value of the payments are forwarded electronically to the customer's and retailer's banks for settlement.

Larger corporations are increasingly using the automated clearinghouse services for bulk payments and are also prime users of cash management services. Small businesses have only recently been taken seriously as a potentially profitable market for on-line financial services. There is mounting evidence that they are more enthusiastic customers for simple cash management ("home banking") services than are private

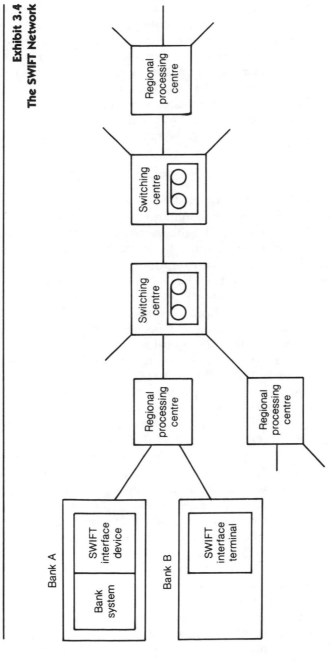

Exhibit 3.4
The SWIFT Network

individuals. Some small businesses, particularly lawyers, accountants, and brokers, regularly make high-value payments.

Individuals may benefit from four main types of electronic funds transfer services: cash dispensers and automated teller machines, front-office services, and home banking. In addition, they may be users of EFTPOS services. Payments they make on a regular basis may be processed by retailers using automated clearinghouse facilities to operate standing order and direct debit procedures. Increasingly, banks are cooperating by sharing ATM networks or allowing their networks to interwork with those of other banks. They see convenience to the customer as more important in marketing terms than a proprietary network.

3.7 SUPPORT FROM MIS/DATA PROCESSING

As discussed earlier, most of the burden of establishing integrated systems is now falling on the shoulders of the corporate MIS group. They are responsible for establishing the overall corporate integration goals, strategies, and implementations. Basically, they have to deal with a number of differing levels of computing needs. Individual, group or department, local offices, branches, or corporate headquarters all have differing needs for computing power and data storage and retrieval. Corporate policies of centralized versus decentralized management add to the diverse job of planning and implementing office systems. Obviously, the more strenuously overall standards are enforced, the less problem there will be in the integration strategy, but even ad hoc solutions must be used to meet the goal of integration.

MIS must face a number of problems in getting the connectivity desired and demanded. Accessing data from a mainframe is not simple even after the technical issues of connectivity are addressed. The desired data may be on disks or tape or in files under index or database managements systems. The data have to be retrieved, processed, probably reformatted, and the data code converted before transmitting to a personal computer or other terminal. In addition, mainframes generally transmit in synchronous, while PC communications are usually asynchronous, and often without error detection and/or correction. Different software packages have different format needs. And once the data have been manipulated on a personal computer, sending it back to the mainframe presents another set of hurdles. The personal computer user needs to know what processes are available on the mainframe he or she is accessing and then must be able to request data appropriately.[8]

Security to prevent inappropriate or unauthorized users from gaining access to valuable corporate data is a major headache that is poorly addressed by most off-the-shelf linkage software. And the access to the corporate mainframe cannot be accomplished at the cost of creating disruption to the ongoing work of the corporate MIS department. Some users try to address these problems by simply having in their office both a personal computer and a terminal linked to the mainframe. But this is far from ideal and leads to duplication of effort and hence unreliable information because of the lack of controls.

Another type of connectivity problem rarely addressed is the organizational procedures necessary for proper connectivity and integration. With most energy spent by firms on the technical issues, not much has been done on correct manual procedures for the use of the integrated system. Users of electronic mail systems, for example, need to develop procedures for prioritizing their mail, as frequently a message of little or no importance can distract the recipient from one of greater urgency. And procedural constraints need to be placed on users to avoid monopolization or abuse, even if inadvertent, of the system.

The introduction of "information centers" and "PC support shops" has made it easier to use office systems. Both are attempts by the MIS group to bridge the gap between corporate systems and the end users. Both assume that the user wants to become directly involved and that what is needed is the right tool and some assistance.

The information center in today's corporate environment is normally an integral part of MIS and provides a consulting and service facility for users. The center may also give users access to business-related data. The in-house shop for users of personal computers is usually an area where the users can familiarize themselves with the technology, often coupled with training courses. The shop frequently serves to control the acquisition of computer equipment by setting standards, specifying approved vendors, obtaining volume discounts, and providing support, among other functions.

Servicing the integrated system is another task for the MIS group. According to a report commissioned by the Association of Field Service Managers, one of the fastest growing areas of service will be office automation systems. The study predicted that by 1990 this type of service will surpass mainframes and minicomputers as a source of revenue.[9] In addition, the study noted greater reliance on self-service by users and predicted that users will become integral to the service decision-making process. Indeed, large corporations frequently have repair as part of their PC shops, and repair staff are becoming increasingly sophisticated. In multi-vendor environments, self-service could alleviate a lot of time-wasting finger pointing, but as yet vendors are still the primary source of service for their products. Third-party service firms are emerging to offer one-stop shopping for firms with multi-vendor products installed.

3.8 BUILDING QUALITY SYSTEMS

Most organizations rely heavily on their information systems, and so the quality of these systems will affect the successful and efficient running—and often the control—of the business. It might therefore be expected that the pursuit of quality would be a major preoccupation of information systems departments. Undoubtedly, most departments strive to deliver the best systems they can within the constraints of time and budget, but the systematic and rigorous pursuit of quality is not usually evident.

At present, the success of a system tends to be judged on three things: (1) whether it "works," (2) whether it was delivered on time, and (3) whether it was delivered within budget (ignoring the fact that most of the real cost will not be incurred until after the system has been implemented).

Quality control is usually equated with rigorous testing, though whether a system does what it was specified to do is only one aspect of quality. Quality assurance, on the other hand, is often not even understood, let alone practiced.

This lack of understanding is partly a legacy of the early days of data processing, when systems often were delivered late and did not work properly. It also stems in part from inadequate attention being given to quality because the effects of poor quality are not always immediately apparent. It is also a consequence of managers not appreciating just what can be done routinely to improve the quality of systems.

To achieve quality in its goods and services, an organization needs to be aware of three things:

1. The need to make quality an important and generally recognized goal of the firm
2. The mechanisms by which quality is produced
3. The measures by which quality can be assessed and evaluated

In an industrial context, the word *quality* refers to the evaluation of a product or service. To define quality, it is therefore necessary to think in terms of the use to which the product is put, and "fitness for purpose" is a commonly used definition.

Formal industrial standards describe the quality of a product or service as "the totality of features and characteristics that bear on its ability to satisfy a given need." These standards also describe the respective determinants and measures of the quality of products and of services.

The formal definitions imply that quality is so important that it might need to be assured, controlled, or improved. For these reasons, it is first necessary to be able to evaluate quality. The definitions also require the features that determine the "fitness for purpose" of a product to be identified. These will include economic factors as well as characteristics such as specification and design, maintainability, and availability.

Users and suppliers of a product have different perceptions about its quality. The user is normally interested only in the quality of what he or she receives; whereas the producer or supplier is interested also in the reasons for poor quality and the ways to correct the shortcomings.

Quality assurance can be defined as the activities and functions that are concerned with attaining quality. It is not concerned only with the provision of proof of quality, as implied by the word *assurance*. Thus, quality assurance includes the determination to achieve quality, the mechanisms for producing it, and the means of assessing it.

Quality control is the aspect of quality assurance that is concerned with the practical means of ensuring product or service quality as set out in the specification. It is concerned with the operational techniques and activities that ensure the product is produced to the quality specified in the requirements. The techniques may be applied either to the system of control or to the product or service being controlled.

When a computerized system is being developed, it may be regarded as a product. Thus, its quality might be perceived in terms of conformance and reliability. Indeed, the software engineering approach encourages this view. However, in the hands of the user, the software and hardware, together with the way it is operated, create a service. So a system that may be viewed as a product by the data-processing department will be viewed as a service by the users.

To complicate matters further, the firms' customers will perceive the computer system as a facility which affects the service provided by the user department. The problem facing system developers is that they need to consider all the features of the system that will satisfy three quality-related perspectives: (1) the engineering-type product view, (2) the user-type service view, (3) and the customer-type facility view. All of these features need to be included in the original objectives and requirements for the system.

Sometimes it is difficult to define the requirements for commercial systems precisely and completely. In turn, this makes it difficult to build systems to meet the requirements. As a result, the quality of commercial systems is normally specified in terms of their efficiency—how well they support the company's operations, for example, and how easy it is to adapt them to changing circumstances—rather than in terms of reliability.

The factors most often quoted as relevant for the quality of computerized systems are

- Correctness, which is the extent to which a system satisfies its specifications and fulfills the users' objectives.
- Reliability, which is the extent to which a system can be expected to perform its intended function with required precision.
- Efficiency, or the amount of computing resources required to perform a function.

- Integrity, which is determined by the extent to which access to the system by unauthorized persons can be controlled.
- Usability, or the effort required to learn, operate, prepare input for, and interpret output from the system.
- Maintainability, which is measured in terms of the effort required to locate and fix an error in the operational system.
- Testability, or the effort required to test a system to ensure that it performs its intended function.
- Flexibility, which is the effort required to modify an operational system.
- Portability, which is measured by the effort required to transfer a system from one hardware configuration and/or software system environment to another.
- Reusability, or the extent to which a system can be used in other business environments or applications. This factor is related to functionality, packaging, and scope of the functions from which the system is built.
- Interoperability, which is the effort required to couple one system with another.

There are no universal measures for these factors because the relative importance of each one is subservient to the overall characteristics of the system in question.

In addition to conforming to functional objectives, a high-quality system will also be easy both to change and to adapt to changing requirements. A system designed to satisfy a fixed, static specification might initially be acceptable, but, inevitably, it will need to be modified in some way or other. Systems quality can therefore also be defined in terms of how easy it is to change a system.

It is not sufficient to include as an objective "ease of modification." Such an aim is far too general to be helpful. Yet it is not possible to translate terms such as *flexibility* and *changeability* into meaningful elements of the specification, because these requirements can be met only by the process of design. The focus therefore needs to be on the design stage, not on the functional specification stage.

Designing a high-quality system requires an understanding of the problems of complexity and structure, in addition to understanding the technology. Real understanding and real utility occur when the number of "things" to interrelate is relatively low. From the human standpoint, simplicity is the most important prerequisite for good design.

There are three interrelated means of reducing the complexity of systems. First, the system should be partitioned into identifiable and understandable parts, where each part is defined by an inherent purpose, objective, or function.

Second, the part should be interconnected by a structure that provides order for command and control of the partitioned parts. Third, the independence of the parts should be maximized by minimizing their interdependence.

The first two are aids to comprehension, and the third is the key to flexibility. A system composed of simple, well-defined parts that interconnect loosely with each other is relatively simple to change. Changes are effected by decoupling from the structure parts that will remain the same, adjusting the structure, and placing new, simple parts to it.

Two consequences arise from treating the parts and the structure separately:

1. A bug or error in the system cannot easily corrupt the whole system because its effects will be localized.
2. Maintenance and enhancement are two separate activities. Maintenance is concerned with repairing faults in existing modules. Enhancement is concerned with making changes to the structure and replacing or discarding or rearranging modules. Clearly, these enhancement activities cannot be carried out without first reanalyzing the whole structure. In other words, system modifications must be preceded by analysis and design.

During the development stages of a system, there are many opportunities to influence the quality of the first system. However, the impact of not specifying or measuring software quality during the development process shows up much later in the systems life cycle.

Quality circles are problem-solving forums for those who are involved in the day-to-day operation of the business. They are based not on cash reward but on satisfaction and recognition of achievement. A quality circle is a group of people who meet voluntarily and regularly to identify and solve their own work-related problems—and then implement their solutions with management approval (Exhibit 3.5).

Experience has shown that quality circles do not work when the idea is imposed from above, although management's attitude is very important for their successful operation. Beyond improving quality and reducing costs, quality circles also improve communications between staff and management. Quality objectives usually cannot be divorced from the overall management objectives of an organization.

Most companies are structured in one or more of the following ways: groups by occupational level, by subject of specialization, according to project or according to the phase of each project. These existing groups are likely to be a governing factor in deciding whether to establish a specialized quality department. Where a department has been set up, its title can cause difficulties. For example, where the term *quality control department* has been adopted, an undue emphasis on the word *control* can lead to interdepartmental difficulties if other departments suspect there is a move to usurp their functions. It is therefore rarely sufficient merely

Exhibit 3.5
Mode of Operation of Quality Circles

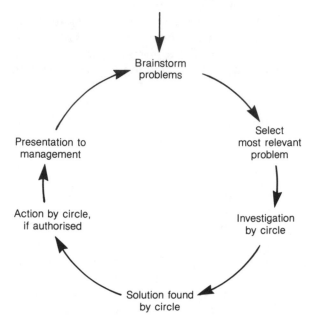

to change the name of an established inspection department to quality control and then assume that the quality objectives of a firm will be attained.

Quality in systems is associated with three separate characteristics: goals, methods, and performance. Goals can be stated in terms of achieving the objectives of both systems users and the total organization. The goals of the organization are primary; the goals of systems users are secondary. If the user requirements conflict with the goals of the firm, the systems quality assurance function must point this out. The goals of any one user also should be in harmony with the goals of other users.

Standardized methods are needed to perform the systems function (see Chapter 6). These methods manifest themselves as policies, procedures, standards, and guidelines.

Performance is concerned with optimizing the use of computer hardware and software when implementing applications. This requires relevant business analysis, proper systems design, the use of appropriate programming and systems techniques, and the best use of the available hardware and software.

Goals or users' needs can be better satisfied if appropriate quality standards exist. But methods should not interfere with goals, nor should methods reduce performance. And goals should not override performance. It is only through the use of appropriate standards, however, that the proper balance among goals, methods, and performance can be achieved. If the organization fails to set quality standards, technical staff will set their own. Far too often, management relies on technical staff setting standards but provides them with little guidance on overall objectives. As a consequence, management later reprimands the technical staff for poor performance.

The role of quality assurance in today's systems environment is essentially to assist system developers to face many differing challenges successfully. The role is seen to be much wider than that normally associated with quality control.

In addition to providing guidance, the systems quality assurance function can undertake three broad roles:

1. Applying the quality controls, which should apply both when developing new systems and when enhancing old ones. Irrespective of the way in which quality assurance is implemented, the goals, methods, and performance of each system must be evaluated.

2. Building an environment in which higher-quality systems can be developed. Reviewing a single application can only improve the quality of that application; creating an environment that encourages quality can improve the quality of all applications. Such an approach also places the quality assurance function in a position where its contribution is more visible.

3. Reviewing applications and systems. Ideally, the quality assurance function should review all systems in depth, but in practice this is rarely possible. Formal reviews should be carried out at the major decision points of system development. Systems should also be reviewed at the early stages of development because this is the best time to influence the quality of systems.

Problems encountered in setting up a systems quality function include the following:

- Lack of management commitment. Quality functions appear to be particularly at risk in MIS departments with a strong focus on keeping deadlines. The general level of management commitment is not a problem in those firms that have introduced quality programs from the top.

- Management attitudes and understanding. Even in firms with senior management committed to a companywide quality program, management understanding can be an inhibiting factor. Quality programs attempt to draw attention to areas in which people may be failing in order to initiate corrective action, but people do not talk happily about these areas, particularly if the failings influence the next performance appraisal.

- Attitudes of development staff. The problems of getting managers to be open about quality failures is also evident in development staff. Few organizations have an "ego-less" environment.

- Lack of influence. Many systems quality functions would like to have more influence, in order to prevent development projects from proceeding when quality failures have been identified. This issue is of particular concern to companies operating a quality control process in which reviews or inspections are undertaken. Recommended corrective action is not always carried out because, typically, deadlines are regarded as more important.

• Motivating systems quality staff. Some firms recognize that the lack of a career path for systems quality staff is a problem, but some look upon a period in systems quality as an important aspect in general staff development.

• End-user computing. There is yet no satisfactory answer to the problem of assuring the quality of systems developed by end users, as enthusiastic as they might be.

NOTES

1. The Gartner Group, as quoted by John Riley, "Mainframes Are Growing Idle," *Computer Weekly* (May 9, 1985).

2. *EDP Analyzer* (May 1986).

3. "Distributed Data Processing and Messaging Systems," *Data Communications* (May 1986): 105–106.

4. Fortune Market Research Survey, "DDP Decisions" (Feb. 1981).

5. Chris Yalonis and Anthony Padgett, "Micro-Mainframe Links: Order Emerging from Chaos," *Software News* (Oct. 1985): 55–71.

6. Bill Harts, Charles Teets, and M. David Stone, "Micro-to-Mainframe Connections: Remote Possibilities," *PC Magazine* (Sept. 16, 1986): 251–274.

7. *Datapro Reports on Minicomputers Newsletter* (May 1986).

8. *EDP Analyzer* (May 1986).

9. As quoted in David Steinbrecher, "Automation Outlook," *Office Administration and Automation* (April 1985): 64.

REFERENCES

Buchanan, Jack R., and Richard G. Linowes. "Understanding Distributed Data Processing."*Harvard Business Review* (July-Aug. 1980): 143–153.
Butler Cox Foundation. "Building Quality Systems" (Feb. 1985).
Butler Cox Foundation Report. "Information Technology and Cash" (Jan. 1986).
Datapro Research Corp. "The Integrated Office System" (August 1983).
Datapro Research Corp. "Office Automation Systems" (June 1986).
Datapro Research Corp. "Perspective: PC-Mainframe Linkage: The Five Connections" (May 1985), from N. Dean Meyer and David Litwak, *Today's Office* (Jan. 1985).
Datapro Research Corp. "Supermicrocomputer Systems" (Aug. 1985).
"Distributed Data Processing and Messaging Systems." *Data Communications* (Mid-May 1986): 105–106.
Knowles, Anne. "The Supermini Showdown Enters IBM's Backyard." *Electronic Business* (Feb. 1, 1986): 55–58.
"Mainframe Software Makers Have Seen the Future—And It's Rugged." *Business Week* (Dec. 23, 1985): 60–61.

Panko, Raymond R. "EMS: Electronic Mail for Managers." *Office Administration and Automation* (March 1985): 40–43.

Riley, John. "Mainframes Are Growing Idle." *Computer Weekly* (May 9, 1985), quoting a Gartner Group study.

Taylor, Paul. "The Desperate Struggle to Stay in the Race." *Financial Times* (April 22, 1986).

4

Communications—Pulling It All Together

Communications among different information technologies has become increasingly important with the influx of personal computers into corporate life. Personal computers are only one part of a corporation's workstation milieu. Terminals, word processors, telex, telephones, mainframe computers, and so forth comprise the dizzying array of equipment that potentially can be linked. In order to understand how to integrate all these systems, it is essential to understand the available options with their advantages and limitations.

While connecting terminals, smart or dumb, to a mainframe or mini-computer is one of the major avenues for integrating systems, there are others. One of the most common solutions is to use bridges between different units. Front-end processors take over most of the host computer functions. Products such as the NCR Comten provide a means for connecting a variety of terminals to different networks. Also, many software packages provide gateway, bridge, and link capabilities, while the use of minicomputers as gateways between local area networks and wide area networks is also becoming popular. Use of the private automatic branch exchange (PABX) system to provide connectivity is an interesting option. Of course, local area networks are becoming increasingly efficient and sophisticated.

4.1 THE PABX SYSTEM

The PABX is the central piece of communications equipment, providing telephone connection between both internal office users and the public network. A PABX differs from a simple switchboard in that it provides additional functions for the telephone user with the aim of improving service and control over voice communication costs. Since the break up of AT&T, the selection of this crucial system has become increasingly complex and competitive. Several major information technology vendors now own telephone equipment companies, such as IBM's purchase of Rolm, and are actively developing marketing strategies to sell "the whole works," from personal computers to mainframes to PABXs.

Basically, a PABX provides free connections between its terminals, enables users to contend for scarce resources such as the facilities provided by the common carriers, and provides a gateway to application information located elsewhere. Everyone can have a terminal regardless of their office location. If you need a whole building of staff to share data, or even several departments, this is a more economical way than with a local area network because you already have the telephone system in place. Functionally, the PABX operates in three major areas: switching, signaling, and transmission. Switching is the means by which a user can be temporarily connected to another user; this is the heart of all modern communications networks. Transmission allows an electrical signal to be physically conveyed from one place to another, and signaling is the means whereby the user interacts with the network, and vice versa. Signaling has always been the limiting factor in any network or system.

The addition of special software to the PABX has provided the user with an impressive array of call-management functions. For instance, camp-on facilities allow the caller to key in his or her phone extension number for a call-back if the number the caller has dialed is busy. PABXs are continuously being developed to provide improved voice facilities and compatibility with other office systems and data networks. The most significant of the new voice facilities is the store-and-forward voice-message system which allows speech messages to be stored on the system. To exploit new facilities, PABX vendors are increasingly moving away from conventional telephones to featurephones, or voice and data workstations, which provide function keys and thin-screen window displays.

The new type of telephone handset can be connected to the PABX by digital or analog means. A digital connection provides the opportunity for end-to-end compatibility with the new digital trunk circuits. A digital channel also uses spare bandwidth for data transmission. As a result, data and voice handling can be integrated into the same circuit and switching system. Many PABX suppliers now offer different terminals of variable sophistication that can be connected together, and to other devices, through PABX products.

For end users with a PC or a terminal who need to send limited amounts of data at low speeds (below 2400 baud), the digital PABX is the ideally preferred integration method. Unfortunately, software to tie all of these needs together seamlessly is far from ideal at this time. To link a special digital telephone into a PABX can be costly—some experts have estimated $1,000 per user. And data communication is a much smaller percentage of a company's communication needs than voice. A digital PABX is quite useful to firms with many terminals or PCs and several mainframes, as it would allow the users to have switched access to each of the mainframes via the telephone PABX. The PABX provides the gateway to external computers and data bases as well. The PABX is less geographically constrained than a local area network and can be quite flexible.

The voice-data integrated PABXs that are now available provide independently switched voice and data circuits. The data circuit can carry data at up to 64 kbit(kilobyte)/second. Calls may be made local to the PABX or can be extended across wide area networks that include packet-switched networks. Protocol converters can be provided which will make communications possible between otherwise incompatible terminals, host computers, and networks, including high-speed local area networks. And extra processors can be attached to the telephone system to provide electronic messaging and voice-messaging facilities.

The falling cost of switching logic allows electronic switches to be distributed around the site being served. This approach has been adopted for the most modern PABXs. Typically, the distributed switching units are connected to a central controller by cables, usually co-axial or optical fiber.

Nonvoice communication in today's office is used for accessing applications data stored in mainframes and ultimately accessing people's own internal data bases. The nonvoice communication needs of the MIS department are not identical with those of the rest of the company. With more and more intelligent terminals on desktops, the traditionally inviolate boundary between the function of the MIS department and the rest of the firm is slowly shifting. The desire for non–data-processing staff to want links into a host creates transmission problems distinct from standard DP issues. First, the data originated by the user must get to and from the data switch. Then the switched data must get into the computer, disk server, or other device. Distances for non-DP users are frequently greater from the mainframe source, so a transmission device is necessary.

PABX suppliers do provide features that support data communications in the office. These have not been widely accepted because of the additional costs involved. Modems are still required for off-site connections; data transmission rates provided are too high to be fully used by most terminals but are too low for file transfer purposes; and high-speed digital transmission cannot be extended to the public telephone network.

There are basically three types of connections: direct terminal to resources, a remote resource accessed for ordinary telephone lines, and signaling through the telephone network. One of the big differences between systems integration requirements and data-processing requirements is the very nature of the desktop devices and the shared resource. The MIS needs are for dedicated terminals, usually connected to a dedicated host with little need for terminal-to-terminal connections. An integrated system needs not only this terminal-to-terminal connection but also a powerful terminal-to-host connection where several hosts with different signal requirements may be accessed during the course of a day.

Telephone system suppliers are addressing these issues in the so-called fourth generation PABX. All forms of communications—voice, data, video, and telemetry—are facing international standardization. The Integrated Services Digital Network (ISDN) PABX will offer a range of applications processing services. It is possible that it will even offer generic forms of word processing, text messaging, and storage facilities at some point. The implementation of this new generation product will take years before becoming totally available in the United States. In essence, analog will be replaced by digital communications, and a single digital line may contain multiple channels of information in effect allowing for a voice channel, a data channel, and a channel for signaling—all on a single pair of copper wires. International standards will allow for direct interface to these channels rather than via such costly and cumbersome devices as modems or multiplexers. Advantages to users include transmission quality, reduced costs for equipment and channels, international interface standards, and the integration of all communication functions on the pair of wires.[1]

Development of common signaling standards and a packet-oriented central office switch are key to realization of ISDN. Additional services such as teleconferencing, integrated voice and data mail, videotex, and others will come via software defined by the user.

The most important feature of this new generation will be the integrated local area network. This will essentially provide the capabilities of purpose-built local area networks, but will be integrated with, or have access to, the voice network. In some cases, this is already being provided by computer connections or by an Ethernet option, one of the best-known baseband local area networks. Modern PABXs are digital and hence can switch between any peripheral equipment connected to them and offer a host of signaling features and terminals. These terminals will grow in intelligence allowing for greater use in integrated systems. It seems probable that the PABX and purpose-built local area network will coexist for several years to come, but the PABX will remain the less popular option for local office systems communications except where (1) cabling costs and complexities are very significant; (2) other features and fourth-generation PABXs justify their use, and the cost of the integrated local area network is small by comparison; or (3) portability within the office environment is important.

Vendors of both telephone equipment and local area networks are recognizing the need to work together to complement each other. The advantages of a PABX (the access to remote computers, use of existing wiring, user confidence, ease of moves and changes, call accounting, and combined voice and data) complement the advantages of the local area network (high-speed, data protocol conversion, lower cost for small groups, available file servers). Both avenues of systems integration need to be considered.

4.2 BUYING A PABX

While this book is not intended as a point-by-point guide to the purchase of a system as complicated as a PABX, a manager needs to know certain relevant pieces of information when considering such a purchase. It used to be that new phone systems were purchased when firms moved to new locations, expanded dramatically in their old setting, or when the contract for the existing system ran out. With the breakup of AT&T and the ensuing competition in the telephone market, managers now are examining telephone systems based on favorable trade-ins of current models, availability of new features and facilities that would justify premature retirement of an older switch, or falling prices from the intense competition.

The selection process can be broken down into three general steps: preselection information gathering, selection of the system, and future considerations for upgrades (Exhibit 4.1).

The preselection process can be broken down further to answer questions about features and facilities available and why these different product techniques might be valuable to your firm.

Most telephone switches have a variety of time-saving facilities, such as save-and-repeat to allow retrying a number, abbreviated dialing for frequently dialed numbers, and ring-back-when-free, among others. There are also a number of facilities to reduce unanswered calls, such as call diversion to an unbusy line, call forwarding, call transfer, or call pickup. The more public-service oriented a firm is, the more important these types of services become to ensure good client service.

In addition to time-saving facilities, there are now available a number

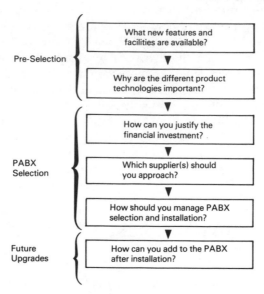

Exhibit 4.1
Selecting a Standalone PABX

of cost-control features that managers find vital to controlling the costs of telephone usage. Route restriction allows selective barring of unnecessary calls and can be used to provide progressive levels of network access. This is extremely complicated to work out on a large system and frequently introduces inappropriate restrictions which can be annoying to the users. However, restriction does have the advantage of limiting private phone calls and easing access to telephone operators.

Call-detail recording provides management with detailed records of all outgoing calls, including originating extension, duration, time of day, and so on. However, charging-back involves review by managers of hundreds of telephone calls and can be counterproductive in its use of time. (It does, however, allow abusive calls to "dial the weather," "dial a horoscope," or to off-track betting to be spotted and curbed.) Call-detail recording should be viewed in perspective. It is not an effective way of imposing discipline on an individual, nor are individual call details of interest to most managers. However, summary departmental costs can be usefully applied against budget, and exception reporting can identify serious incidents of call abuse, such as evening cleaning staff making overseas calls.

The modern PABX offers a wide range of facilities to improve the overall day-to-day operation and management of the telephone service.

For the switchboard staff, electronic switchboards improve call handling, and consoles can be ergonomically pleasing to use. Some are more elaborate than others allowing for variations in individual taste and job needs. For management, system features aid telephone service management. There are facilities for monitoring the telephone service, facilities for controlling costs, and facilities for running the service. Least-cost routing allows the call to go over the cheapest route available automatically. Before installing a new PABX, a suitable extension numbering plan needs to be prepared. This may be identical to an old one, but installation of a new system provides a good opportunity to revise or amend an outdated numbering system. At the same time, there is the need to allocate facilities by assigning a class-of-service to each extension. After installation, a move-and-change facility allows for ready updating and facilities records.

On the subject of maintenance, modern PABXs can locate and diagnose faults without human intervention. Indication of a fault appears at the operator's console. A trained engineer can then communicate with the PABX via the service printer to obtain a listing of faulty components. In most situations, the manager will contract out to a supplier or distributor for system maintenance. It is worth asking the service firm how it undertakes regular maintenance, including spot checks on equipment performance, and how emergency calls are answered. Things break down, but bear in mind that as with a car, there is usually a break-in period with a new product although most PABXs are more reliable than most data-processing facilities, or cars.

There are four elements basic to modern PABX:

1. The switching sub-system, which contains a set of switching circuits, or physical links, which connect one phone user to another.
2. The line interfaces, which connect users to the switching sub-system and include ring tone generation, and so forth.
3. The control sub-system, which takes over the role of the human operator for outgoing and internal calls and contains the computer hardware and software necessary to activate switching circuits and monitor performance.
4. The signaling sub-systems, which interpret incoming dialing pulses and multifrequency tones, produced by push-button phones, converting them into computer instructions for the control sub-system.

Switching technologies (Exhibit 4.2) affect the PABX performance in four ways:

1. The traffic a PABX can handle. Traffic is determined by the number of available switching circuits within the PABX.
2. How this capacity is made available. Variations in layout may impose artificial limits on the switching capacity available to each extension. For example, the sales department, which needs to use the phone a lot, may find that its

Exhibit 4.2
Comparison of the Characteristics of Two Switching Techniques

CHARACTERISTICS \ SWITCHING TECHNIQUE	SPACE DIVISION	TIME DIVISION
LIMITATIONS ON TOTAL TRAFFIC HANDLING CAPACITY	Designed to handle 0.1 Erlangs, although can easily be extended to accommodate extra traffic at little extra cost.	Offers a fixed switching capacity (e.g. up to 400 simultaneous conversations) regardless of number of extensions. Can provide up to 1.0 Erlangs for smaller systems (below 500 lines).
AVAILABILITY OF SWITCHING CAPACITY	Usually consists of several interlinked switching networks. Multiple switching levels can mean that extension users may be unable to get a line under unusual traffic conditions.	Because there is a single switching path, access is less complex and there is less chance of being unable to get a line.
BANDWIDTH LIMITATIONS	No direct digital link available for connection in to the System X or digital private networks, although bandwidth limitations are unlikely to be a problem here.	Can make either analogue or digital connection into external networks. However bandwidth is usually limited to 64 Kilo bps per circuit.

allocation of circuits is inadequate while other departments don't make full use of their allocation.

3. Bandwidth limitations. Each switching circuit needs to be able to deal with analog voice signals, but to introduce nonvoice traffic, additional bandwidth capacity is vital.

4. Links to other networks. Compatibility between the signaling procedures used in the switching sub-system and external networks could in the future determine the number of network options an organization can choose among.

The control sub-system is responsible for carrying out the switching instructions received for either an extension or a trunk circuit, via the signaling sub-system. It also has the task of performing background administration and error diagnostics for the telephone network. The control sub-system is a direct replacement for the telephone operator in a manual switchboard where internal and outgoing calls are concerned. The control system includes one or more general-purpose computers and a set of operating instructions (software) stored in the computer memory.

The kind of control system you choose (such as a minicomputer) has a direct effect on the PABX's performance. It affects reliability, system flexibility, system performance, and product uniqueness.

When choosing a PABX, these are the critical questions to ask about the control sub-system:

- Is there spare processing capacity to enable the PABX to be upgraded to provide more voice and nonvoice functions, or is the processor running flat out?
- Can the main memory be expanded to enable new features to be added, or is it fully stretched?
- Is the computer designed to accommodate disk storage? This affects the range of processing functions that can be added.

While hardware faults are simple to diagnose and correct, software faults occur less frequently but are more difficult either to predict or track down. They may be the result of an untested sequence of instructions executed by the computer in response to several extension users requesting different facilities at the same time. It is almost impossible to fully test concurrently every set of user conditions likely to be encountered in a busy office.

The purchase of a new PABX can involve substantial capital outlay for medium to large firms. The decision to buy is often a result of the existing system reaching the end of its useful life or the desire to take advantage of new features and facilities. The move toward fully electronic, computerized PABXs has brought improvements in operational efficiency which, if used to full capacity, can result in real savings. Fewer operators are needed, outgoing call charges can be lowered, the private network can be better used, and there are lower administrative costs. Cost reductions also include reduction in running costs, reduction in telephone bills, and reductions in staffing costs.

Although the modern telephone system offers many tangible cost savings when used both alone and as part of a network, a dramatic reduction in outgoing call charges through improved management is unlikely because control of individual dialing habits is both expensive to carry out and unacceptable to most office employees. Also, a modern telephone network is easier to use, and therefore encourages people to make more calls!

Only in the case of large networks is the return on investment attractive to a business. Typically, a change to an electronic PABX can provide a two- to three-year pay-back period.[2]

4.3 LOCAL AREA NETWORKS

The proliferation of personal computers has created new communications problems because they were originally designed to operate independently. Now there is a need for them to transfer information, share

data, and so on. In addition, as personal computers become more numerous, the total cost increases. Sharing expensive peripherals can be a way
to get these costs down, and this creates a further impetus toward communications.

Office systems built on shared minicomputers do not have a local
communications problem because all communications are channeled
through the computer, which functions in a sense as a local network
controller.

As noted earlier in this chapter, one solution to the local communications problem is the use of the PABX. It has always been possible to use
modems to put data calls through a PABX. The alternative is the use of
the local area network (LAN) which can link computers, workstations,
and terminals in one physical location. It also permits simplification of
the connectivity requirement of the configuration of traditional computers and consequently reduces cost.

LANs are communications networks which can carry voice, data, and
text in a restricted geographical area. They are internal to the corporation
and do not use public carrier lines, although they can be connected to
external networks and to PABXs. In the last few years, a wide selection
of high-speed local area networks has emerged. These networks allow a
number of different devices, such as computers, printers, and disks, to
be shared by all the terminals attached to the network. LANs give devices
access to the whole capacity of a high-speed channel. To avoid a communications overload, attached devices must make intermittent use of this
channel. Consequently, LANs are particularly appropriate for handling
the high-speed bursts of traffic characterized by communications between computers.

A typical local area network consists of the computers or terminals that
serve as network workstations, cabling, a hardware interface connection
for each computer to be hooked into the LAN, networking software
(including an operating system), a file server such as a hard disk drive
and a dedicated computer for managing the network's file operations,
peripherals that are shared (printers, modems), and ideally, network-
ready applications that take advantage of being shared across the network. The network file server is a hard disk drive that acts as the
storehouse of the network—all systems and applications are installed on
it and shared by the other PCs connected via the LAN.[3]

There has been uncertainty in many organizations about whether voice
and data transmission should be integrated via a PABX network or via a
LAN. The requirements for digital interactive speech transmission are
easily met by the types of systems used in computerized PABXs. A few
LAN architectures can meet the requirements of voice communication,
but most LAN architectures constrain the network to transmit speech in
packets. This increases the transmission time, which is disruptive to

Exhibit 4.3
Combined PABX and LAN Networks

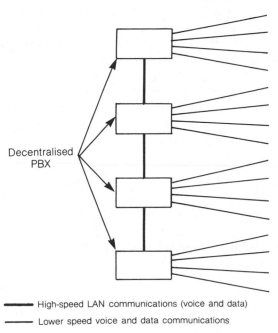

Decentralised PBX

▬▬▬ High-speed LAN communications (voice and data)
───── Lower speed voice and data communications

interactive speech, if the LAN has digital devices connected for use with other applications. This situation can generate a high level of packets, which in turn creates data congestion. Recent product offerings by digital PABX vendors now use LAN techniques to communicate between nodes (Exhibit 4.3).

4.4 LAN NETWORK OPTIONS

In practice, three possible types of communication networks exist: single-frequency, baseband, and broadband. The single-frequency option is the traditional approach and is used for telephones and PABX systems. It is fully transparent to the user devices. The wiring can be unshielded or shielded twisted-pair cable. There are several disadvantages: Its relatively low speed makes it inadequate for high-speed data transfer and high-speed graphics; its susceptibility to electrical interference can cause relatively high data error rates; and troubleshooting and fault isolation can be a problem. One-to-one connection between several hundred workstations is possible with single-frequency networks and a PABX.

Baseband LAN simplifies the wiring by putting all communication on a single channel in one cable. It works at high speed and allows each connected unit to take turns at transmitting, thus effectively providing the high-speed connecting link. (Be aware, however, that vendors' claims for bandwidth speeds are the theoretical maximums the network can achieve. In reality, the actual speed is much slower depending on the number of terminals, the distance between them, the use of signal-repeating devices, and the protocols in use.)

These systems work very well for small installations in a limited office area, and most popular LANs are of this type, including the IBM Token Ring and PC Networks, AT&T Starlan, Novell Netware, Nestar Plan 3000, Corvus Omninet, and Appletalk. These are the drawbacks:

- Only a single channel is available. Units take turns at communicating over the relatively high-speed channel, but file transfers or other larger operations can impact other users.
- Baseband systems are limited to 4,900 feet (1,500 meters) unless repeaters are used.
- The links, or taps, to wire individual offices are prone to interference.
- Interfacing with other networks requires special equipment.

Current baseband LANs can connect up to 1,200 workstations, although most are in the eight to fifteen workstation range.

Broadband communications networks overcome many of these drawbacks by carrying several hundred channels over a single co-axial cable. They can also provide additional video, voice, and data channels. With standard cable television repeaters, the network can extend up to about 40 miles (65 kilometers). However, the need for more complex electronics makes these networks most cost effective in installations that have large terminal populations or encompass multiple buildings or many floors in one building (see Chapter 7). About 100 workstations can be connected with existing broadband networks. Xerox's Ethernet system is the most widely known of this type of network.

Standard cables are not the only choice available for connecting office systems. Fiber optics are potentially the best medium for a LAN, but because of the lack of a satisfactory solution to "tapping" the fiber optic link, it has to date largely been restricted to point-to-point applications, such as linking PABXs. Only about five workstations can be connected with this type of LAN currently.

Essentially four main network configurations are used in LANs (Exhibit 4.4):

A star configuration connects end-users' terminals point-to-point to a master computer or controller. The end points can be intelligent or unintelligent terminals and can be oriented to data, text, or even voice. The approach is similar to a shared-logic work-processing system, which

Exhibit 4.4
LAN Configurations

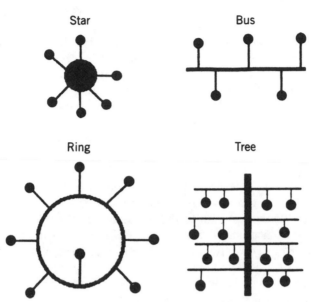

Star   Bus

Ring   Tree

relies on a centralized computer to mastermind the operation. The star configuration is the oldest and least reliable type of network configuration. The central switch can be a minicomputer or a PABX system. Since all end-user devices must be connected to the central control unit, the star system uses a great deal of cable, and failure of the central control area knocks out the whole system. AT&T's Starlan uses this configuration.

The bus configuration is not centralized like a star, since the system has defined end points that can be added to. All devices are connected directly to the main bus line. A signal originating at a terminal or processor propagates away in both directions along the bus line. Each connected device "listens" for its address on the bus. Recognizing its address, it accepts the data transmitted. Control of a bus network system resides in each individual terminal. The Corvus Omninet/Omnidrive LAN uses the bus configuration.

The tree configuration offers an expanded version of the bus configuration, by turning the bus to a vertical position and extending its branches. Tree-type LANs use processor bus technology, which is typically co-axial-based. As such, applications processors are attached to the pathways that provide access to all resources on the system. Terminals are spaced along a central "line" and communicate with devices called "servers" that provide electronic mail, disk storage, and printer facilities. A cable TV network is an example of a tree network.

The ring approach is based on token passing, essentially a continuous path without defined ends. Signals pass around the ring and are pushed along by each device as they pass. Terminals or other devices that recognize the signals access them. (In October of 1985, IBM made a series of major product announcements, including its token ring network using common telephone wires or other twisted-pair wiring. Given IBM's hold on the existing LAN market, this announcement will probably increase its dominance. A detailed discussion of the merits of this system can be found later in this chapter.)

Transferring a million bytes of information from a mainframe to a PC would take about 20 minutes over PABX lines, while only a second or two with a LAN. Engineers, financial firms, payroll departments, accountants, and inventory departments all use large amounts of data which would take too long to transmit over the slower PABX. Local area networks are particularly useful to the work group of up to ten users who work nearby each other. For example, engineers creating bit-intensive graphics can share drawings and data more productively with a LAN.

A concurrent voice-data system is currently being beta tested in Europe and could become available in the United States by late 1987.[4] Putting a LAN on a voice digital system requires a system structure capable of accepting the simultaneous internal existence of several system architectures. The ITT 5700BCS is an integrated voice and data system that can be seen as an electronic multifunction telephone system, a data transmission system, and a LAN, all operating simultaneously as one system.

The ITT 5700 user station has all the usual telephone facilities such as call pickup, hold, and ring suppression, as well as a diary, telephone directory, and date and time. A Data Module attached to the station permits the connection of data terminals or personal computers. The Data Module can be either a 10NET or RS–232 module. The 10NET module is an interface board developed jointly by ITT Spain and Fox Research of Dayton, Ohio. It is designed to be installed in an IBM PC or compatible and transforms the ITT 5700 into a 10NET local area network. A string of 10NET personal computers can be attached to one PC that contacts this 10NET Data Module. This PC is, in turn, attached to the ITT 5700 ring by connecting the 10NET Data Module to a 5700 user station. The ITT 5700 acts as a transparent medium for the LAN yet provides the concurrent voice capability.

The RS–232C Data Module attaches to the data port of the ITT 5700 user station. Point-to-point or multipoint communications can then be established between any number of existing ITT 5700 RS–232C data ports.

Because of the high costs involved in rewiring older buildings and manufacturing sites, the cabling issue has risen in importance. For buildings more than ten years old, no one probably knows where all the wires go! Adding new wire means testing for "crosstones" such as electronic interference from other wires. This can be costly. In addition, capacity must be checked. Data transmissions overloading the voice and data network can prevent the CEO from making a voice call.

One of the goals of newly constructed office buildings is flexibility, and many of the new offices today are built around the "open plan" because of this need for flexibility. Walls are movable, furniture is modular, lighting is task ambient, ceilings and floors lowered or raised to accomodate wiring. All the wires to support today's power-hungry equipment are usually hidden in the ceiling or floor, running under room dividers and through partitions. Architects and space planners must address the wiring issue very early in the planning stages. They must be able to install the appropriate capacity wiring that allows for optimum flexibility at lowest cost that is easily moved and unobtrusively placed. Use of a raised-access floor costs approximately $5 more per square foot installed,[5] and major buildings going up today are including this option, as it allows for air-conditioning distribution as well as cabling. Older sites, unfortunately, too often suffer from the myriad of wiring needs creating unsightly, dangerous, and often counterproductive environments. (Crossed or kinked personal computer wires, for example, can block data transmission.)

Local area networks can be configured using one of three types of transmission cable or wire. Each of these differing cable types has a number of advantages or disadvantages. However, no one type of cable currently supports all the applications data in either analog or digital form.

Twisted pair wire is the most frequently used type of cable. But because it is not shielded from outside interference, it is subject to outside electromagnetic problems and can be intercepted fairly easily. It is not used in high-performance LANs where speed is important because of this problem. Transmission for unshielded pair wire is limited to slower transmission rates, although it is the least expensive wire for use in LANs.

Shielded wire is found in two basic types, shielded twisted pair and co-axial cable, although there are a number of variations of shielded wire available. Shielded twisted pair wire eliminates the interference/intercept problems of twisted pair wire by covering the wires with a wire/insulation coating to reduce interference and to permit faster transmission rates. The one disadvantage is that electronic impulses within the wires tend to decrease over extended lengths of wire, and line amplifiers are required to boost data along longer distances.

Co-axial cable is similar to the shielded twisted pair cable but generally has only one wire encased in a protective sheath. It is available in a variety of forms, the most common of which is a general-purpose, single conductor type. While this cable is effective, it is also somewhat expensive and can cause space constraints because of the physical size required to install both send and receive wires within walls and ceilings.

Fiber optics are useful for very high-speed, high-capacity communications applications. This cable is essentially glass-based, made from two types of glass, one for an inner core, the other for an outer layer. Since the two different glass types have different indexes of refraction, this combination prevents light entering one end of the fiber from passing through the fiber's outer surface. The fiber itself is cased in a protective sheath to lend structural integrity. Fiber optics cable transmits signals in the form of light. While it is immune to the electrical and cost problems of other types of cable, at present too few people understand how to install it. Further, connection costs for end-user devices is more expensive than for wire.

4.6 IBM'S TOKEN RING LAN

Although IBM's PC Network has been available for some time, in late 1985 the company announced its local area network product: the Token Ring LAN. While many had hoped this would solve all the problems of device interconnection in the office, at least for IBM equipment, this has turned out to be far from the case. Indeed, the Token Ring appears to be a product designed to fill a gap in IBM's product line. In the long run, however, the significance of this "seal of approval" is likely to be great if only because of the dominance of IBM in the personal computer marketplace. The Token Ring LAN is of strategic importance because it forms a central part of IBM's thrust into the office. It defines a new family of standards underpinning a new architecture and ability to support a wide range of applications. Because of the open nature of the standards and their wide applicability, IBM will promote competition among a variety of other vendors, eventually leading to a much greater choice of products.

The IBM Token Ring must be considered in conjunction with the IBM Cabling System, which has to be installed before the Token Ring LAN can be used, and with two network software packages, NETBIOS and APPC. NETBIOS was developed by Sytek for the broadband PC Network and provides the resource sharing expected of a LAN. APPC is an implementation of a type of Systems Network Architecture (SNA) for the

IBM PC. The Token Ring LAN has been designed to support both software packages.

The IBM Cabling System is a product for the complete wiring of buildings. Like telephone and power wiring, it is best installed during building construction, though it is not mandatory. It must be installed according to IBM guidelines, and it must be constructed from IBM-approved components, which include the wiring closets, intercloset wiring, station cables, faceplates, and device attachment cables. Any manager working on moving the company to a newly constructed site would be wise to have an IBM cabling expert attend construction planning sessions.

Each wiring closet contains racks and has a distribution panel for data (Exhibit 4.5). The distribution panel allows rapid and convenient reconfiguration with no need for cable pulling or splicing. The wiring closet may also contain a distribution frame for telephone wiring, wiring concentrators for LANs, cluster controllers, and other communications equipment. One closet is generally the origin for up to 250 station cables. The intercloset wiring depends on the mixture of devices to be supported. For 327x terminals, for example, co-axial cables will be needed if the cluster controllers are in the computer room, but co-axial cables, twisted pair, or fiber optic cables can be used if the controllers are in the wiring closets.

Several alternative types of cable can be used for the station cables, but Types 1, 2, and 3 are the most important. Types 1 and 2 are based on two shielded twisted pairs, intended for data transmission, and Type 2 also has four twisted pairs intended for telephone use which are placed outside the shield but within the outer sheath. Type 1 and 2 cables are thicker and stiffer than ordinary telephone wire and thus are more difficult to install; it may sometimes be necessary to install special conduits to accommodate these cables, which can be costly if the work is a retrofit. Type 3 cable is defined as "good quality" telephone wire and is cheaper both to buy and to install, but its signaling properties are not as good, so it can be used only for short distances and low transmission rates.

An appropriate drop cable (device attachment) is needed to attach a terminal or host to the Cabling System. At the terminal end, drop cables terminate in a Cabling System faceplate in each office or next to each desk. If Type 2 cable is used, a second faceplate for telephones will also be needed. Fewer faceplates could be installed, but this would make it more difficult to move or add equipment. Every drop cable terminates in a hermaphrodite plug that is inserted into the faceplate to match a similar plug behind it.

The IBM Token Ring LAN is designed for IBM PCs, particularly for use in buildings that have been prewired with the IBM Cabling System, or

Exhibit 4.5

Components of the IBM Cabling System

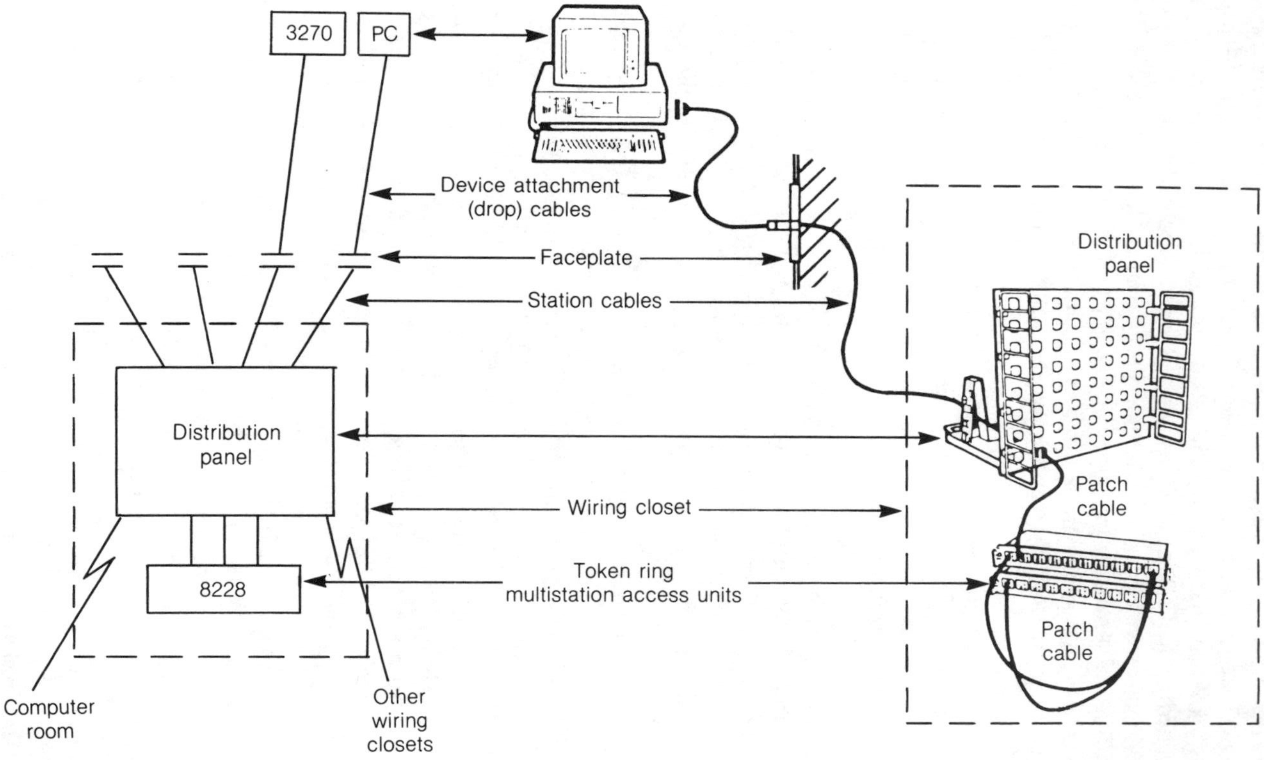

Distribution panel

Patch cable

Patch cable

Device attachment (drop) cables

Faceplate

Station cables

Wiring closet

Token ring multistation access units

Other wiring closets

PC

3270

Distribution panel

8228

Computer room

(Adapted from material provided by IBM)

installed on an ad hoc basis. The Token Ring runs on twisted pair cables laid in a star-shaped ring through multistation access units located in wiring closets. A special bit pattern, the token, circles the ring continuously. When a station holds the token, and only then, it can transmit a single packet of data. It must then release the token for use by the next station. The product has a signaling speed of 4M bits, but higher speeds can be expected. It is primarily a data transmission product and supports neither voice nor full-motion video.

The Token Ring's network management functions continually monitor the ring's operation. When a ring segment fails, the station receiving from that segment detects the loss of signal and transmits an error message around the ring to the preceding station—the station that should be transmitting onto the failed segment. That station then removes itself from the ring and tests its link to the wiring closet. If that link is defective, the station remains off the ring, enabling the ring to operate correctly. If the sending station's link is operating correctly, the receiving station then removes itself from the ring and tests its own link to the wiring closet.

At present, the network management functions are defined for a single ring and are not integrated with SNA network management in a wide area network, even an SNA network accessible from a Token Ring. So far, there are no independent performance measurements for the Token Ring LAN, but IBM claims speeds of up to 300k bits. This responsiveness falls as the total load on the LAN increases, but at high loads the performance is markedly better than that of a contention LAN running at the same speed. LANs, however, normally operate at relatively low loads, where the performance advantage lies with contention networks, and in most circumstances, the overall performance of a LAN depends more on the speed of the personal computer and the efficiency of the software than on the characteristics of the network.

The two proprietary software packages are distinct and independent software environments above the data link layer. The NETBIOS environment requires IBM's PC Network program and provides economies by allowing the sharing of peripherals and the exchange of information on the LAN. These are the main services provided by the NETBIOS software:

- File service. PC files can be transferred across the network and applied to a shared disk unit. Files, directories, and data volumes may thus be shared by several PCs.

- Print service. Output for printing is written to a spool file and may be printed later by another PC.

- Message service. This provides an inter-PC message mechanism that is purely local and is not compatible with anything else in the IBM range.

NETBIOS can be used in conjunction with separate software that allows the LAN to access IBM 370, System/36 and System/38 computers, and with special hardware and software for access to Series 1 computers. Developed by Sytek for the broadband IBM PC network, the protocols are proprietary to Sytek. Applications using NETBIOS may be transferred between broadband and Token Ring LANs.

APPC (Advanced Program-to-Program Communication) is an implementation for the PC of the most recent SNA standards, including PU2.1, which provides peer communications rather than master-slave working, and LU6.2, which defines a clean interface with higher-level protocols and includes advanced functions such as synchronization.

In effect, these standards have created a new version of Systems Network Architecture that provides peer-to-peer working, interprogram communication, and a layered architecture free of device dependencies that IBM now admits were included in previous versions of SNA. The SNA network can now be seen as a system in its own right and not merely as an adjunct of a mainframe.

While the IBM Cabling System and Token Ring products are sound, they do have some serious shortcomings:

- The Cabling System is expensive to install. The use of the star topology requires up to ten times as much cable as a simple ring. Also, cable needs to be carried to every desk. Per outlet costs of $700 for a retrofit installation are not unusual.
- The Token Ring does not support 327x terminals, its largest user base. However, the benefits of connecting 327x terminals to the Token Ring would be minimal, as the lack of intelligence in this terminal would not allow for use of all of the Token Ring facilities. In the near future, IBM has promised to provide Token Ring interfaces for the System/36, /38 and 5520 Administrative System.
- The Token Ring does not support voice-data integration. This has serious limitation given the costs involved in installing the Cabling System. The alternative to the wholesale replacement of cables would be to retain separate voice and data networks.

This discussion of the IBM Cabling System and Token Ring LAN is not meant to either endorse or repudiate the product, but rather to provide a basis of understanding of one product that can be expected to play a major role in the LAN marketplace. A recent Datapro survey indicated that 11 percent of the respondents used some type of IBM LAN, although the DEC DECNet also was used by 11 percent of the respondents. Increasing competition leads to price reductions, and low-cost manufacturers based in Taiwan, Korea, and Hong Kong can be expected to dominate the market in the future.

4.7 WIDE AREA AND EXTERNAL COMMUNICATIONS

Packet-switched networks address a number of different requirements resulting from disadvantages of public and private switched telephone circuits. These systems used for data transmission have high error rates;

the total bandwidth of the circuit is occupied for the duration of a call; and transmission speeds and call set-up and clear-down are slow. Data traffic is sensitive to errors and often occurs in short bursts. Error detection and correction is therefore required on data circuits, and economies can be achieved if the capacity of a circuit is shared among a number of users. High transmission speeds are required for many applications, and short set-up/clear-down times are desirable when small amounts of data are transmitted.

The CCITT (Comité Consultatif International Télégraphique et Téléphonique) has defined the X.25 packet-switched protocol for use on public data networks. The CCITT is responsible for developing recommendations for the design and operation of telecommunications equipment and services; members are nominated by national governments. The designation X.25 defines the connection between a terminal or computer and a public data network. It also defines the service offered by the network. Data pass the X.25 interface in the form of packets of not more than 128 bytes of data. Each packet is addressed to another device attached to the network, and, as in a telephone system, a connection must be established between the devices before any communication can take place. X.25 packet-switched networks have been developed in a number of European countries, Japan, Canada, and the United States.

The main benefits of packet-switched networks, compared with other data transmission options, are lower transmission error rates, greater flexibility, lower costs, and switching, which cannot be achieved easily on dedicated leased-line networks. Packet-switched networks can be used as an integral part of many network architectures. Thus the software environment exists within which the packet-switched network option can be used. There are great potential benefits to office systems users because of the low volumes of intersite traffic likely in most circumstances. However, it should be emphasized that the precise combination of wide area communications facilities chosen is very much a function of the specific needs of the user.

Integrated Services Digital Networks (ISDN) are a developing trend that do or do not yet exist in mature form, depending on whom you talk to. Basically, telecommunication experts are in broad agreement about the general nature of an ISDN. The ISDNs that are being developed include the following functional requirements:

- A variety of data speeds
- Economic transport of bursts of data as well as continuous data
- Fast call set-up and clear-down
- Computerized trunk and local exchanges
- Low error rates
- Low data transfer delay times
- Different levels of security for transmission

When an ISDN is fully implemented, each subscriber will have one or more lines. Each line could be connected to a digital telephone, an answering machine, a data terminal, a facsimile device, a computer, or a multifunction workstation. Standard protocols will ensure that messages are delivered only to devices that are able to interpret them properly. It is specifically intended that one ISDN-compatible line should be able to service both a telephone and a data terminal concurrently. The ISDN interface provides both circuit-switched and packet-switched access to the local exchange.

Satellite developments have played an important role in the exponential growth of telecommunications traffic. Demand for satellite capacity is growing as fast as it can be provided. Telecommunication satellites are used primarily for television transmission and long-distance voice and data communications, and their main users are telephone companies, broadcasters, industry, business, and government. Telephone companies lease capacity on the different satellites and serve as common carriers themselves or provide specialist services. In business, the main market is in larger dispersed organizations in manufacturing, finance, and government, as well as in computer service companies.

The future of satellite communications for long-distance voice and data traffic, including private network services, seems assured. Although the costs of land-based cable networks will continue to fall, particularly with the widespread installation of optical fiber cable and the digitization of the telephone network, these networks will tend to be used for local traffic and to feed long-distance satellite links. The greatly increased bandwidths and line speeds made available by these technologies may even stimulate the growth of image-based products and services in business, such as slow-scan TV, facsimile, and teleconferencing.

Cellular radio technology is primarily designed to provide many more simultaneous mobile telephone conversations than is now possible. Where conventional mobile telephone service can handle about 700 subscribers, introduction of cellular radio could increase this to about 100,000, eliminating delays and offering more reliable service and clearer reception at a lower cost. The key to cellular radio technology is the central computerized automatic switching system within a metropolitan or rural area in which the service operates. The total area is divided into cells, each of which contains a base station transmitting only to radio telephones within its boundaries. As the user moves from one cell to another, the conversation is automatically switched to the next base station by the central switching system. Because it allows frequencies to be re-used, many more calls can be handled within the area, which, in theory, could always be subdivided into more and smaller cells, providing almost unlimited capability for the system (Exhibit 4.6).

Cellular phones can offer automatic direct-dial connections anywhere

Exhibit 4.6
The Cellular Radio Principle

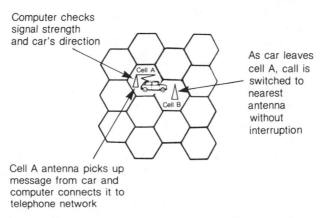

Computer checks signal strength and car's direction

As car leaves cell A, call is switched to nearest antenna without interruption

Cell A antenna picks up message from car and computer connects it to telephone network

in the world. The phones can also provide stored numbers for high-speed dialing and can even be used for data, telex, and videotex transmission, via a modem. Although cellular radio technology is usually thought of as a car-based facility, portable phones and terminals can also use this technology. Cellular radio offers a potential means of supporting mobile office workers or providing field service workers and sales staff with office services. The simplest application is voice mail. The mobile telephone can be used to leave or listen to voice messages, or a portable terminal could be connected via cellular radio for electronic mail use.

A value-added network service (VANS) is a service based on a telecommunications network by which messages (voice, data, text, and/or image) are given additional value in the process of transmission. Protocol conversion, electronic mail, and on-line database retrieval, for example, are three different ways in which value can be added in a network. For example, GTE's Telenet offers a range of services for IBM devices to allow users to access multiple host computers, as well as a specialized data base and electronic mail service to the medical and health-care professions developed in conjunction with the American Medical Association.

The future trend in VANS is toward more comprehensive, integrated, and intelligent services. They will also move from general services to more specialist services, such as industry-specific electronic ordering systems. Common in other sectors of the information technology market is the trend toward greater competition and choice, including VAN services for the consumer market such as property-for-sale data bases.

4.8 ELECTRONIC MAIL

The communication of textual and graphic material has become a necessity in today's office. Information is input electronically, then transferred and received for output at a remote site. Anyone who is on the system can send and receive mail and messages from anyone else, and mail includes memos, general administrative memos, or longer textual documents or reports.

Computer-based electronic mail systems are becoming the most common type of electronic mail system. Standards for this format are being developed by the National Bureau of Standards Specification of Message Format for Computer-based Message Systems. In theory, adherence to this standard could allow any system to hook up with any other system to transfer messages or data. In general, computer-based electronic mail systems exist as networks with local and/or remote access to processors to conduct the mail functions. Terminals, usually smart, are located at user sites while a central computer or processor handles the processing of the traffic. Some systems have access to common data bases and files, and some provide such advanced features as store-and-forward. Individual users have an individual "address" and a "mailbox" as well as an on-line directory of other users' names and addresses.

Computer-based electronic mail systems allow for creation, editing, and other functions at the user terminal, either by way of word-processing features in the terminal or through the software for the electronic mail system. For example, users of the Wang Mailway system can create a document in the Wang word-processing mode, transfer it to Mailway, and then distribute it to the appropriate parties. Some systems also allow for scheduling, calendaring, and database access.

In-house electronic mail systems can be created by either upgrading existing equipment or purchasing an entire system and installing it. Departmental systems using local area networks are being developed for electronic mail. A communications processor is at the heart of any system. It consists of a processor, an interface to the host computer, a communications multiplexer for the control of data, interfaces to other peripherals, and software to control it all. Some processors are for data transmission only, but some digital PABX systems can also control data and text traffic.

The in-house electronic mail system must have text-editing features at some point, as well as code conversion capabilities. The ability to upgrade the conversion capabilities of the communications processor will allow a wider range of terminals to be accessed. The ability to upgrade the on-line storage capacity is also important to allow for additional filing space and mailboxes.

Public electronic message systems are a flexible and popular way to access remote sites or public data bases even if your firm lacks a computer or network. By using an off-site third party, computer users can take advantage of text processing and other facilities designed for different user populations. A teletypewriter or data terminal communicating over telephone lines is all that is needed.

Vendors of communication facilities, such as GTE or Tymshare, offer remotely accessed electronic mail services. While their primary business is the movement of data and text over their own non-Bell facilities, the addition of user services such as electronic messaging has proven to be a popular marketing strategy. Using these remote services allows you the benefits of electronic mail without the costs of installation, although of course you do pay for accessing these services.

Managers are particularly enthusiastic electronic mail users, whether they use it personally or delegate it. It saves tremendous time, is accurate, flexible, and relatively inexpensive. The price of public message systems is continuing to fall and soon may undercut postage costs. For example, depending on the length of the document, the number of recipients, and the charge of the service, a message may cost under $1. On AT&T Mail, a 400-character message created off-line will cost forty cents to transmit. Composition on-line adds twenty cents. There is no charge for checking your mailbox for messages.

Several dozen vendors offer some form of electronic message system via the telephone or data networks. In 1985, electronic mail services delivered about 13.5 million messages.[6] All allow for composition, transmission, and reading of incoming mail. In addition, the ability to load files from personal computers and word processors using ASCII is available, allowing for document exchange and remote editing. Some personal computer software will automatically check several different electronic mail services for incoming messages, working totally in the background until mail is found.

There are disadvantages to using remote services for electronic mail. It is not inexpensive, although costs vary by distances, rates, and time of use. The remote services offer limited storage and database access and can be slow on input and output. The questions of reliability and data security are not easily addressed, and if the security of data is an issue, the vendor should be screened carefully so you understand the protections offered by the service.

If your firm is looking into using an electronic mail service, good planning is important. Understanding of the communication needs of your users will help you select an appropriate vendor. More than one vendor may be selected because some vendors offer different services such as overseas mail. Some vendors such as AT&T Mail focus on electronic mail to the exclusion of data bases. Other vendors such as Western Union's EasyLink and MCI Mail provide off-net options for transmission of mailgrams, telexes, telegrams, and the like. Other vendors allow you to send messages between competing systems, as with MCI and CompuServe, as well as access such services as the Dow Jones News.

Voice mail avoids the keyboard and provides the user with the ability to deliver voice messages over a touch-tone telephone. Like the much-maligned answering machine, voice messages allow the user to identify the telephone number of the recipient's phone and designate time priorities needed. The message is digitized, forwarded, and converted back to a synthesized voice message for the recipient. If the line is busy, the computer stores the message and forwards it later. Recipients can review their voice messages much as the answering machine plays back the recordings. A minicomputer or processor is accessed through the telephone pad and provides the user with a wide range of control over recording, playback, and forwarding, while ensuring security and message integrity. The elimination of telephone tag alone saves hours of a busy day.

Anyone with a telephone can access a voice mail system, which is a particular benefit for busy senior executives who do not use a keyboard or terminal. Some firms use voice mail for central dictation, and it can be combined with the delivery of hard-copy or electronic messages.

The newer PABX devices are increasingly capable of offering voice as well as electronic mail over their integrated lines. Calls can be sent at all hours and are particularly effective when rates are lower. Most messages are brief and rarely require an answer, and productivity savings can be impressive. Many voice mail systems are now the size of a two-drawer file cabinet using 32-bit chips. Prices range from $17,500 upward to half a million dollars, depending on the number of ports, the number of "mailboxes," and the total disk storage capacity. Dataquest predicts that the market for voice-messaging equipment and services will be $750 million by 1989.[7]

As with electronic mail, there are voice mail service bureaus. While they may lack integrated features such as message waiting indication, call forwarding, or transfer to operator, they can be a cost-effective alternative to an in-house system. A typical rental of the voice mailbox could run about $25 per month plus telephone charges, and volume discounts are available.

Voice mail facilities are particularly useful to firms with extensive off-site staff, such as salespeople, pilots, auditors, and reporters. The voice mail system should have the ability to leave messages for outside and inside callers, store-and-forward at specific times, and automatically cue recipients of messages waiting. A voice mail time-sharing service is now available to subscribers of Wang's DVX and Cellular One's mobile telephone service.

4.9 FACSIMILE

While the use of facsimile equipment is not at the core of systems integration, a brief discussion of the pros and cons of this transmission device should put it in perspective. Use of facsimile for document transmission is relatively slow, although certainly faster than the mail service, and somewhat cumbersome. Because the facsimile device transmits an electrical signal of a document, it includes even the blank spaces and margins, which makes for a slower rate of transmission and can increase cost accordingly.

There are advantages to using facsimile, however. Most of today's fax machines can be installed almost anywhere, and desktop models are inexpensive and easy to use. The fax can transmit every kind of document, from text to graphs to photographs, and can receive these as well. Because of its slower speed, there are fewer errors in transmission, and the equipment is simple to operate reliably.

4.10 CASE STUDIES

Lincoln National is the fifteenth largest insurance company in the United States. It employs 35,000 staff at its headquarters in Fort Wayne, Indiana, and another 35,000 people in other offices. The company has broadened its internal electronic mail system to enable its many clients to link into it via a national private network.

Lincoln moved into the office automation arena seven years ago. It started by developing an internal system encompassing word processing, electronic mail, and personal computing. This has evolved into the present Prime-based system using standard dumb terminals. Users are linked into the Prime system using a local area network. The initial 30 terminals have grown to 17,000 in early 1985 and are used by 25,000 staff.

Lincoln first used an internal electronic mail system—MCI—which provided either hard copies or electronic transfer and receipt of information. Responding to requests by staff, the company then decided to give users the chance to communicate externally as well. For this purpose, MCI Mail Link was used—a specification developed by MCI Digital Information Services. This is a forerunner of an electronic message network interface standard, known as X.400 which is now under development. X.400 provides access to other public and private message networks and to TWX/telex terminals. It also links with laser printers that output hard-copy messages for delivery to those without terminals. MCI agreed to use Lincoln National as one of two test sites (the other was Citibank).

Users decide in what timeframe they want the mail delivered—by normal post, overnight, in four hours, by telex, or electronically. The costs vary according to the choice.

Although most users like the system's new ability to communicate with corporate clients outside the company, the cumulative costs of sending letters at $2 to $3 each are quite significant. However, an internal survey at Lincoln suggests that productivity improvements of 12 percent to 20 percent have been achieved. Also, using the electronic mail link is the only way for letters to be delivered within four hours.

The Hy-Vee supermarket chain in Iowa uses an approach designed to benefit from EFTPOS—electronic funds transfer at the point of sale. The banks provide terminal equipment and networking.

Hy-Vee operates a total of 153 supermarkets in six states, but its 16 EFTPOS stores (with a total of some 240 checkouts) are in Iowa. They use the Iowa Transfer System, a network supporting ATMs (automatic teller machines) and EFTPOS which has been developed jointly by Iowa financial institutions and whose use is shared by them. The bank providing the EFTPOS equipment varies according to the grocery store's location.

The store equipment is all NCR-based, with NCR 2552 scanning systems connected to NCR 8200 store processors. Upgrading to EFT required the addition of a 10-key pinpad and bank card reader. Only debit transactions are accepted. The system operates on-line, and the customer's account is debited and Hy-Vee's credited the same day.

NCR EFTPOS equipment was initially made available to Hy-Vee on a pilot basis several years ago. The pilot phase was completed, and EFTPOS is now being introduced in other stores. EFT currently accounts for about 10 percent of payment transactions in the stores where it is installed. Only a minority of check transactions have been replaced by EFTPOS, but there are still over 200 transactions per day for which the worry of bad checks has been alleviated and which yield substantial time savings at the checkout. For a period of time, congestion on the Iowa Transfer System network and the consequent slow response prevented realization of these savings, but the capacity of the Iowa Transfer System network is being increased to solve the problem.

An unexpected result of the Hy-Vee trials was that customers paying by debit card spend more on average than other customers.

Marketing the service at the point of sale has proven important. Illuminated signs have been displayed at the checkouts, but the cashiers play the most important role in encouraging customers to use EFTPOS. Hy-Vee has found that people are reluctant to trust the system initially but become enthusiastic once they have used it two or three times. Tying customers to Hy-Vee if they wish to pay by debit card is seen as one of the most important benefits of the system.

Hy-Vee has relatively few costs to offset against the benefits. The bank owns the EFT terminals, which cost about $2,500 per checkout, and pays for installation, communications, and maintenance. The financial arrangements governing the use of the Iowa Transfer System are such that the debited bank pays ten cents per transaction, six cents of which goes to the Iowa Transfer System, with the remainder being shared between Hy-Vee and its bank. In other words, the store also enjoys a reduction in bank charges in addition to the other benefits gained.

Hy-Vee's experience is notable in a number of respects. It has managed to attain appreciable benefits, including a reduction in bank charges, while leaving costs and responsibility for terminal provision to the banks. It has been fortunate, too, in being able to integrate EFT with its point-of-sale equipment because its POS supplier could also supply EFT equipment supported by the Iowa Transfer System. The grocery chain has also learned the importance of actively marketing EFT service at the point of sale and the importance of commitment and enthusiasm by cashiers who promote its use.

A San Francisco law firm installed a WangNet broadband local area network several years ago. It has reduced turnaround time dramatically and resulted in cost savings over individual wiring of terminals. The law firm specializes in government contracts, corporate law, and other business law applications. With five branch offices and over 150 lawyers, the firm has over 200 support staff. When their new corporate offices were under construction, the decision to install the LAN was made. Outlets averaged $300 each as opposed to an estimated cost of $1,200 for using traditional hard-wire technology for connections.

Three Wang VS computers are attached to the system. One is used for accounting, timekeeping, cost records, and billing. Another is dedicated to professional applications such as litigation support. The third is used for office automation—primarily, word processing. There are also over 50 workstations, half a dozen Wang Professional Computers, several PIC image systems, and two modems for telecommunications. There are also six printers. All of the systems are managed by the MIS group, which provides standards and technical support.

The devices now gather data for billing, keep track of telephone calls, document copies, and provide word-processing services. The telephone system computes the cost for a long-distance call using telephone company rates and then matches the call to an account number. This is then communicated, without human intervention, to the Wang VS that is handling client billings. Once stored, the prestored billing format eliminates the processing time of bill preparation.

NOTES

1. Francis X. Dzubeck, "Data Communications," *Administrative Management* (April 1986): 55–56.

2. Roger Camrass, "Buying a PABX," Oyez Scientific and Technical Services Ltd. (1983).

3. *InforWorld* (March 24, 1986): 26.

4. Edmond Kiatapov, "New System Allows Simultaneous Voice and Data Combined with a LAN," "The Automated Office," *Administrative Management* (March 1986): 13–14.

5. Ronald W. Anderson, "Wiring the Automated Office," *Office Administration and Automation* (Sept. 1985): 33–35.

6. Jack Bell, "How to Choose an Electronic Mail Service," *Personal Computing* (Sept. 1986): 60–67.

7. Gail Siragusa, "Voice Mail Takes Off," *Administrative Management* (April 1986): 43–48.

REFERENCES

Crabb, Don. "Major Vendors Differ on Network Approach." *Inforworld* (March 24, 1986): 25–28.

Datapro Research Corp. "Electronic Mail" (April 1986).

Datapro Research Corp. "Facsimile" (April 1986).

Flint, David. "The Significance of the IBM Token Ring." Butler Cox Foundation.

Foster, Lawrence W., and David M. Flynn. "Management Information Technology: Its Effects on Organizational Form and Function." *MIS Quarterly* (Dec. 1984): 229–236.

"Law Firm Finds for LAN in Case of Network vs. Cable." "Systems in Action." *Administrative Management* (April 1986): 16–18.

Lewis, Jamie. "LAN Software Innovations Make the Connection." *Words* (June-July 1986): 23–25.

"Local Area Networks." *Data Communications* (Mid-May 1986): 113–114.

Mortensen, Erik. "One World—One Network." *Administrative Management* (June 1986): 39–46.

Paznik, Jill. "Digital PBX—A Networking Alternative." *Administrative Management* (Jan. 1986): 33–37.

"Users Rate Their LANs." *Data Communications* (June 1986): 114–121.

5

The Impact of Integration: People, Equipment, and Information

5.1 PEOPLE AND SYSTEMS

When discussing the interface between people and equipment, one must take into account the physical, psychological, and psycho-social characteristics of the people. A person's physical characteristics determine the optimum size and shape of the equipment and the forces required to operate it. Psychological characteristics not only determine the way a person thinks, solves problems, and communicates, but also the motivation to perform a specific task, and the attitudes and values held. These psychological considerations are particularly relevant to the way in which tasks are designed and organized into jobs. But because people do not exist in isolation, a person's psycho-social characteristics determine the way in which people inter-react with one another.

Adaptability of people is a major human strength, especially by comparison with the adaptability of machines. In practice, this often means that a person is left to carry out the functions that a machine is not able to perform. But if too much is expected of the person, then he or she may fail to perform the task, and the equipment will then not be used effectively. On the other hand, if too little is expected of someone, the person may find the task boring and tedious, resulting in a lack of vigilance that may cause errors to be made or even equipment to be abused. And if the tasks performed by the equipment do not match the task needs of the user, the equipment may not be used effectively or at all.

Surveys suggest that no more than 10 percent of senior managers use a personal computer, or indeed even feel comfortable about the prospect of using one or any other type of computing device. So while the personal computer or other workstation will certainly have an impact on what senior managers do, it will be an indirect effect caused by people further down the organizational hierarchy who do use these devices. The principal effect on the few senior managers who have begun to use a terminal has been to blur further the dividing line between home and office. Many of them have an equivalent personal computer at home, and they find it is easier to carry home the corporate budget on a disk than it is to carry large volumes of paper. Another advantage comes from being able to link their terminal at home to the corporate network.

Many reasons have been put forward to explain the low rate of use of business personal computers by top management. The most common are fear of new technology, fear of being seen to be typing and hence a loss of status, fear of making a fool of themselves, fear of not knowing what to do with all the information gathered, and fear of losing hard-won interpersonal skills. Another reason sometimes put forward is that senior managers are deterred by the training time required. However, the most important factor preventing senior managers from using business microcomputers is that these technological marvels have little to offer this level of management, whose work is largely unstructured and not well suited to computerization. Unless or until senior managers perceive real personal benefits from personal computers, they will make little use of them.

All information processing equipment must conform to the physical and psychological requirements of the user, not only in hardware but particularly in software. The cost of tolerating poor software interfaces is even more difficult to measure than the cost of tolerating poor hardware interfaces. Vendors have advanced the hardware ergonomics of the information processing equipment to the point today that almost all keyboards and screens are comfortable and pleasing to use. The software interface, however, still has a way to go in comfort and ease of use. This interface has three basic components: language which the system and the user share, the way in which that language is organized into procedures and operations, and the time base that underlines those procedures and operations.

The ideal solution to the language of the software is to use the natural language of the user without modifying or abbreviating it. If a natural language dialogue between man and machine is to be meaningful, the use and the software need to share the same "world model." Without such a shared world model, the dialogue may be not only misleading, but also dangerous. The user may believe that the system understands what he or she is saying and may then assume that the system has the same inferential powers that a person making the same type of response has. Right now, it is practical to share only limited world models with information systems, and this limitation restricts the usefulness of totally natural language communications. However, many of the task languages that are already in common business use are either abbreviated or condensed subsets of natural language. Indeed, brevity in the form of coded information can facilitate the assimilation of output and reduce the amount of keyboarding effort required.

The language of the interface is organized into procedures and operations. These may be concerned with either the input of data into the system or the display of output or a combination of the two. The most common method of entering data into a computer-based system is by keyboarding, although there has been a stigma attached to the skill of typing in recent years. Many older executives refuse to touch a keyboard, and vendors have gone to great lengths to make more "friendly" touch- or voice-activated interfaces, with limited success for the senior executive market. Most younger executives and managers today are computer-literate and find the exercise of power gained by information preferable to the potential embarrassment of being a poor typist!

The success of a dialogue between user and machine involves sharing knowledge by exchanging information, and restrictions imposed by the communications medium usually reduce the success of that dialogue. The greater memory capacity of equipment today makes this easier and cheaper to achieve than in the past. Electronic mail systems, for example, are increasingly tied to the human speech pattern and thus become more popular even among casual users. As another example, menu selection works well for inexperienced users, but regular users need to be able to take shortcuts.

The timing that underlies the software interface is particularly important to the more frequent user, and the popularity of hard-disk-based personal computers attests to the problem. When a user is engaged in solving a problem, delays are disruptive to the thought processes, and the time the user is willing to wait for a response from the system is a function of the user's perceived complexity of the request he or she has made to the system. Booting up a dual-disk personal computer rather than turning on the machine and having it ready, although it only takes about one minute, can seem endless and frustrating to a preoccupied worker intent on solving a problem.

One solution to the complex problems of personal computers has been user groups. At present, there is no formal association among the diverse personal computer groups, although there is an informal exchange of newsletters and software. These groups have been formed by individuals who have congregated to get the best out of their brand of personal computer. While many groups get aid and cooperation from the manufacturer, this is not universally true. The exploding personal computer magazine industry also offers detailed assistance to readers.

5.2 USER MOTIVATION

One of the attractions of an individual personal computer or workstation is its immediacy. Equipment can be installed in days or even hours, and useful applications can sometimes be implemented in a similar time scale. It is this characteristic of the information technology equipment that is focusing users' attention on the potential benefits of integrated systems.

Another attraction is the feeling of independence that is provided. Users like to feel in control of their destiny and, indeed, are often reluctant to allow their terminals to be used by others, even though they may use the terminals themselves for only a couple of hours a day. They like to feel that the equipment is available for their own personal use as and when it is convenient for them. This is part of the territorial attitude that humans have and applies to business telephones and desks as well as terminals.

Without a doubt, the main user motivation for acquiring a personal computer or connected workstation is the perceived business benefits that the machines will provide. The general attitude among the managers and professionals using this equipment is to accept the machines as a worthwhile aid that can be used when appropriate to help the user do his or her job better. There are, nevertheless, subtle pressures also at work. Peer pressures, both within an organization and within professional groups, are also prompting many managers to realize that they too can benefit from using information technology.

This benefit is hard to measure. A number of articles in the press have questioned the "value" of information technology products, and the issue of payoff has been raised. While it is indeed possible to measure productivity improvement in certain jobs, such as clerical or typing, the use by professional and managerial staff is less clearly defined. Information technology products are tools that improve the value and quality of the work these staff produce, and when the work is better, the whole corporation benefits tangibly.

5.3 MANAGING THE HUMAN IMPACT OF TECHNOLOGICAL CHANGE

Office systems are more susceptible to problems in human motivation than traditional data processing because of the greater variety in the types of users and the often significant degree of discretion users have in deciding whether and how they will use the systems.

One school of thought suggests involving employees at the initial planning and testing stages to get early commitment from them. This is an attractive idea, but its success depends on the history and culture of the organization. It is not always the best approach, as staff may attempt to exploit the situation, taking advantage of minor problems to reject the new systems completely, before the systems have had a chance to prove their benefits.

Essentially, the shortcomings of the traditional approaches result from their technical emphasis and the imposition of the chosen solution on the users. This manifests itself in several ways:

- The designers put most effort into the technical aspects of the system, such as screen dialogues, communications protocols, performance prediction, and so on.
- When deadlines are tight and corners have to be cut, the human aspects are often the last items on the planned list of activities that are considered. These activities are concerned with testing, training, and other user-related tasks and, although last in planning lists, are essential to ultimate success.
- Existing work organization and job content are not seriously challenged. Manual procedures in offices have a tendency to become more complex over time, and the exceptions that gave rise to the complexities in the first place have been long forgotten, while the procedures, forms, and methods live on. The result is that the new systems are expected to fit the organization without any changes. Moreover, users often ask for 100 percent automation, not realizing that automating the 20 percent of the work that requires 80 percent of the effort is often the best approach. You do not need a word processor for three-line memos.
- Systems are not consciously planned to provide feedback and to permit change if necessary. Plans are rigid and inflexible and only allow for one possible outcome.
- Training and education are limited to one-way communication from designer to user.

Despite the shortcomings of the traditional approach, designers and planners have usually paid at least lip service to involving users in the process of design and implementation. These users are normally the managers and supervisors in the offices concerned. But even where other levels of employees are involved, this involvement has often just taken the form of interviews to ascertain how the job is done today, not how the job is to be redesigned. This is perhaps an extreme view, but most managers will recognize the familiar elements of the traditional analyst's approach in this description.

Effective technological change requires the involvement of those affected. Change then becomes something that they are part of, something that belongs to them, and something that they want to succeed. Owner-ship has been established. Small problems then become challenges, rather than insurmountable obstacles. The end user will become a source of ideas rather than a source of complications and complaints. In practice, however, involving users is seldom easy, for some of these reasons:

- There are penalties to be paid in involving users, mainly in time and cost increases. The discussions take time, conflicts and disagreements need to be resolved, and everybody involved needs time to learn to work together posi-tively and productively.
- Users have jobs to do. Working on planning a new system, however exciting and interesting, lessens the time they have to do their jobs, thus increasing the pressure on them.
- The user organization's values may run counter to participative approaches of this kind. Not all supervisors and managers will be comfortable with a con-structive approach to resolving difficulties that arise.
- User expectations may be raised too high. Designers and planners may end up with a "wish list" that is impossible to meet.

The short answer to these difficulties is that, despite them, user involve-ment is essential to the success of an integrated systems project and that new ways must be found to overcome them.

There are two approaches that meet the requirements outlined for user involvement. The first is what might be called the participative approach, where end users and their managers and supervisors are included in the design process and in steering the progress of planning and imple-mentation. The overall aim is to encourage users to participate throughout the design process, creating a "window" for user contribu-tions to the design.

The second approach suggests that user involvement should extend beyond the participative approach to incorporate limited use of small-scale systems that provide a learning environment for users, whose experience is then fed back into the design process. Learning then be-comes an evolutionary process, as a series of individual projects allows the organization to reduce the options gradually and hone in on the right kind of system for its needs.

Obviously the approach that is adopted depends on the type of ap-plication being considered. For conventional or back-office systems ap-plications, the degree of technological change demanded of the organization is not so great, and the impact on the organization may well be limited. The participative approach will function adequately in this context, and the involvement of users at this level should be sufficient to achieve commitment. Provided that the changes are explained in terms of what they are going to do for the organization and the benefits to the users, and by downplaying the technology aspects, it will be possible to motivate staff to want office systems.

Strategic or front-office systems—or systems that mean major changes in the way the business objectives are to be achieved and the nature of the work people do—will usually require the second, evolutionary approach. In this case, the specific impact of the office systems themselves is unclear to most users. The organization not only wants to gain the commitment and involvement of users, it needs to find out what the systems are capable of, how they can best be used, how they fit in with existing systems, and so on.

A word of warning. Trial systems and pilot systems can be used as an excuse to bypass normal business investment rules. The organization becomes gradually and unknowingly involved in a project that grows and grows, and it suddenly finds itself irrevocably committed, financially at least, to a major office system project. Therefore, although the learning element in initial office systems projects needs to be acknowledged, such projects should have defined objectives as well. They should be carefully controlled, have a clear start and end, be designed to achieve specific goals, be of short duration, and be evaluated formally so that the lessons can be learned and applied to subsequent projects.

5.4 TRAINING AND EDUCATION

In recent years, a great deal of importance has been attached to providing adequate training for office system users. In general, however, organizations have not invested in high levels of training and support. Typically, after an initial training and education effort, during which large general-purpose office systems were installed, the training and support effort fell to quite low levels.

Some firms, granted, have well-established in-house training centers, but on the average, only a small percentage of the corporate budget for automation goes toward training. Managers requesting, or being given, personal computers or other terminals are frequently left to learn while they work—an expensive training method. Indeed, this lack of follow-up and service can frustrate users to the point where they refuse to use the equipment originally requested and certainly attempt no further exploration of the potential information possibilities.

Key staff involved in planning and installing integrated systems often stress the need to carry out an initial large-scale education exercise to ensure that the early office system installations are successful. Once any early psychological barriers have been overcome and successful systems installed, user demand for office system facilities, together with assistance from colleagues already using the system, typically overcome any limitations in the formal training programs. Even if formal training is inadequate, if the system is widely accepted, users will learn.

For examples, one company employed one person to support more than 1,000 electronic mail users, while another firm used five staff to support more than 2,000 users of a multifunction general-purpose office system. A senior vice-president at a major brokerage, who worked an average 70-hour week, most of it traveling, asked for a personal computer. When it arrived, she had to teach herself from the literature that accompanied the software package. The exceptions to this training laxity are either systems that require quite intense but short-term training, and senior management training, which is usually demanded and given individually.

In-house training has a number of advantages beyond the obvious disadvantages of being labor intensive and time-consuming. It is probably less costly than hiring an outside trainer, and it can be tailored to meet specific corporate needs. Having such instructor-intensive training allows flexibility of training to meet the abilities and needs of the different staff being trained. The investment in personnel and materials to establish an in-house program probably pays for itself quickly in large firms with extensive installations. Post-training testing of proficiency is also easily accomplished with in-house training. In-house staff also allow for preinstallation training as well as ongoing refresher courses designed for new applications and needs.

Training is available from avenues other than in-house staff. The vendors of the hardware often offer complete training programs, as do independent firms who either train on their site or yours. Computer-aided instruction is another way to teach staff, although the human interface is usually necessary at some point. Many firms today have begun writing their own training programs with the aid of authoring software. These programs offer flexibility to create programs that firms are unable to purchase and to tailor them specifically to their needs and applications.

Vendor programs for training can range from simple to complex and can cover either the general system or the specifics of one or two applications. These courses can be costly, and it is possible to arrange group rates in some instances. The vendors can often handle the training at your location if proper equipment and space are available. Vendors usually have adequate equipment for hands-on training, where independents may not because the necessary investment is high. Vendor training offers little in the way of back-up support or follow-up, and the demand on them is such that many firms may not be able to schedule timely training sessions. Also, vendors who provide free training often provide only limited services, and you may find that additional "help" must be purchased.

There are hundreds of independent firms offering computer training. Some firms who sell hardware and software find that their customers demand support during the initial setup phase, and refreshers to keep them current on software changes. For example, in New York City, Businessland will help you plan, select, and install a local area network, then provide your staff with training and service support. Some firms specialize in training only on specific software applications. These firms are usually small businesses, although some of the major employment services in the United States now offer staff training, particularly for word-processing and spreadsheet applications. One advantage of independent training firms is their impartiality: Because they do not sell equipment, they can give a more balanced view overall. Independents can often be more flexible in offering finely targeted training or a variety of training locations. However, this type of training can be costly, and once the training is complete, you have to re-hire the trainer the next time you need such services.

When dealing with integrated systems, the level of knowledge of the training staff must go well beyond that of the general PC user. One of the difficulties of implementing successfully integrated systems is that many people find learning such systems as SNA or DISOSS extremely difficult. Hence, few competent staff are available to train others in the use of the system. And the independent training firms cannot offer state-of-the-art training in systems for which the vendor cannot offer adequate training to begin with, even though the vendors created the system.

Many vendors now have training films, video cassettes, and printed training manuals. While these are extremely costly to produce, they do allow flexibility in learning times, so that staff can work at their own pace. Some companies feel, however, that self-training is time-consuming, expensive, and not as productive as classroom tutorials. Most people are more used to classroom learning and prefer it to watching a video or reading four hefty manuals, which are frequently poorly written. Computer-aided instruction—wherein the computer screen literally "talks" you through the learning process—is becoming more sophisticated and user friendly but still assumes a basic understanding that may or may not be present.

Part of any user training must be an education and understanding of some of the legal technicalities of software ownership. While many firms pay little attention to this issue, software vendors are particularly sensitive to unauthorized copying and use of their proprietary packages. Most software comes with the license agreement attached to the outside of the off-the-shelf software package, but few take the time to read it. Some software firms stringently enforce their "no back-up copy" rule, and management would be wise to understand these rules before they purchase the products.

Many vendors of larger software systems only license end use of their product, and backing up this type of software is usually illegal. Guidelines should be established to keep software inventories by serial number to protect the firm against theft and bogus copies. Including this kind of education in training programs will serve to protect the firm while dispelling the idea that unauthorized copying is condoned.

5.5 MONITORING AND AUDITING THE USE OF OFFICE SYSTEMS

Office systems present a challenge to any company that wants to monitor and control their use. This challenge arises from the inherent characteristics of office systems themselves and from the office environment in which they operate:

- Because office systems are distributed on desktops throughout the company, responsibility for their efficient operation tends to be diffused.
- Office system costs include a large fixed component, and, as a result, management attention tends to be focused on the acquisition costs.
- Except in large-scale clerical operations, such as those in banks and insurance companies, work measurement and predetermined work standards are rare in offices. Versatility is encouraged, and the organizational relationships are more dynamic than they would be in a factory, for example. Therefore, any measurement is more difficult, and the results limited in applicability.
- Office system users, particularly managers and professionals, have a good deal of discretion in when and how they use a system.

It should be emphasized that in many instances comprehensive methods for monitoring and control are not required, and there may be a danger of using overmeasurement as a substitute for clear, well-defined objectives. Setting clear objectives and measuring a limited but relevant set of criteria is important, despite the fact that for most user companies, the use of office systems is still in its early stages. But this very newness of office systems makes it all the more important to learn from any experience gained already, however limited.

Controlling the acquisition process and work measurement are both valid approaches to controlling office systems, but they do not fully address all the control requirements normally specified by management—namely, effectiveness, efficiency, and economic acquisition (Exhibit 5.1).

Effectiveness is concerned with the contribution of the office systems to the goals of the firm. Does the system meet its objectives? Is the value received consistent with the cost of the system investment? The control requirements for effectiveness can be subdivided into two groups—strategic goals and operations goals. The strategic goals are the business goals to which the system is to contribute such as to increase the

Exhibit 5.1

Relationship of Control Methods to Management's Control Requirements

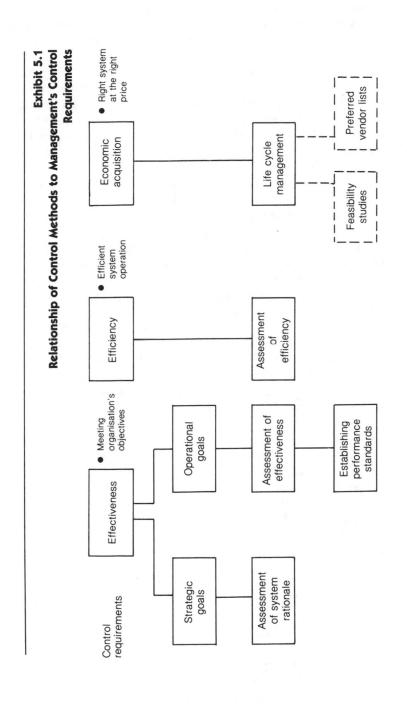

share of customer's orders or to improve clerical productivity. The operational goals are related to more immediate system parameters such as the backlog of documents for word processing, electronic mail messages sent/received, and time spent on different system tasks.

The control methods for effectiveness are *assessment of system rationale* (a periodic review that examines the basic rationale for the continuing existence of the system in relation to the strategic goals set by the company) and *assessment of effectiveness* (periodic or ongoing assessment that monitors the performance of the system). Baseline standards need to be established ideally when the system is first installed or, subsequently, by reference to other systems or to published standards.

Efficiency requirement is concerned with the efficiency of the system. Could the same results be achieved at lower cost? Is the system used properly? The control method here, *assessment of efficiency* of office systems' operation, is concerned with access to the system (are some of the workstations underutilized?), with system operation practices (back-up files, hours of operation), and with the cost and effectiveness of maintenance services, technical support, and so on.

Economic acquisition requires correct management of the office system life cycle and acquisition of equipment, software, and related services under terms and conditions favorable to the company. Is the need for the system clearly identified, and are the specifications defined in such a way that the acquired system will meet user needs in an economical manner? Is the maintenance service cost-effective?

The appropriate control method is *life cycle management*: an ongoing process that begins with the initial identification of the need for a system and ends with disposal of the system at the end of its useful life. Current management practice focuses on two aspects of life cycle management: the feasibility study, which establishes the economic and technical justification for the system, and preferred vendor lists, which is the visible part of a policy that seeks to ensure compatibility between systems and to simplify and improve the purchasing procedures for office systems.

A detailed review of the four types of control systems should provide guidance in their use.

5.5.1 Assessment of System Rationale

A general view of the system is taken in an attempt to decide if the benefits received are worth the cost to the company (Exhibit 5.2). This type of assessment is usually carried out periodically and may be triggered in a number of ways. A reorganization, replacement of obsolete equipment, a cost-cutting exercise, new management—these are all circumstances that may lead to the reexamination of the basic rationale for the continuing existence of the system.

Exhibit 5.2
System Rationale Issues

Type of issues	Basic assessment questions
Systems rationale (Is the value received worth the cost?)	Are the original reasons for the system still valid? Are the results achieved by the system consistent with the original intentions and the intended impacts and effects?
Impacts (What results have been achieved?)	What has happened as a result of installing the system? Does it duplicate, overlap or work at cross-purposes with other systems?
Goals achievement (Has the system performed as expected?)	Did the system meet its original objectives?
Alternatives (Is there some different approach that is less costly or better for doing the job?)	Are there more cost-effective alternative systems? Is there a non-systems alternative?

In many ways, this kind of exercise can be looked at as a reverse planning exercise. Here, the system is already in place, and one attempts to construct a business case that will either justify the continued existence of the system or suggest an alternative, should the result of the assessment be unfavorable.

The steps involved in an assessment of this type are as follow:

1. Understanding the system. The first step is developing a good understanding of the system and the office environment in which it operates. This process involves (a) identifying the background and general structure of the system, (b) checking the general consistency of the system with its objectives, (c) determining the relationships between the system and the business results it is intended to produce, and (d) confirming these details with the appropriate managers.

2. Identifying the purposes of the assessment. The users, the purposes, and the triggering factors for the assessment all influence the focus of the work. For example, some users may require a greater level of precision and more tangible evidence of the results than others.

3. Establishing the assessment criteria. Ideally, this step should comprise two stages. In the first stage, the concerns expressed by the various users or recipients of the assessment results, as they relate to the value of the system

and its cost to the organization, are translated into specific criteria. In the second stage, these criteria are discussed with the users so that priorities can be assigned and the relative importance of the criteria established.

4. Determining the measures to be used. At this point, the way the contribution of the system is to be assessed needs to be determined. If the original purpose was to increase the success rate of customer quotations, for example, or to reduce the effort required to produce monthly statistical reports, then the need is to know how results can be measured. In the absence of direct measures, what proxy measures can be used? The latter may take the form of operations measures (for example, time now taken to turn around a quotation, compared with the time it used to take) if the impact on the business is too difficult to measure, or where a direct cause-and-effect relationship between the system and its intended effect is too difficult to establish. If such data are not readily available, then a data collection program may need to be set up. This will usually take the form of a "snapshot" of the current performance and costs. In the absence of any norms or previously established standards (frankly, a more typical situation), the performance will have to be assessed against current needs.

5. Analyzing the information. Once the information has been collected and any additional survey completed, it must be analyzed to provide answers to the questions addressed by the assessment. This analysis may include the following types of issues: describing the office workers and sites included; referring to the sources of information used and their reliability; specifying the assessment criteria, which might be in tangible or intangible terms; relating the system to the impact it has achieved and to its original goals; estimating the effects of the system and its value; identifying the reasons for the effect achieved or the failure to achieve effects; relating the costs to the value received from the system; or generalizing the results to the total set of workstations/systems, if only a sample was looked at in detail.

6. Examining alternatives. Where the balance of cost and value is unfavorable, alternatives need to be identified. Specific questions that need to be considered here include these: Can the system be eliminated altogether? Does it do more than is necessary for its basic purpose? Are the standards achieved really necessary? Could the system be replaced by an external service or be combined with a system elsewhere in the company? Does the system duplicate an activity carried out elsewhere?

7. Formulating conclusions. The results of the assessment are documented, reviewed, and discussed with the users of the assessment.

8. Developing recommendations. The typical assessment of system rationale provides recommendations for further action where necessary. In particular, a study of the effectiveness of system operations may be suggested.

5.5.2 Assessment of Effectiveness

The assessment of effectiveness is designed to determine how well the operational goals of the systems are being met. Any assessment of effectiveness and productivity will be concerned with performance measure-

Exhibit 5.3
Assessing the Effectiveness of an Office System

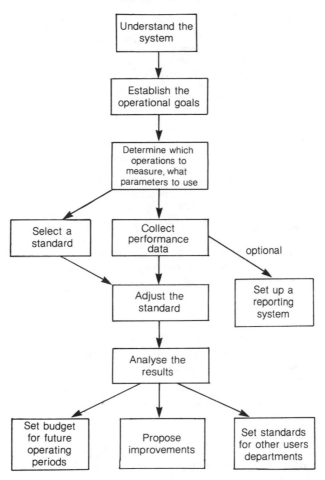

ment and with establishing performance standards. As a general rule, the scale of benefits expected should considerably exceed the cost of undertaking the assessment of effectiveness, which can be substantial. The steps in the assessment follow a logical pattern, but it must be emphasized they may lead to setting up permanent systems for measuring performance, and they may therefore represent an ongoing commitment (Exhibit 5.3).

Exhibit 5.4
Sample Parameters of Office Systems Effectiveness

Productivity
- Hours worked per activity
- Documents completed
- Requests for information handled
- Number of records processed
- Revisions to spreadsheet file
- Client contacts in period
- Overtime worked
- Idle times

Service levels
- Work backlogs, work in process at key points
- Time to process transactions
- Hours of the day when service provided
- Ratio of worst delay to average delay
- Time to handle priority cases

Quality control
- Number of recycled transactions
- Proportion of spot-checked transactions
- Number of spot-checked transactions with errors
- Complaints received

1. Understanding the system. The system's role in the user company is clarified. The organizational relationships and paper flow are documented. Forms and sample inputs and outputs are collected.

2. Establishing the operational goals. User goals are identified and translated into operational goals. These are verified against the original system objectives.

3. Determining which operations to measure and what parameters to use. Measures are chosen which best reflect the operational goals. This means deciding what operations shall be measured and identifying units of work that can easily be counted (see examples in Exhibit 5.4).

4. Selecting a standard. A standard is required for each operation. Service levels, productivity, and quality control all require that norms be established. Where such norms were not established at the time the system was set up, there are two choices available: Predetermined standards can be used (based on data for several hundred offices that provide standards for typical office operations, these have been developed by several office systems consultants). Or standards based on estimates or post-production measurements can be used (this requires that a baseline study be made to accumulate performance data).

5. Collecting performance data. Survey forms and interviews are used to collect performance data for each of the parameters. The size of the sample and the

length of time over which data are collected depend on the reliability required and the scope of the assessment.

6. Setting up a reporting system. Supervisors of large operations may want a continuing means of measuring how well staff are performing against the standards, or compared with previous periods. This requires regular production reports normally limited to a few key parameters (although reports are not required in all cases).

7. Adjusting the standard. Before using the standard, allowances need to be made for personal time and other variations peculiar to the office or company being measured.

8. Analyzing the results. The results of an analysis of performance data and of standard performance levels are assessed. Significant differences are analyzed in detail so that explanations for variances can be prepared. Actual details of the analysis will vary with the operational goals and parameters used. Three subsequent steps may follow:

   1. Setting targets for future operating periods. The results of the assessment can be used to set targets for future operating periods, either to maintain existing performance or to improve performance.

   2. Proposing improvements. Detailed analysis may reveal ways in which the system could be improved, either through new equipment and software or by changing user procedures.

   3. Setting standards for other users or departments. The assessment provides the basis for new or revised standards. These can be used for planning purposes or for assessing other users and departments.

5.5.3 Assessment of Efficiency

The emphasis of an assessment of office system efficiency will be on the cost and effectiveness of support services, the efficiency of operational practices, and the provision of access to the system. The benefits are not likely to be major in terms of financial savings, but improvements could affect effectiveness quite significantly.

Actual levels of equipment utilization are frequently a secondary issue in assessing the efficiency of office systems, unlike the data-processing environment where this is a major concern. Checklist items to consider in reviewing system efficiency include the following:

1. Support services. Are systems adequately documented? What are the training policies for new staff? What maintenance services are provided? Is technical support available to users? Are tests made of new software packages before distribution to users? What is the cost of support services? Could it be reduced? Is the level of support services consistent with real user needs?

2. Operational practices. Are file back-up procedures in place? Have security needs been addressed? What arrangements have been made for emergency repair or provision of replacement equipment? Is equipment insured?

3. Provision of system access. Are there sufficient workstations to meet user needs? Are they convenient to user work locations? What are the hours of operation for common services such as electronic mail or voice mail? What about access to printers or other peripherals? Are there superfluous workstations? Could alternative access be provided at less cost?

5.5.4 Life Cycle Management

Any individual office system can be considered to have a life cycle consisting of five stages (Exhibit 5.5). Each of these stages must be properly managed, and decisions must be supported by good information if value is to be obtained when acquiring equipment and software. These are the five stages:

• *Definition of needs*. The basic need for the system should be clearly defined in terms of what it is going to do for the company. The level of the need must also be defined, such as how many offices will be affected, for example.

• *Specifications*. The specifications translate the needs into a description of the system that is required to meet those needs. They define how many workstations will be required, where they will be located, the software, ongoing support, and so on.

• *Acquisition*. This stage covers the acquisition of the equipment, software, and services, including purchase, lease, and rental.

• *In-service*. During the service life of the system, maintenance and support will be required, software and equipment will be updated, and management will need to keep track of equipment performance—how it is used and where it is located.

• *Disposal*. This step covers the sale, trade-in, or other disposal of the equipment no longer needed, obsolete, or unserviceable.

An important aspect of life cycle management, especially with large numbers of user sites, is the regular gathering of information on usage, user profiles, and user problems to help with the decisions that need to be made at each stage of the life cycle.

Most user firms are very conscious of the need to manage the first three stages of this life cycle. This is consistent with the way in which office system costs are incurred, with a high fixed cost at the acquisition stage. The areas most in need of attention are the provision of repair and maintenance services, and keeping records of the performance and utilization of systems, particularly personal computer-based systems.

How can control be exercised effectively over the system life cycle? The answer is straightforward: The organization needs to recognize the ex-

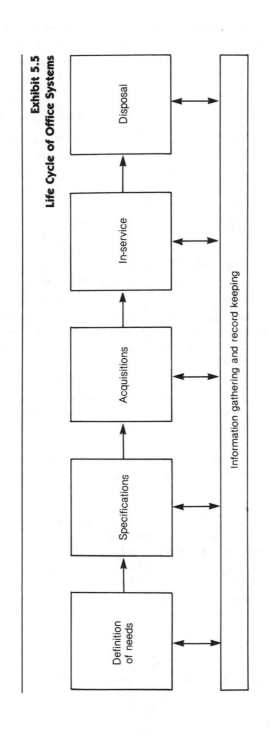

Exhibit 5.5
Life Cycle of Office Systems

Definition of needs

Specifications

Acquisitions

In-service

Disposal

Information gathering and record keeping

istence of the stages described and take steps to ensure that procedures are in place to govern the management of each stage. These could be as simple as a requirement that the conclusion of each stage is signed off, with a standard checklist to be completed in each case.

5.5.5 Setting up Control Systems

A reporting system can be of great assistance in ensuring that planned-for benefits are achieved, because of the feedback to the responsible managers. Setting up such a system can be a formidable task, depending on the nature of the intended benefits and how they were stated in the first place. The more strategic benefits can be especially difficult to assess in retrospect, which is why organizations frequently abandon any attempt to assess them. It might also be argued that the money is already spent on the system; therefore, no amount of reporting will help matters. This latter argument misses the point that the system may be costing money, or that adjustments might bring greater benefits.

At the heart of management's difficulty in these cases is the way in which the system was justified and planned in the first place. If the prime system benefit was stated in such general terms as "improving customer service levels," then management faces a difficult task indeed. A proxy, or substitute measure such as "number of messages sent/received via the electronic mail system" would be more readily assessable. Therefore, the answer lies in expressing the system objectives in precise terms. These will not always be measurable in a strict numerical sense but should certainly be visible, or capable of being assessed, even if only subjectively.

The manager seeking to set up a reporting system to ensure that benefits are being achieved has three options, all of which may be applied:

1. Periodic surveys of customers or staff, for example, to determine whether improvements have been observed in the target areas. These surveys can be on a sample and can ask respondents to rate the results on a scale. By compiling and comparing the results for each period, managers can determine if the planned-for benefits are being achieved.

2. Direct measurement of results or, where appropriate, use of an operational measure such as work backlogs.

3. Formal performance measurement exercises (Exhibit 5.6). Consulting firms are frequently called upon to carry out this type of study. Such a study would normally lead to recommendations for remedial action and might lead to major changes in the system or its replacement. It is common to use consultants for this type of impartial review, but too often the consultants are used as scapegoats as well when suggested changes do not work as projected.

Exhibit 5.6

Carrying Out a Sample Study of Office System Performance

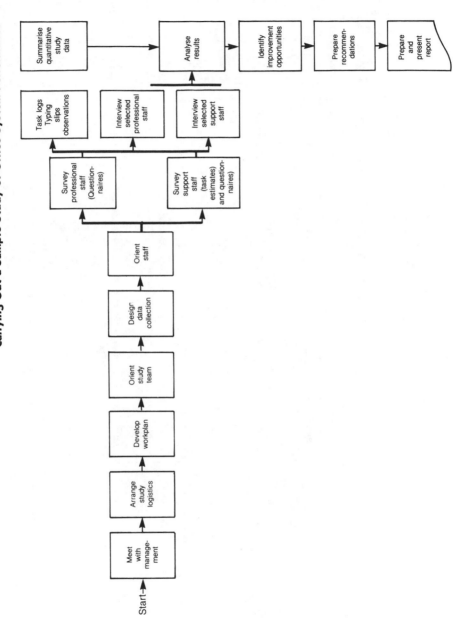

Exhibit 5.8
Typical Results of a Performance Measurement Study

- *Staffing allocations and costs:* derived from salary and staff information provided by the department liaisons. Other target areas analysed/developed from this information could be:
  — Overall department support costs
  — Professional-to-secretary and clerical staff ratio
  — Cost per professional
  — Average annual salary
  — Profile of permanent/temporary help.

- *Distribution of secretarial and clerical staff time:* derived from the daily task logs. Staff equivalents and costs for the distribution of time are derived by analysing/comparing staff costs with time distribution. In addition, the following subject areas are highlighted under this heading:
  — Breakdown of activities, e.g., clerical, secretarial, document production, other, etc., and definitions
  — Unit costs by activity
  — Allocation of staff by time distribution (number of workers by activity).

- *Professional/secretarial and clerical staff time estimates:* derived from the task estimate sections of the staff questionnaires. This can be used to compare staff estimates to actual distribution of time from daily task logs. Also included under this heading are:
  — Comparison of task logs and estimates
  — Professional/secretarial perception of how time is spent
  — Agreement/disagreement and validation of task log data
  — Any perceptions which directly apply from interviews.

- *Service levels:* derived from the task logs. Typical areas that would be highlighted are:
  — Backlog of work (average, daily variations)
  — Turnaround time to respond to external requests for information, and to complete support tasks (e.g., typing). This will be classified by type of work and priorities.

- *Profile of typed documents:* derived from a typing slip summary. It provides an overview of all documents produced. It is used to assess:
  — Turnaround requirements (from professional questionnaires)
  — Volumes of high/standard/low priority work
  — Satisfaction with typing support (from questionnaires)

- *Observed distribution of time:* derived from an observation summary. It provides observations on time distribution and identifies idle/away from desk time. Areas under this heading would include:
  — Cost of away from desk/idle time
  — Validation of results from task logs.

(Exhibits 5.7 and 5.8 summarize typical forms used and results gathered by consulting firms.)

Quality control is normally intended to control the incidence of errors. For example, in office paperwork there are several ways in which errors can arise. The frequency of occurrence will vary, and there may be a question about exactly what constitutes an error in a particular office operation. For example, the impact of spelling errors might be relatively minor in an invoice, whereas a numerical error might be very significant indeed.

There are three parts to any effort to control quality:

1. A decision must be made on what is to be checked. This poses a question of the impact of errors. If the impact of errors is great, then a large sample (perhaps even 100 percent) needs to be checked. Few quality control reviews cover 100 percent of the items processed, and a sample is nearly always used.
2. Work needs to be spot-checked. This is normally done by the supervisor, in accordance with a predetermined frequency.
3. A formal quality audit of work may be carried out, usually by the internal auditor of the organization-and-methods group. If financial records are involved, the external auditors may audit a transaction sample and review system controls.

The need for quality control can be much reduced in an office systems environment, particularly for applications that involve numerical data. By designing appropriate transaction controls into the system (like using batch controls), errors in key fields can be detected upon input. The system could maintain price lists and customer address details, reducing the possibility of error. Such controls are commonplace in data-processing systems.

Because office systems are not always formally designed in the same way as data-processing systems, managers should be sensitive to the possible lack of these controls and the resulting potential for error. For example, clerical staff may use a personal computer data management package such as dBase III to maintain records about clients. The only verification may be visual inspection of the screen as information is entered, or an inspection of a printout of the file contents. Spot checks by a supervisor may therefore be desirable so that the likelihood of errors can be assessed, and reduced.

The institution of organizational policies and procedures is designed to set the ground rules for certain aspects of the management of office systems. Thus, one of the most frequently used such policies is the use of preferred vendor lists. The intention of the company is usually to enable office systems to be mutually compatible. For example, a policy frequently encountered prescribes that only personal computers compatible with the IBM personal computer may be purchased. To ensure that such a policy is carried out, the purchasing department may have instructions to review all purchase orders and to refer purchase orders for other types of personal computers to the MIS department. This procedure is designed to implement one component of the company's office system policies (although it causes considerable anguish among non-IBM personal computer manufacturers!).

The use of formal procedures is well suited to ensuring that system life cycle management is effective, particularly in the early stages of needs identification, specification of the equipment, and acquisition. Later stages of the life cycle are less visible, and any procedures are correspondingly difficult to enforce.

On the question of effectiveness and efficiency controls, formal procedures can be used to specify the circumstances under which assessments will take place and their frequency and scope. These are the limitations, however, in the use of such procedures:

- They are applicable only to certain aspects of the control of office systems.
- Procedures depend on cooperation in all parts of the organization, and their effectiveness may well be highly dependent on the status and power of the department that issues them or is responsible for seeing that they are enforced.
- The procedures may be seen by departmental managers as conflicting with their own objectives. With office systems, individual expenditures on items such as personal computers can be relatively small. Therefore, departmental managers may decide to bypass normal purchasing procedures to achieve an immediate short-term objective.
- Management is usually aware of the risk concerning general policies. Effective applications or the economical acquisition of office systems may result in specific procedures that are counterproductive if rigorously applied in every circumstance. Unfortunately, the response to this problem tends to lead to bureaucracy by making the procedure more complex, with various exceptions and eventualities taken care of by sub-clauses, footnotes, and so on.

A budget is a specific plan of action against which progress can be measured over a specific period. The focus of the budget is on the cost of the office system rather than on the results.

By dividing the costs by project or by program, it is possible to determine how costs are being incurred, and to use cost targets for these items as a means of control. In reality, this will only work fairly if all office expenses, including staff, are included in the budget and the cost calculations. Thus the impact of the office system on total office costs can be assessed. If certain goals are associated with different office system projects, progress toward these goals can be assessed, usually qualitatively, providing input for a management decision on the value received.

Exhibit 5.9

Example of a Project or Program Budget

Item	Current month			Year to date			Results Achieved
	Budget	Actual	Over (Under)	Budget	Actual	Over (Under)	
Projects/Programmes							
A. Document production	$10000	$11500	$1500	$50000	$58000	$8000	— 2/3rds of documents turned around in less than 1 day.
B. Monthly sales reports	$3000	$2500	($500)	$15000	$12500	($2500)	— Ready by third working day etc.
. . . other items							
Total							

As an example, the project budget in Exhibit 5.9 is for document production. A target for monthly costs is set at the beginning of the budget period, and in the example, these costs have been exceeded. However, the results column shows that two-thirds of documents are being turned around in less than one day, which provides management with feedback on the results achieved in nonmonetary terms.

The key rationale behind the use of budgets for control purposes is that a budget focuses on costs. If some of the desired results can be expressed in the same terms (such as staff savings and expense reductions), then this is helpful. However, simply categorizing costs into meaningful line items can help by making these items more visible. Management is then in a better position to examine what has been achieved.

As an alternative, an office system budget can be used in conjunction with work measurement, with the work items set out as targets to be achieved, usually in terms of volumes to be processed. Costs may not even be included in this case.

5.6 THE USER EXPERIENCE—CASE STUDIES

The next section will review some case histories of users' experiences with office systems. Some overall lessons emerge:

- Progress involves changes, and organizations may need to change both current policies and management responsibilities to achieve controlled progress in the office. In the early stages of development, departmental managers and staff set the pace in developing new systems. As this process gathers momentum in different departments, the level of aggregate cost and the risks of proliferating the incompatible sub-systems both become obvious. Management action needs to be early, decisive, and firm.
- Users need support, often much more basic and fundamental than is often supposed.
- Progress takes longer than expected, and simply plopping a terminal on 100 desks does not necessarily accomplish the goal of systems integration.
- Cost displacement is irrelevant to some applications, so no single yardstick of cost-benefit appraisal is useful in every case. Applications with a specific functional target, as noted earlier, usually fall into the back-office category and often produce clearly identified cost reductions. In other application areas, such as electronic mail, tangible cost savings have been harder to pinpoint and may in any case be somewhat irrelevant to the main purpose, as the real benefits may lie in better decision-making or faster response to clients.
- Communication is a big problem, as the inherent incompatibilities of hardware and software become apparent when they are to be linked.
- Every answer creates new questions. Short-term actions toward systems integration need to ease rather than obstruct transition to longer term objectives. Even a dim perception of the distant goals is better than none.

- Believe only half the promises, because not all technical solutions are equal to the task and suppliers still fail to deliver as much as promised.
- There is no universal solution to systems integration. No single method of planning, developing, and implementing office systems is right for all organizations. Nevertheless, a planning framework (see Chapter 6) can form the nucleus of a successful approach.

The Chase Manhattan Bank is one of the largest banks in the United States. It has over 300 branches, 50 major international subsidiaries, and 600 correspondent bankers, as well as 36,000 employees and $81 billion in assets. In 1979, Chase made a commitment to develop its office automation arena to the extent that in 1983 it invested $40 million in office automation.

The first issue to be addressed was whether to centralize or decentralize office systems decision-making. The company resolved this issue by developing an innovative tier approach, which directly involved individuals contemplating automation of their departments. These are the three tiers:

- Tier 1: Projects needing a corporatewide strategy and corporate-level implementation.
- Tier 2: Projects needing corporatewide strategy, but which are implemented at the sector level, such as arranging access to data bases.
- Tier 3: Projects needing only corporate guidelines and standards, with their implementation accomplished independently by the user sectors, such as individual professional workstations.

Chase considered several areas to be crucial to success, including interpersonal communications, executive, professional, and administrative support, environmental and human factors, and networking access. The company also placed a great emphasis on projects that provided the earliest productivity gains—namely, expanding administrative support, developing an electronic mail system with a high level of penetration among users, and tailoring executive support to unique business needs.

Today, Chase's office system base is substantial. It embraces both Wang and IBM systems, and several thousand personal computers, major Wang equipment, a Wang Mailway electronic mail system with thousands of mailboxes, and a Wang network. The electronic mail system was designed to overcome communications problems with Chase's overseas operations, especially the U.S.-Europe link. The original system used a pouch with a four-day turnaround. The present Wang Mailway system provides overnight turnaround. The electronic mail strategy is only about half complete with over 4,000 mailboxes in place. Some of these are used by more than one person, for example in Sweden, where 12 to 15 people can share one mailbox.

Chase is now looking at integrated voice/data terminals, has made some investment in voice store-and-forward systems, and has established a local area network linking several of the bank's downtown Manhattan facilities.

Lederle Laboratories is a manufacturer of pharmaceuticals and over-the-counter drug products. With revenues of nearly $1 billion, it is the largest subsidiary of American Cyanamid. There are approximately 4,000 staff, and about one-fourth of them are involved in office work. The medical research division has led the corporation in computer technology and applications since 1977, when it bought a Digital Equipment Company mainframe and five VAX superminicomputers. They later added DECmates for word processing, and eventually desktop personal computers.

The personal computer influx allowed end users to develop their own applications. But it soon became clear that the personal computer held the potential for unnecessary duplication of both information and processing resources. A mechanism was needed for central control of information systems that would at the same time allow the business groups autonomy to develop and implement their own office system applications.

Lederle's response to managing the proliferation of personal computers is indicative of the company's philosophy and reflects how the company has since organized to meet its information requirements. The corporate information services group issued vendor-of-choice lists for personal computers and word processors. These included the vendors with whom Lederle was already doing business, personal computers that could interface with the installed base of equipment, and the names of vendors who could reasonably be expected to remain in business after the expected shakeout in personal computer manufacture.

In 1981, management consultants were retained to conduct a strategic planning study for information systems within the Cyanamid Group. This study helped to initiate the thrust toward further decentralizing information services functions. Each of Cyanamid's business groups was given its own information services group, who had responsibility for implementing its own programs. Central control for information service planning and administration was placed in the corporate information services group. An office automation committee was established in 1982, consisting of members from information services and some end users.

No single body has responsibility for the full range of office automation activities and applications at Lederle. Telex and facsimile services are provided through a corporate services wire room, while print and photographic services are handled through a corporate service center. The company has not yet integrated data and voice systems, but it plans to introduce digital switching for voice and data communications in the near future. At present, Lederle uses a variety of office systems, including an automated project management system, a word-processing center with two satellite systems, distributed word processing and personal computing, electronic mail, and computer-assisted information retrieval. Preliminary trials have been conducted in new applications such as voice mail and local area networking.

Pharmaceutical companies have been leading users of voice mail, especially in field sales, where traveling salespeople need good links with their base. In late 1983, Lederle conducted a pilot study in voice mail. Users were provided with access to a time-sharing service through their standard push-button telephones. Each user has a voice mailbox, which can send, receive, reply to, and redirect voice messages. Messages may be sent with a single call to one voice mailbox at a time or to a group of voice mailboxes. When a user receives voice messages, he or she has the option of discarding them, saving them, replying immediately, or redirecting them to others who may need the information.

The users have responded in various ways to the voice mail system. The field sales support staff was highly enthusiastic. These agents had previously relied on telephone and written messages for communication with their home office and with delays resulting from telephone tag. Voice mail allowed them to keep informed without reducing time spent on sales activities. Clinical field agents were equally positive about the application, which they used for communicating between hospitals or universities, where clinical studies were being conducted, and the main corporate research offices.

Outside the field sales and clinical areas, however, user response to voice mail at Lederle was more restrained. As about half of Lederle's income is derived from international sales, the medical research division relies on a high volume of international communications. These are currently handled through long-distance telephone communications, written messages sent by special couriers, and electronic mail using Tymnet and VAX-Mail. Voice mail has not yet been linked to international telephone systems, which limits its applicability for this group. Even so, Lederle's information system management hopes to bring the voice mail system in-house because of the success in the clinical and field sales areas. The information services staff is also exploring the possibility of linking voice mail to the PABX, once the company upgrades to digital switching.

A major U.S. engineering company started its office systems effort in 1980 with a project in its information services group, which handles companywide and scientific data-processing services. The aims of the office system project were to create documents, to send mail electronically, to prepare schedules, to analyze spreadsheets, and to create personal files all on one system.

IBM's menu-driven PROFS software (see Chapter 3) was chosen because, at the time, the company felt it had both the widest range of software and the greatest potential for expansion. It also allowed the company to keep its existing 2,000+ terminal base in place. PROFS was installed in a phased manner. The preprototype phase had eight users in early 1982, followed by the prototype phase with 30 users which lasted for a month later that year. After that, the system grew more rapidly until the current level of nearly 3,500 users was reached.

The company now uses IBM 3279 color terminals, IBM 3287 dot matrix printers, IBM 7436 letter-quality printers, IBM 6670 laser printers running under the VM/CMS operating system, and mainframes, which were upgraded to the present IBM 3083 system. There are, at present, 1,400 users in the main office and over 2,000 across the corporation. The loading system averages about 200 users at a time, and it is strained during peak use periods.

PROFS is used for internal mail among different departments within the corporation. Each department was given the chance to assess the system and then made requests to participate. During the prototype phase, numbers were limited deliberately, but later, however, departments were free to enter the system if they wished.

One of the major barriers to the system's success has been the lack of direct involvement and support by upper management. In particular, senior managers in the finance and administration areas resisted the introduction of new technology.

Another major problem was lack of coordination over supplier selection. One department uses DEC VAX equipment with ALL-in-one software, although an interface between the VAX and IBM system was effected later through DEC gateways. In addition, there are a large number of Wang users in the company. PROFS use is billed to each department monthly and is an expense item; whereas Wang equipment is bought by each area and is therefore a capital cost, not an operating cost. This policy makes PROFS more expensive for the user and therefore affects the extent of its use. The company hopes to interface the Wang OIS system with PROFS through the Wang VS systems, and two Wang VS have been bought for this purpose, although software has only recently become available.

The experience of a West German law firm provides useful lessons for any potential user of integrated systems, particularly for how professional users can benefit. With some 25 partners and over 100 employees, the firm has a strong commercial practice, and much of its work is international. Typical clients are the German subsidiaries of large, multinational companies, which it advises and for which it executes legal transactions. There are few private clients.

Law firms are information intensive. Because of the nature of its client base, at a law firm, efficiency and quality of work are particularly important, as are good communications facilities. In 1980, the firm installed its first system, a Wang WP25 office system. Further systems were added later and expanded as required. The hardware base at present consists of the original WP25 with three terminals, and an OIS140 office system, also from Wang, with 21 workstations. Standard Wang software is used for word processing, and the different applications are based on packages supplied by Wang. The office systems are used mainly for word processing and communications.

The firm has a digital telephone exchange, supplied by Siemens, which allows the firm to keep sophisticated records of telephone costs. It also uses a high-speed telefax, which transmits at 20 seconds per page, and at slower standard speeds as well.

Each secretarial office has one word-processing terminal shared by two secretaries. The word-processing facilities are used for long documents, for documents that are required repeatedly, and for all telex documents. Ordinary typewriters are used for other types of text. Some of the word-processed text segments have been used over 1,000 times. One of these segments has saved about 500 hours of lawyers' time alone, not to mention the savings in secretarial time for keyboarding the text.

The secretaries usually enter and correct text, but about half of the legal professional staff also use the word-processing workstations themselves for minor corrections—some use the system occasionally and some on a regular basis. The word-processing system is closely integrated with electronic mail. This law firm uses an internal mailbox system, but it also linked its word-processing system to the West German teletex system. The internal mailbox system is not considered to be very useful so far. To make it so, a terminal would be needed on every lawyer's desk, but for now such a move cannot be justified by the firm.

The external link with the teletex system is far more important and successful. Messages can be entered and sent by a secretary directly from his or her desk through the word-processing system. This facility has been used extensively: In the first five months of 1985, 3,000 messages were sent in this way to clients, colleagues, and other business contacts. Over two-thirds were out of Germany. Before the teletex link was introduced, one telex terminal was dedicated to outward telexes and was busy between 8 and 12 hours a day.

Avoiding the rekeying of the texts of telex messages has released time equivalent to about one and a half secretaries for other, more important tasks. In addition are the benefits in quality and speed which have been achieved. For example, two lawyers, each in a different city, worked together on a brief, each writing a part of the document and exchanging drafts via teletex. The system allowed the lawyers to beat a tight deadline by writing and editing the brief, printing it, and getting it to court, all within a few hours.

Toybrary is a lending library for children's playthings and adult toys and professional and recreational gear in Vermont. The Novell LAN links just two personal computers, but eliminates the chore of having to swap disks between the two computers and of frantically trying to figure out which disk has a needed file.

The LAN can be expanded to grow with the business—a capability all new business owners hope to need. The PCs, AT&T model 6300s, are used for back-office operations such as spreadsheet analysis, word processing, and database management. With thousands of franchise queries needing to be followed up, the computers have been quite useful. And the franchises themselves use computers to run the Toybraries, keeping track of the 3,000-item inventory in each branch as well as determining who has borrowed an item and for how long.

I/Net, of Michigan, has made a business of capturing full-color pictures, storing them in a mainframe, and then transmitting them to clients throughout the country, particularly real estate multiple listing services. This way prospective buyers can look at a home before making a trip unnecessarily. Another client, Childfind, helps locate missing children.

I/Net uses two IBM System/38 computers as repositories for the pictures. A slide, photograph, or other illustration is digitized with a special device, compressed, and then transferred to a mainframe computer for storage. From the mainframes, the photos can be sent to customers on regular telephone lines. Each image uses between 4 and 7 Kilobytes of the computer's storage space, and one floppy can store about 40 images.

I/Net is currently developing an application to computerize all active passports in the world. Customs agents who question someone's identity would type in the passport number which calls up a picture of the actual passport holder, thus avoiding fraud and potential terrorism.

American Gold Key, of Washington, provides free 3M Whisperwriter teleprinters to its clients who check out prospective renters of apartments and houses through credit ratings, employment histories, and previous landlord references. Prospective renters go to the houses or apartments, fill out applications that list pertinent information and references, and then pay a processing fee. The building's manager or owner then types the applicant's information into the teleprinter and sends it over telephone lines to a teleprinter at American Gold Key. Application information takes about 20 minutes to communicate verbally, but about ten seconds to send over the teleprinter.

After American Gold Key staff check the references, they prepare a report on the prospective renter's history and enter it into a Molecular computer. A client wishing to retrieve the completed report calls the computer's modem, and the file is sent to the teleprinter. Linked to the computer are three personal computers—an NCR Model 6 and two ITT Xtras—which all communicate over a Novell LAN.

The firm is pleased with the process of entering the information via a PC and storing it on the computer for customer access. Six incoming telephone lines for customers have replaced two ITT personal computers used to store and access reports. The old setup severely limited the utility of the personal computers for other tasks, as they had to await client calls. The next step, according to the owner, will be to install a multi-use computer system to allow people to enter information into the computer as each step is completed, rather than waiting until the report is completed.

A British subsidiary of an American multinational firm used to use a forklift to transport their records to the computer. In addition, they spent several thousand dollars a year on services supplied by an IBM computer bureau. They have now switched to a networked computer system to help control production of their products. Although the systems that they purchased may be unfamiliar to American users, the lessons remain the same.

The system they purchased was called Micross, supplied by Kewill Systems. It uses HiNet to transmit the data to the firm's four main buildings. Almost all data traffic is transmitted by the network among the seven terminals and two printers that are connected to it. An IBM PC and a Sirius are also linked into the system.

HiNet is a multidrop network providing 500-baud data transmission. It can support up to 32 users and can address up to 255 others. Data protection is by a "mimic master"—a back-up network master reads all the data that passes through the functional network master, in effect duplicating its data files. Should the functional network master fail, the mimic takes over immediately.

The firm feels that production control benefits are multiple. The prime advantage is production scheduling, as the equipment they manufacture is complex, and usually no two pieces are precisely the same. This means that the route through the factory is probably different each time, and components that are needed to make any particular item are also different from the previous requirement. Now production controllers can input new schedules twice a day if things need to be changed that often. In addition, the firm derived better stock control because the computer always gets the totals correct and because usable stock can be salvaged from obsolete stock. The personal computer searches the stock list for a match and quotes the relevant stock level if it finds one.

The firm also found that the system helped with job costing, as the cost of any job is known more quickly and can be priced more accurately. Finally, bottlenecks can be spotted earlier by clerks using the system, providing them with reasonable time to arrange for sub-contracting or other ways to ease congestion.

The installation was completed with little negative reaction from the 300 staffers, as unconditional assurances were given that the new equipment would not cause redundancies or layoffs. As the staff got used to computers controlling production, keyboard resistance was nil even from people such as drafters who had had no previous experience using terminals. They need only make a few keystrokes to get the answers to their questions. When the system is at its busiest, the response time does not exceed two seconds. Daily back-up on a fast tape streamer is done in a few minutes.[1]

NOTE

1. *Communications* (June 1985).

REFERENCES

Benwell, Nick. "Local Area Network in Metal Manufacture." *Communications* (June 1985): 46–47.

Betts, Mitch. "OA Productivity Requires More Emphasis on Training." *Computerworld* (June 24, 1985):18.

Butler Cox Foundation. "Cost-Effective Systems Development and Maintenance" (August 1983).

Butler Cox Foundation. "The Interface between People and Equipment" (August 1980).

Butler Cox Foundation. "Managing the Microcomputer in Business" (Sept. 1984).

Butler Cox Foundation. "Office Systems: Applications and Organisational Impact" (Dec. 1984).

Felix, Robert G., and William L. Harrison. "Project Management Considerations for Distributed Processing Applications." *MIS Quarterly* (Sept. 1984): 161–170.

Johnson, Bonnie. "From PCs to Integrated Systems," *Words* (June-July 1985): 16–17.

Kliem, Ralph L. "In-House Training for Microcomputer Users." *Administrative Management* (Dec. 1985): 50–51.

Kliem, Ralph L. "Overcoming User Resistance to Microcomputers." *Administrative Management* (May 1986): 52–54.

Steinbrecher, David. "Computers Are Rapidly Changing Business Methods." "Automation Outlook," *Office Administration and Automation* (May 1985):10.

"Training for End Users." *EDP Analyzer* (August 1982).

Williamson, Arthur R. "OA Ergonomics . . . Changing the Workplace to Fit the Worker." *Words* (Feb.-March 1985): 19–22.

6

Planning for Integrated Systems

Over a period of 30 years or more, the data-processing community has evolved a methodology designed to bring the planning and implementation of data-processing projects under its control. This methodology now exists and is widely used. While data-processing projects do still go badly, the explanation is that the methodology is simply not used, or used incorrectly, not that it does not exist. For most of the period in which advanced office systems have been sought, no equivalent methodology actually existed. The tried and tested tools for the control of data-processing projects could be applied to office projects, but they often proved of limited value.

Now that MIS departments are becoming more concerned with integrated systems, if they wish to discharge this responsibility effectively, it is essential that they develop and apply suitable planning and implementation tools. Moreover, this must be done quickly. The evolution of planning tools for integrated systems over a 30-year cycle is not going to be good enough.

The development and adoption of the planning tools outlined in this chapter is a serious and challenging management task, involving both management time and cost. But it is a key task for any manager becoming seriously involved in integrating systems. Without such a planning framework, success will be haphazard, with consequent risks for both the individual and the firm. Office systems are continually evolving, as is the understanding of their capabilities and potential. Users do not need, or even want, a monolithic plan for integrated systems that acts as a constraint on action, rather than providing a positive environment in which successful office systems can be identified, planned, and implemented.

6.1 METHODOLOGIES FOR PLANNING OFFICE SYSTEMS

The requirements for a workable, integrated system planning method may be summarized as follows:

- The planning method must allow for shifts in goals and systems, to reflect experience gained in the organization and changes in the available technologies.
- It must provide room for a mix of standard office solutions and custom-built systems. Where necessary, it must provide for office systems that complement the information systems of the organization.
- It should take advantage of the individual manager's enthusiasm and commitment and encourage initiatives within the organization. Different rates of advance should be possible.

A wide spectrum of potential office systems applications must be provided for, from radical applications that involve major resource commitments and risks, to operational improvements that reduce costs and improve productivity.

There are several ways to plan for integrated systems: productivity-focused planning, information systems planning, and two-level planning. Each has benefits and drawbacks, as will be discussed, but the two-level approach probably is most suitable for comprehensive systems planning.

Productivity-focused planning usually takes as a starting point an analysis of how time is spent by office workers, and then targets the information system at the most labor-intensive activities. This allows identifying the potential time savings to be made. The inherent strength of this method is that it provides a rational, analytical route to identifying office systems that pay off. The weakness lies in the built-in assumption that office systems are only about productivity.

Information systems planning methods are now well established and might appear to offer an alternative approach to more comprehensive office systems planning. Two well-known methods are the Critical Success Factors method and IBM's Business Systems Planning method.

The Critical Success Factors method is for eliciting user requirements. Users are asked to define the factors that are critical to success in performing their business functions or in making decisions. The information needs critical to achieving success are then identified and used as a starting point for planning the integrated system.

The Business Systems Planning methodology, developed by IBM, derives information requirements from the objectives of an organization in a top-down fashion by starting with overall business objectives and then defining business processes (for example, in purchasing or quality control). Business processes are used as the basis for data collection and analysis exercises in which executives are asked to specify key success factors and to identify problems. Logically related categories of business processes and data are then identified and related to business products. Following the definition of an information architecture, application priorities are established and data bases planned.

The primary purposes of these information system planning methods are to define an overall information system, to specify a portfolio of applications and data bases, and to define the detailed information requirements for each application. The approach reflects the way in which traditional data processing works, aiming to automate entire business functions. However, in the context of integrated systems, this approach is not usually the best, as it often makes more sense to automate that 20 percent of office work that yields 80 percent of the benefit. Also, the information requirements of integrated systems represent more than just data—they also include text, voice, and graphics. These considerations limit the use of information systems planning techniques in the office systems context.

The shift to distributed systems, the diffusion of systems throughout the organization with more local autonomy and control over systems, and the integration issues created by increasing penetration and proliferation of information systems have revealed shortcomings in the old central planning processes. To avoid the rigidities and the complexities of coordination, there has been a shift to establishing an appropriate framework or architecture, within which detailed planning can take place.

Corporations are finding that the first priority of successful information systems planning is getting the architecture right, but relying on individual operating units to identify the projects that will meet their business needs. This approach is also applicable to integrated systems planning, which has an important user-driven, or bottom-up, component.

The planning approach derived from this thinking is a two-level one:

1. First, the company sets out a broad definition of aims and tasks and specifies the target areas for information systems. This is the master plan. The technical architecture, the business rules, and the organizational framework are part of

Exhibit 6.1
Thinking Big, Starting Small, and the Role of the Master Plan

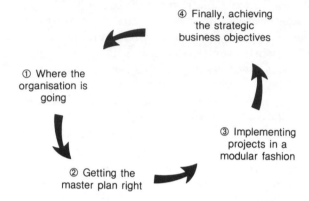

④ Finally, achieving the strategic business objectives

① Where the organisation is going

③ Implementing projects in a modular fashion

② Getting the master plan right

this step, which has as its underlying objective the creation of an environment that will facilitate the individual projects.

2. Next, the individual office system projects are undertaken to meet specific needs as and when they are identified. Each project must be consistent with the master plan.

This type of two-level plan is becoming increasingly common in data processing, office systems, and telecommunications—all the keys to integrated systems (Exhibit 6.1). The main reasons are that a good master plan allows for initiative and flexibility at the local and end-user levels, while recognizing the broader concerns of the organization, the total investment involved, compatibility and communications requirements, and the deployment of technical resources. The philosophy behind this approach is "think big, start small." Having established the master plan, the organization can proceed with considering specific projects that are consistent with the objects of systems integration set out in it.

Individual projects can be tested against the overall rules and criteria outlined in the master plan. Some of these projects will be approved, some not. The aggregate of specific projects is then the total portfolio of office systems. For larger projects, a formal feasibility study will usually be required. For smaller projects, more informal methods of assessing their feasibility will often be more appropriate. The master plan will also evolve under the pressure of business needs and as a result of technologi-

Exhibit 5.7

Summary of Forms Used in a Typical Performance Measurement

Use	Name	Purpose	Completed by	Frequency
Data collection	Principal questionnaire	Obtains qualifiable and quantifiable data regarding the services provided by secretaries and clerical staff	Professionals	One time
	Secretarial/clerical staff questionnaire	Solicits secretaries and clerical staff observations and comments about their daily work activities	Secretaries/clerical staff	One time
	Task estimate sheet	Determines, a priori, how the secretaries and clerical staff estimate their workweek is spent	"	One time
	Daily task log	Records time spent on tasks each day	"	Daily
	Typing slip	Records time, volume, priority, document type, and input source of all typed material for establishing document profile and productivity	"	Daily for each document typed
	Observation sheet	Records observed activity of secretaries and clerical staff according to established schedule	Study team	Daily
	Interview guides	Provide a standard structure for obtaining specific information from interviews with secretaries, supervisory staff	"	Each interview
Tabulation	Summary sheets	Data submitted by survey participants for summarisation and tabulation	"	

Exhibit 6.2
The Logical Planning Cycle

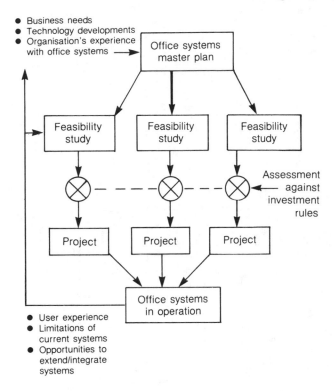

cal developments. The result is planning, rather than plans, and the flexibility to react to changing circumstances as they arise (Exhibit 6.2).

6.2 ELEMENTS OF THE MASTER PLAN

The master plan can be seen as a process that comprises two elements: One resolves the strategic issues involved for the organization, and the other provides the planning infrastructure for the future (Exhibit 6.3).

The strategic level divides readily into four steps:

1. Defining the organization's needs, both long- and short-term goals, should include any threats posed by competition, constraints due to resource or technical shortcomings, and any other key issues that might conceivably be resolved in some way by the use of integrated systems.
2. Identifying the office system opportunities is an iterative process, as the

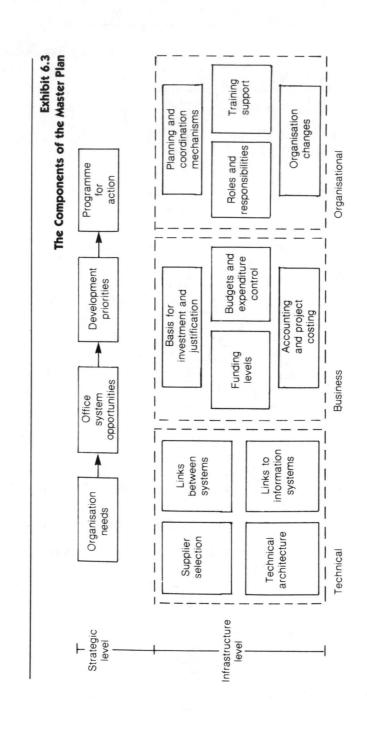

Exhibit 6.3
The Components of the Master Plan

search for opportunities works both top-down, starting with the organization's objectives, and bottom-up, starting with potential technology solutions.

3. Establishing the development priorities needs to be worked out to allow decisions to be taken. Some opportunities provide a greater payoff than others. Some cost more or are riskier and more complex or depend on the prior implementation of other system components. The approximate costs and benefits and system interrelationships need to be worked out.

4. Developing a program for action is not intended to produce a detailed step-by-step plan for every office in the organization. At the same time, the desired results will not happen by themselves.

The program for action is concerned with setting up the essential infrastructure—technical, business, organizational—and with setting out the work program for the first planning period in overall terms.

The other part of the master plan provides the blueprint for the infrastructure. A good infrastructure will allow considerable flexibility at the individual office or group level in terms of types of systems and applications. This will depend on the following:

- The significance of office operations to the business of the organization
- The size of the organization, the number of departments or work groups, and the composition of the work force
- The experience of the organization with office and information systems and the available in-house resources
- The relative autonomy of managers within the organization and the diversity and geographic scope of its operations
- The scope for and impact of office systems
- The level of sophistication of the plans for office system technology
- The need to link the systems with one another and with the information systems

The key issue involving the technical infrastructure is the requirement for and the ability of office systems to link and fit together both with one another and with the organization's information systems. In addition, they must have the ability to grow over time to meet user needs, and the suppliers and in-house technical staff must be able to provide support. The need to meet these requirements has led many users to choose a one-vendor policy. However, the organization may pay a considerable premium for such a policy, which is not necessarily warranted by the benefits achieved.

Nevertheless, there may be a case for choosing such a policy, or for limiting the number of vendors. A statement of policy of supplier selection, and any requirement for MIS/data processing (or the responsible manager or steering group) to approve exceptions, should be a part of the master plan infrastructure.

The basic thrust of the master plan will in many cases be a mixture of front-office and back-office projects—the former designed, for example, to give a competitive advantage and to improve directly the service offered to customers and clients, and the latter designed to improve productivity and to achieve cost savings.

The master plan must specify the rules for investment in these projects—how they are to be paid for, the pricing of common internal services, and the pay-back periods. Equally important, the master plan should establish the funding levels and how budgets and expenditures and the measurement of benefits will be controlled.

The mechanisms for planning and coordinating the master plan will need to be set up and roles and responsibilities assigned. Some reorganization may be required. At its simplest, this may require only the setting up of a small project team to provide training and support, or an expansion of the existing technical support team in the MIS department to cover integrated systems. But some strategic front-office applications may require a major restructuring of customer services or of marketing and sales departments. For example, a factor often underestimated by technical planners is that the organizational effort required for such restructuring may be as great as or greater than that needed for the technical infrastructure.

6.3 SCALE OF THE MASTER PLAN

The level of effort required in setting up a master plan will vary according to the scope and size of the systems investment being considered. It will also depend on the size of the organization considering investment in integrated systems. Therefore, the stages involved in setting up the master plan will vary according to organizational and system parameters.

The five stages of the planning sequence are illustrated in Exhibit 6.4. Needs definition and opportunity identification activities are combined into stage 1 as these are iterative in nature—that is, one depends on the other. Stage 5 will usually start while the master plan is still being finalized. These different stages are flexible to some extent and can be omitted, or combined, depending on the scale of system envisaged. A total integrated office system plan for an organization would require moving through all the stages in a complete and thorough fashion.

A simple expansion, however, of an existing base of office systems will not normally require a fresh look at the strategic needs of the organization; the focus is more likely to be on improved ways of using the systems already in place. Likewise, where the existing office systems are to be linked to the information systems, only technical infrastructure issues

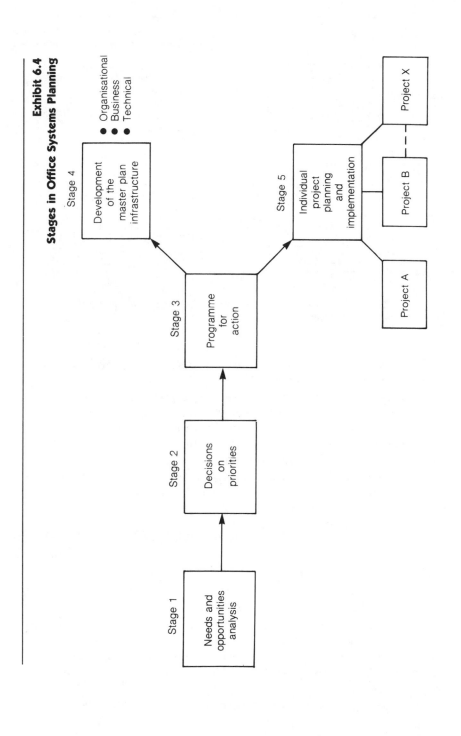

Exhibit 6.4
Stages in Office Systems Planning

Stage 1

Needs and opportunities analysis

Stage 2

Decisions on priorities

Stage 3

Programme for action

Stage 4

Development of the master plan infrastructure

● Organisational
● Business
● Technical

Stage 5

Individual project planning and implementation

Project A

Project B

Project X

Exhibit 6.5
Organizing for Office Systems Planning

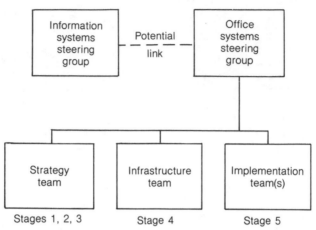

Note: Number and size of teams will depend on scope of plan and
organisation size.

will normally be involved, and the effort required to produce a master plan can be modified accordingly.

Similarly, small and medium-sized organizations, or individual departments, can usually combine some of these stages or scale down the effort and elapsed time required. No elaborate intermediate reviews are really necessary in the smaller organization, because there are fewer organizational interests involved, and agreement can be more readily reached. In a larger organization, this process usually takes much longer, and the intermediate reviews are essential to gaining the necessary commitment by all parties.

6.4 ASSIGNING RESPONSIBILITY FOR PLANNING AND IMPLEMENTATION

Getting the organization right for doing the job is just as important as having the right plan. One way of setting up an organization for an office system planning project involves teams, although for smaller projects the different responsibilities may be assigned to just one or two teams or even individuals (Exhibit 6.5).

A strategy team concentrates on the ultimate objectives that the office system will be designed to achieve. The strategy team should ideally be led by users.

An infrastructure team is concerned with resolving the technical, business, and organizational issues. Ideally this team will be led by someone with strengths in both office systems and systems and telecommunications issues, generally, and who is familiar with the technical standards and policies of the organization.

A series of user-led implementation teams would be responsible for implementing the individual projects. MIS and data-processing departments will normally contribute technical expertise to the individual projects.

A separate steering group will be desirable for very large plans, both to oversee the activities of the teams and to provide a formal link to the MIS department or DP systems steering group. The responsibilities of the planning, infrastructure, and implementation teams are different in type and scope from those of the office systems steering group. Not all organizational cultures are comfortable with steering groups and committees, and some see these concepts as bureaucratic, to be eliminated or kept in check where possible.

Whether or not such a culture is strong within an organization, it is essential that the steering group avoid adopting a bureaucratic stance or taking on the job of challenging proposals put forward to it. In a sense, it should not steer at all but act as a feedback mechanism and as a facilitator. It is very easy for individual users to focus on a narrow front and to ignore the organization's broader objectives. The members of the steering group should wear the "corporate hat."

6.5 SPECIFIC ASPECTS OF PLANNING AND IMPLEMENTATION

Once the opportunities have been identified and assessed, a business case must be prepared to support the action proposed, to enable decisions to be taken on priorities, and to set out the infrastructure issues. The business case will refer to the technical and organizational issues that need to be resolved, but its primary purpose is to present as completely as possible the advantages of the proposed course of action. In addition, attention must be paid to the steps that should be taken to ensure success and the provision of adequate support. A discussion of these essential steps follows.

Cost-benefit analysis is not an easy task. Unlike the factory, there is no strong tradition of efficiency improvement in the office, and office output is not easily measured. It will not be possible to measure all elements in similar terms, such as money. Some costs and benefits cannot be evaluated specifically, such as disruption of office routines during an implementation (Exhibit 6.6). In addition, changes which benefit one part of the organization may incur costs in another. Judgment will be required in allocating benefits. It may be necessary to test the sensitivity of the results to changes in these allocations.

Exhibit 6.6
Checklist—Cost-Benefit Analysis

The classic cost-benefit analysis attempts to express both cost and benefits in the same terms so that the relative advantage of a course of action can be assessed. This will not always be possible (or even desirable) for office systems. It is essential however to clearly establish the beneficial effects of the office systems (preferably in quantitative terms) and to establish the corresponding cost of achieving these benefits.

TYPICAL BENEFITS	COSTS
Time savings	**One-time costs**
Productivity improvements	Equipment
Service improvements	Software
Reductions in work-in-progress	First-year software maintenance
Cost savings	Installation
Reductions in accounts receivable	Initial training
Increased market share	Custom software development
More prospects converted to customers	File conversion
Increased geographic scope of business	Parallel running
	Building facilities
Shortened distribution chain	Power, air-conditioning
New products and services	Cabling
Increased return on assets	Shipping
Increased profits	Insurance
Flattening of management structure (fewer middle managers)	Learning time
	Management time (negotiations, supervision, morale)
Reductions in meetings, travel time, travel expenses	Audit review (if accounting systems involved)
More effective deployment of field sales, field service staff	Temporary help
	Consultants
	Purchasing, legal
Reductions in queues, service times, for customers/clients	Systems analysis
	Data processing (if links to be established)
Reduced cost per transaction	Setting up cost and benefit Tracking systems and procedures
Higher quality of service, take-up of benefits (social agencies)	**Recurring costs**
Higher number of outputs produced per period and/or reduced cost of planned outputs	Hardware maintenance
	Software maintenance
	Software licences
	Supplementary systems analysis, consulting, training, etc.
	System manager, operators
	Supplies
	Share of business overheads

Selecting a supplier, another step, involves more than just product selection. Given the volatility of the technology marketplace, such issues as vendor stability, business strategies, and general business practices must be considered as well. The office system business is still very much technology driven. Suppliers are not equal, nor are their products equally suitable to every application.

Therefore, choosing a one-vendor strategy can be risky and can result in the user paying a premium when equipment and software has to be adapted to a purpose for which it is not ideally suited. At the same time, a one-vendor strategy has the advantage that few decisions have to be made by the user organization on technical architecture issues, as these will be made by the vendor.

In either event, the nature of computer technology makes it very difficult for the user to switch suppliers, because of the enormous investment in equipment and software of only limited compatibility (if at all) with other equipment and software on the market. In addition, the staff training time and, in some cases, the time devoted to customized software must be considered. Selecting the right supplier therefore can be a key decision in any integrated systems plan because it may close off many future options (Exhibit 6.7).

Specify your requirements to only a short list of suppliers. Not only is it costly for the supplier to respond to complex requirements documents, but the supplier will also put in a better effort and be more responsive knowing that he or she has a reasonable chance of obtaining your business.

Ways of developing this short list of suitable suppliers include searching published case studies and trade journals to identify a suitable list. The existing data-processing system supplier should be included among the potential candidates when considering integrated systems. For a large project, sending a brief questionnaire to a large number of suppliers and developing a short list based on the responses is a good idea. You might also investigate the solutions implemented by other users in your industry and include their suppliers in the short list based on their recommendations.

In principle, the requirements themselves should be expressed in terms of what is to be done, not how it is to be done. This may, however, not always be possible. For example, where standards for communications or operating systems software are already in place, these put inherent constraints on the requirements. A further consideration is the extent to which itemized requirements are mandatory or desirable. It is important for the vendor to know this distinction so that different options can be quoted, where appropriate (Exhibit 6.8).

Detailing the program for action is the next essential step to control the momentum most projects acquire. A sequence of the typical activities

Exhibit 6.7
Checklist—Selecting a Supplier

ONE SUPPLIER OR MANY SUPPLIERS?

Has the organisation the technical know-how to deal with the potential integration problems arising from more than one supplier?

Can one supplier meet all the organisation's needs?

Is there a premium to be paid for dealing through one supplier?

THE SUPPLIER'S BUSINESS

Is the supplier committed to the office systems business?

How long has the supplier been in business?

How big is the supplier? Is there local support? Is the supplier going to be around for the lifetime of the system?

How effective is the supplier's maintenance and support operation?

THE SUPPLIER'S STRATEGIES

How broad is the supplier's involvement in office systems?

Does the supplier have an office systems architecture that allows for integration of his present and future products?

Does the supplier conform to Open Systems Architecture or IBM's Systems Network Architecture? What about other standards such as Ethernet, IBM's Document Interchange Architecture (DIA), etc?

THE SUPPLIER'S PRODUCTS

Does the supplier have the software and hardware combinations required to meet user needs?

Is software readily available from third parties to meet specific user needs?

What stage of their product life-cycle have the products reached? Will they become obsolete or be superseded in the near future?

Can the products be readily 'fitted in' with existing office systems, data processing systems and voice communications systems?

involving the program for action is shown in Exhibit 6.9, although no indication of the actual time involved is shown, since this will vary considerably for different types of projects. This type of linear approach is often subject to criticism because it can lead to long periods before any payback is received. For this reason, the time frame may be telescoped by starting several sub-projects before agreement on all details of the master plan is reached (Exhibit 6.10).

The difficulty with this approach is the risk of an early implementation that turns out to be a technological white elephant, or that is found to be inconsistent with the directions determined during development of the

Exhibit 6.8
Checklist—Specification for Suppliers

BACKGROUND TO REQUIREMENTS
— Why this specification
— Brief company background
— Importance of system

BASIC REQUIREMENTS
— Business purpose of the office system
— Scope (users, locations, functions and data included)
— What the system is

APPLICATIONS REQUIREMENTS
— Standard applications packages
— Applications to be developed
— Workloads, growth rates, processing cycles, etc
— Links to other systems
— Reliability, responsiveness required (should be kept realistic)

HARDWARE AND COMMUNICATIONS REQUIREMENTS
— Number of workstations
— Peripherals (storage, printers, etc)
— Links required
— Standards applicable (eg organisation standards, links to other equipment, compatibility with systems, software)

SUPPORT REQUIREMENTS
— Training
— Installation
— On-going support, maintenance

COST INFORMATION REQUIRED
— One-time and recurring costs
— Cost of optional items
— Cost of future expansion
— Need for building changes, power, air-conditioning, etc.

SUPPLIER INFORMATION
— References
— General information (eg size, history, geographic spread)

ADMINISTRATION
— When a response is required
— How proposals will be reviewed and the criteria for making a decision
— Whom to contact for further information, clarification

Exhibit 6.9

A Sequential Approach to Planning for a Large Office System Project

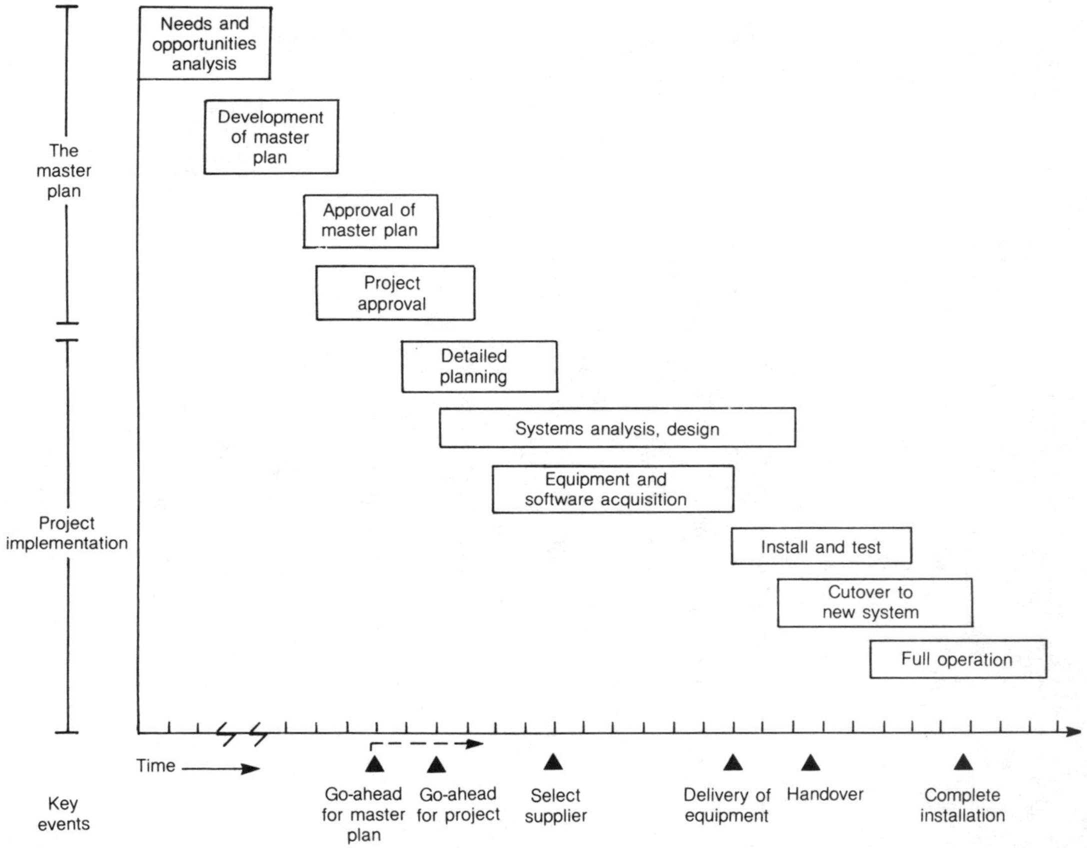

Needs and opportunities analysis

Development of master plan

Approval of master plan

Project approval

Detailed planning

Systems analysis, design

Equipment and software acquisition

Install and test

Cutover to new system

Full operation

Time →

The master plan

Project implementation

Key events

Go-ahead for master plan

Go-ahead for project plan

Select supplier

Delivery of equipment

Handover

Complete installation

154

Exhibit 6.10

A Parallel Approach to Planning for a Large Office System Project

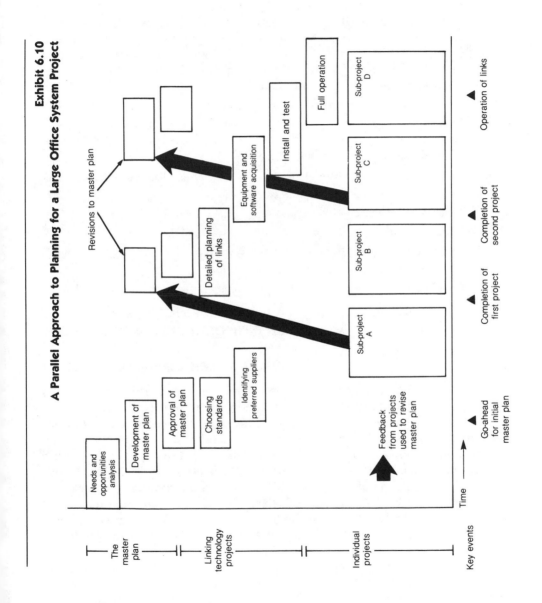

master plan. For these reasons, early projects should be limited in scope, and a very short pay-back period should be specified.

Detailed implementation planning for the individual office projects or sub-projects is similar to that for traditional data-processing projects. Project activities should be broken down to a sufficiently detailed level to enable progress to be tracked and responsibility assigned. As a rule of thumb, activities should not be broken down to less than about two weeks, or the equivalent of ten working days. Included should be the following major activities and events:

- Definition of working procedures and methods
- Purchase, delivery, testing, and installation of all equipment, software, and communications facilities
- Physical installation and building changes
- Purchase of office furniture, supplies, and other miscellaneous smaller items
- Planning of the time scale for the work
- Assignment of responsibilities and reporting structure
- Budgets and expenditure control
- Criteria for assessment of the success of the project
- Provision for training and education
- Coordination with other departments, customers, data processing, and so on

6.6 THE PHYSICAL OFFICE ENVIRONMENT

6.6.1 General Considerations

Complaints from office workers about the working environment in which their office systems are installed might be perceived as a symptom of their resentment of change. Nonetheless, the physical office environment is a major concern for many office staff and an issue periodically raised by unions and staff representatives. Estimates of white-collar unionization are that complaints will increase fourfold by 1993 with governmental regulations of white-collar working conditions increasing, particularly at the state level. Where the office system is perceived as being genuinely relevant to the task of the workers and where it helps them achieve their objectives, ergonomic considerations are seldom a problem.

A study by the Buffalo Organization for Social and Technological Innovations found that a well-designed office environment can affect job performance and satisfaction and increase productivity by as much as 15 percent of a worker's annual salary.[1] However, several main points need to be considered:

1. Ergonomics. An adequate working surface, adjustable equipment position-ing, and good seating are perhaps the three most important aspects of desktop ergonomics. The importance of these requirements is generally accepted for word-processor operators and clerical staff. Managers and professionals are often forgotten or left to make do with inappropriate furnishings from the presystems era. Sadly, it is not uncommon to find a personal computer, telephone, fiche reader, and printer piled on a standard L-return secretarial desk.

2. Air Quality. Air conditioning is no longer the problem it once was as most office systems are fairly robust in this respect, although disk drives and printers can be sensitive to temperature and humidity changes. As a general rule, an office temperature of between 68 degrees F (20C) and 72 degrees F (22C) is advisable with a maximum humidity of 50 percent. Keep in mind, however, that even a small personal computer does emit heat, and several pieces of equipment in a closed, poorly air-conditioned environment can make workers extremely uncomfortable.

3. Lighting. Use of furniture-integrated or task ambient lighting has been shown to increase productivity while decreasing energy costs. Display terminals should be positioned to avoid glare or reflections from lighting and windows. Some glare shielding for lights and control over direct daylight, using curtains or blinds, may be required. Also, keeping the display terminals clean will reduce glare as well.

4. Noise. One disadvantage of the open office plan is noise. Planners fail to take into account good acoustical design when preparing the work environment, and remedial measures can often cost more than the proper construction in the first place. Incoming speech is distracting even if coming from next door. Acoustically treated furniture panels, a sound-absorbing ceiling, and a sound-masking system will aid in providing speech privacy in the open plan. Acoustic covers, cumbersome though they are, are essential for impact printers in offices. Laser printers, however, are relatively noiseless. Keep in mind if considering customized acoustic covers that room must be provided for an exhaust fan mechanism.

5. Space. Proper space planning is probably the most important ergonomic factor in achieving successful use and acceptance by users. Planning for space al-locations, work-flow arrangements, and associated furniture and equipment needs should be an important element of the detailed planning process within each project. The location of shared equipment, such as printers or facsimile machines, should be particularly carefully considered. No detail is too small—for example, one installation of a new system was considered a partial failure because the desktops stuck out about two inches beyond the room dividers. The popular open office plan, while flexible, lacks visual and acoustical privacy and is costly to install. Many employees perceive a loss of status associated with a move from a conventional office to the open space. Pressure to make offices smaller due to increasing office rents exacerbates this problem, although future reduction in paper filing systems could offset this.

6.6.2 Wiring Options

As the number of individual office workstations increases, the problem of office wiring becomes more and more acute, particularly when planning for integrated systems. The main problems encountered are cost, multiple networks, and delay. On some sites it can be as expensive to install and connect a new workstation as it is to buy one. Many organizations now have three, or more, data communications networks on a single site (such as ASCII, 3270, and telex). And it often takes days or even weeks to install a new device or to move an old one. Users therefore feel an increasing urgency for a universal wiring scheme that will enable them to support all their current and anticipated future office equipment at an acceptable cost.

Regrettably, there is no such scheme yet. Instead, there are four options: twisted pair, the IBM cabling scheme, broadband cable, or Ethernet-type systems and other proprietary local area networks (as described in Chapter 4 and illustrated in Exhibit 6.11).

Twisted pair cable is the most common cable found in offices, but it comes in a variety of forms. The cheapest is the unscreened cable used for telephones. For data, however, heavier and more expensive cables, often with shielding, are used. Twisted pair is a well-understood medium and has the great advantage that it is sometimes possible to use spare pairs on the telephone system, thus avoiding the need for new cable installation. The twisted pair medium, however, has several characteristic limitations:

- It is suitable for terminal support but not for the resource sharing that may be needed between personal computers.
- It cannot be substituted for the co-axial cable used to support synchronous terminals.
- Voice and data are not integrated.

The IBM cabling scheme announced in 1983 had the objective of providing a universal solution to the wiring problem. The scheme being promoted provides, in a single jacket, wires for both data and telephone, with the option of including optical fibers as well. However, the scheme is expensive. For instance, a 250-outlet IBM cabling scheme network was installed at Carnegie-Mellon University in 1983. The installation was technically successful but cost $400 per outlet. The university has calculated that it would cost between $7 million and $9 million to wire the whole campus, and that 40 rooms would have to be used as wiring closets. Other options are being considered.

Broadband cable systems comprise a tree of co-axial cables, usually with frequency converters and network management equipment at the cable head-end. Broadband cable installations need not be expensive, but

Exhibit 6.11

Comparison of Local Cabling Options

Feature	Telephone cable	Shielded twisted pair	IBM cabling scheme	Broadband	Ethernet
Material costs	Low	Moderate	High	Low	Moderate
Labour costs	Low	Moderate	High	Low	Low
Can individual offices be pre-wired?	Yes	Yes	Yes	Yes	No
Do individual offices have to be pre-wired?	No	No	Yes	Yes	No
Terminal-to-host costs	Low	Low	Moderate	Moderate	High
Micro-network costs	n/a	Moderate (proprietary)	Moderate (Pronet)	Moderate	Moderate

they do require fairly skillful planning and management. This is the system used by the popular IBM PC Network, by Sytek. Although the wiring and installation for a broadband system aren't necessarily expensive, the electronics often are. As a consequence, a broadband LAN is more expensive than a baseband system operating at the same speed and providing the same functions. However, under favorable conditions, a broadband system may be cost-competitive with a switched, twisted pair network.

The greatest advantage of Ethernet is that it is now a standard. There are at least 200 suppliers, offering products ranging from personal computer interfaces to public network gateways. Thousands of Ethernets have now been installed worldwide. Against this background, the arguments about the relative advantages and disadvantages of the actual technology are of no consequence. A majority of the installed Ethernets are used to support resource sharing between personal computers, and Ethernet is now a leading LAN for personal computer networking. Although badly matched in purely technological terms, many successful pc terminal networks are now based on Ethernet.

There are also proprietary LANs provided by a wide variety of suppliers. These products may be divided into two groups: those delivered as integral parts of an application system, and those designed as communications products. System-based LANs have been devised to support resource sharing among attached computers. These computers may be ordinary personal computers, or machines specialized for applications such as office automation or computerized design. They are thus a necessary, though often minor, part of the total computer system. These LANs are often poorly designed from a communications viewpoint, with little thought having been given to wiring and management aspects. And they are almost all nonstandard. However, they include some exciting technologies and form the basis of many successful installations.

Communications-based LANs have been designed to support the terminals that have already been installed in user sites. They fall into two groups:

1. Inexpensive systems which allow a small number of terminals to be connected in a limited area. These products can be very cost effective provided that their limitations are recognized and accepted.
2. Highly functional and costly systems which are usually well engineered, but are not often cost effective.

6.6.3 Installation

The first installation of office system facilities usually represents the beginning and not the end of the total undertaking. Even so, the installation is likely to be spread over weeks or even months.

The following activities will normally need to take place before the system is fully installed:

1. Purchase and delivery of all office systems equipment and facilities
2. Purchase and delivery of all physical environment facilities, such as furniture
3. Purchase and delivery of other equipment such as communications equipment
4. Physical installation of infrastructure facilities, such as wiring, power, and desks
5. Definition of time scales for installing the equipment and detailed allocation of responsibilities
6. Provision of training and educational facilities including the ordering or preparation of manuals
7. Modification of standard equipment or facilities, where required
8. Definition of working procedures
9. Testing of equipment and facilities

The number of queries and problems is likely to be highest immediately after an office system has been implemented, and the training staff and analysts should be continuously available to provide help and advice during this period.

Integrated systems will usually be introduced in a phased manner, with the number of users increasing steadily with time. Such a phased implementation can cause either an initial lack of the required critical mass to make the system really useful or an imbalance between related user groups. These effects should be recognized quickly, and suitable action should be taken to overcome the problems. One possibility is to hold a limited amount of equipment and facilities in reserve, so that unexpected imbalances can be overcome quickly. Holding some equipment in reserve may also be advisable in medium-sized and large installations so that a rapid response can be made to any equipment failures, particularly during the early stages of an implementation.

6.7 PLANNING FOR LOCAL AREA NETWORKS

When considering the installation of a local area network, several questions need to be answered before beginning:

How many terminals and other simple digital machines must be supported, and what interfaces and protocols do they use? If the terminals are widely scattered, a network based on existing wiring (most likely telephone cabling) is probably the best choice, as cabling costs, as discussed earlier, are quite high. If usage is high, a dedicated data network is indicated rather than an existing PABX.

How often will these terminals be moved, and how quickly must they then be reconnected to the network? If terminals are moved frequently, or must be moved at short notice, then a network which can be installed in every office is probably the best choice, although this is costly with baseband networks.

What is the speed required of the network? Is there any need to support computers and workstations that need fast file transfer or speedy resource sharing? The LAN chosen must provide interfaces over which the required services can be accessed. Many vendors offer such compatibility aids as protocol conversion and file format conversion.

How many host computers must be supported and with what interfaces? Networks can provide a data circuit service supporting interactive terminals, facsimile transceivers, and computers that emulate these devices. Circuit-switched networks usually offer only the basic data communications service; therefore, some network choices may sharply limit the scope of interface services. The way in which the data circuit service may be used is also a concern. Most circuit-switched networks, and some LAN-based networks, require network addresses to be specified through a convenient access code. Though acceptable for small networks, this approach is frequently unsuitable for large networks or where terminals are shifted or moved with any frequency. The more sophisticated local networks provide a name server that accepts the name of the required computer or network service and converts this to a network address.

Does the overall location need several incompatible networks in the same area? This need probably exists in large organizations with diversified businesses. A broadband LAN on which one or more frequencies can be reserved for each network may be useful. In most cases, any network that can provide data circuits which have their own access control mechanisms can be used.

Is there a need for voice and data integration? Most current LAN users have little need to integrate voice with data, and these systems will probably not develop until much later in the decade. However the use of the PABX is attractive to avoid the need to install new cables, and it provides economies in switching logic and network management.

What are the requirements, if any, for video communications, and must these be integrated with other communications? A cable TV network is upgradable to a broadband data network for a modest cost. If there is no cable TV network, it will not cost much more to install separate cable TV and baseband LANs if done at the same time.

What are the security requirements of the data? Ease of use is a prime feature of LANs, and security can be difficult at best. While some vendors are addressing this issue, LANs can still be fairly easily jammed and data destroyed. If security is important, the LAN should be kept separate—if necessary with a secure bridge or gateway to screen out unwanted signals.

Several specialized needs can also dictate the type of local area network solution selected. For instance, does the LAN need to operate in industrial areas with high risk of fire or explosion or electrical interference? If so, the use of optical fiber should be considered. Does the LAN need to support specific items of equipment such as an Apollo CAD system, which requires installation of a Domain LAN for compatibility. Indeed, several high-resolution CAD/CAM terminals can generate as much traffic for a LAN as ten times the number of word processors. Is there a need for very high network availability, which can be met only by networks that can support multiple independent routes between devices with automatic re-routing?

The checklist illustrated in Exhibit 6.12 will help you in determining your LAN needs and installation requirements. The need for careful planning for any LAN installation cannot be stressed too much. Planners must not be swept away by impressive speed rates or large numbers of terminal devices accessible and must plan for failures as well as growth. Poor planning can leave an office with a cabling system that needs to be replaced too soon, or with no spare parts. Local area networks are still in the developmental stages, and no one network will satisfy every user. Indeed, no network will satisfy every need within one user group, which may explain the hesitation companies have shown in embracing this technology. In addition, there exists a decided dilemma in choosing to obtain all components for an integrated system from one vendor or mixing and matching products. Where one has the advantage of simplicity, it may not offer the features and price advantages of the other while locking the firm into a major hardware and software investment.

The technology is constantly improving, and the cost of the LANs will fall over the coming years. It is interesting to note that an overwhelming majority of building contractors are planning for the development of "intelligent" buildings that offer data circuit services to tenants (see Chapter 7).

6.8 USING A CONSULTANT

It is commonplace in the data-processing environment to conduct audits, either performed by internal auditing staff or external consultants. Top management relies on an audit to verify the effectiveness of internal controls and the reliability of data-processing results. This role is a logical extension of the internal auditor's traditional role; however, the job of the internal auditor has changed.

Internal auditors can no longer audit "around the computer" because

Exhibit 6.12
Network Selection Checklist

1. Choose your application software first. This is the most frequently violated rule. Too often a network is selected on the basis of benchmark results and performance, only to be found unusable by virtue of its inability to run the perfect application program for the job at hand. This includes knowing what you want the network to do as well. Do you need outgoing asynchronous gateways, 3270 SNA gateways, inter-network communications, electronic mail, printer spooling, PC file sharing, etc?

2. Limit the systems examined to those that adhere to accepted standards (IEEE 802 specs, DOS 3.1, NetBIOS, etc.). This will help avoid potential obsolescence of the system as new systems are developed. Some of the most exciting features are available from some of the smallest and least known vendors, but if they do not have the resources to keep up with a new development that is required to implement a new hardware or software feature, the utility of the network may be severely compromised.

3. Examine the possibility of using existing wire. The single greatest expense in a local area network installation is the cost of cabling and the labor required to install it. Using existing cable can be a source of significant savings.

4. Ignore benchmark test and performance statistics. There is a great deal of discussion today regarding the virtues of one system versus another. The real difference between two systems, however, is of purely scientific interest. A user at the workstation will rarely, if ever, experience more than a 1- or 2-second difference in response times.

5. "Test drive" the system. If your supplier does not have a demo system running, request the names of other clients that are currently using a configuration as close to the proposed system as possible. Talk to the users of this system. Ask them the following questions:

    What is the response of the system like?
    Does it run all the applications you need?
    Is it reliable? How frequent are failures?
    How well does the system recover from errors?
    How long did it take to learn how to use the system?

6. Purchase your network from a reputable supplier. Be sure that they will be able to support you for the foreseeable future. Be certain that they are familiar with your needs. Ideally a supplier should be able to handle the entire project from cable installation through system start-up to user training.

so many of the controls that ensure the accuracy and completeness of data processing are built into the systems and cannot be viewed and verified through direct observation. Many companies now routinely involve either internal auditors or consultants in the design and evaluation of these data-processing systems and controls, and standard approaches and techniques have been evolved for this purpose. Management consultants, and auditors, typically rely on computer audit specialists to advise organizations in these matters.

Many computer audit techniques are directly applicable to office systems, particularly where numerical data or accounting data are to be processed. Because of the packaged nature of most office systems applications, controls cannot be readily built into the systems themselves, and reliance may have to be placed on controls incorporated in manual procedures.

The consultants' work in this area can be summarized as the appraisal of checks and controls used in office systems for processing financial data. These are the processing controls. The classic statement of audit objectives is as follows:

• To ensure the completeness of data processed by the system
• To ensure the accuracy of data processed by the system
• To ensure that all data processed by the system are authorized
• To ensure the adequacy of audit trails

Consultants and internal audit departments have also traditionally checked many other aspects of the organization's activities, which are neither strictly financial nor connected with the assets of the firm in the accounting system. Therefore, the financial/accounting audit may be a prelude to formulating a case for reorganization, or it may follow a major reorganization to determine whether the sought-for benefits have been achieved. Such an audit typically includes these points:

• Checks on the effectiveness of managers
• Checks on their compliance with company or professional standards
• Evaluation of the reliability of management data
• Evaluation of the quality of performance of duties
• Recommendations for improvements

This type of examination is variously called a management audit, an administration audit, or an operations audit.

The recent development of this type of audit has achieved prominence in public sector organizations. This is known as the value-for-money audit, and in very simplistic terms, it can be described as the public sector's substitute for a profit-and-loss sheet, because it attempts to assess directly the management of the organization.

The ideas behind value-for-money auditing are applicable to office systems for this reason: It can be difficult to draw up a profit-and-loss

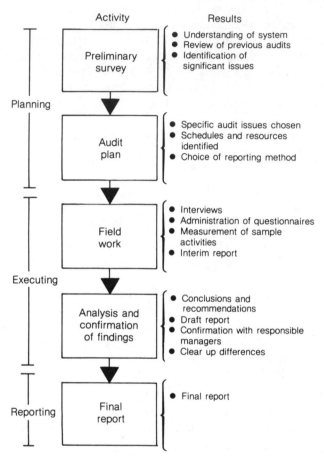

Exhibit 6.13
Phases of an Office Systems Audit

Activity

Results

Planning

Preliminary
survey

- Understanding of system
- Review of previous audits
- Identification of
  significant issues

Audit
plan

- Specific audit issues chosen
- Schedules and resources
  identified
- Choice of reporting method

Executing

Field
work

- Interviews
- Administration of questionnaires
- Measurement of sample
  activities
- Interim report

Analysis and
confirmation
of findings

- Conclusions and
  recommendations
- Draft report
- Confirmation with responsible
  managers
- Clear up differences

Reporting

Final
report

- Final report

sheet for the office system. Therefore, the audit approach draws extensively on the concepts of value-for-money auditing, with the emphasis on the management and administration of the office systems.

The five basic phases to an office systems audit are illustrated in Exhibit 6.13 and discussed in depth here:

1. *Preliminary survey.* The first phase of the audit is the preliminary survey. This is intended to produce an understanding of the office system objectives, working methods and procedures, any previous reviews, and the financial and organizational aspects (costs, users, documentation, manager responsible, technical support, and so on). The survey results in a summary of the main audit issues, their scope, and their

relative importance. These issues are the criteria that will be used to judge whether the office system is being managed properly.

2. *Audit plan*. The audit plan sets out the detailed approach to examining the audit issues. The scope of the audit examination has been narrowed at this point, and all subsequent effort should concentrate on the specific audit issues. The audit plan specifies tasks, schedules, interviewees, sampling schemes, and dates and choice of reporting method. It is often called a work plan.

3. *Field work*. In the third phase, the members of the consulting team examine the issues selected. Typically, the team is putting together evidence to support any comments that will be made at the reporting stage, and to further clarify the issues and the impact of any shortcomings in management controls. Typical audit issues cover

- Effectiveness, including the availability of data to assess system impact, impact on productivity, attainment of business objectives, service levels, and quality control.

- Efficiency, including utilization of equipment, back-up procedures, access to equipment, and time taken to effect repairs, remedy software problems, and so on.

- Economic acquisition, including management of the system life cycle, definition of why the system is needed, how suppliers are selected, and provision for training and maintenance.

4. *Analysis and confirmation of findings*. The fourth phase revolves around the consolidation of the reports on the various issues. A most important part of this phase is the review of the conclusions with the responsible managers and supervisors. Often their reactions to any criticism will be to attack the final report at the detail level, and they will, quite naturally, use any errors of fact to invalidate the overall findings. Thus it is essential to meet this problem head-on by ensuring that the basic facts are right before the final report is prepared. The managers who are being criticized may still disagree with the conclusions drawn from the evidence, but at least the evidence will not be in dispute.

5. *Final report*. This phase includes the final presentation of the consultants' findings and recommendations for any remedial action. It will also include any follow-up work required to respond to the comments of the person or persons who commissioned the study, usually top management.

It is perhaps stating the obvious to say that the consultant is concerned with learning lessons from what has happened rather than with pointing the finger at the guilty. If, for example, there are surplus personal computers in the offices of the firm, the consultant will be concerned to find out why this has happened. It could be that the original need was overstated (in which case the planning procedures may need to be cor-

Exhibit 6.14
Audit Issues

Audit issues — effectiveness

Audit issues	Control objectives	Appropriate control techniques
Effective office systems	— To ensure that office systems meet the needs of the organisation	— Specifications documented and signed-off — Liaison with users throughout development and implementation — Periodic review of office systems already installed
System rationale	— To ensure that office systems are only installed where justified by the relative costs and benefits involved	— Cost-benefit analysis of office system proposals — Management review of proposals

Audit issues — economic acquisition

Audit issues	Control objectives	Appropriate control techniques
Equipment and software	— To ensure economic acquisition of equipment and software	— Use of competitive bids and/or negotiation — Use of bulk purchases to obtain discounts — Life cycle management
Maintenance	— To ensure economic provision of maintenance services	— Periodic review of maintenance contracts — Analysis of need for maintenance contracts for all equipment
Support services (training, consultants, etc.)	— To ensure economic provision of support services	— Specification of work in terms of results to be achieved — Use of fixed-price contracts
Telecommunications services	— To ensure economic provision of telecommunications	— Periodic review of telecommunication needs and service contracts

Audit issues — efficiency

Audit issues	Control objectives	Appropriate control techniques
Operating practices	— To ensure reliable and efficient operation of equipment, software and telecommunications	— Problem log — Configuration control — Maintenance procedures — Clear assignment of responsibilities for remedial action — Software change control
Quality assurance	— To maintain quality control over output, files, procedures, back-up	— Periodic review of system controls — Quality control responsibilities assigned to an individual/group
End-user operations	— To ensure effective operation of systems by end-users	— Documented operating procedures — Technical assistance readily accessible — Training courses for end-users

Audit issues — management of office systems

Audit issues	Control objectives	Appropriate control techniques
Office systems planning	— To ensure that plans are in place — To provide criteria for selecting projects	— Long-term plans — Office system investment criteria
Organisation of office systems support	— To provide adequate resources	— Office systems budgets included in departmental budgets — Support skills requirements periodically assessed
Office systems administration	— To provide control over projects and visibility of office systems costs	— Costing system — Personnel time reporting and allocation
Office systems standards	— To ensure that effective methods are followed in the development, implementation and operation of office systems	— Formalised project management process — Documented policies
Audit and evaluation	— To ensure periodic assessment of office systems activities	— Post facto audit of new systems — Periodic reviews

169

rected) or that there has been a reorganization (in which case the equipment should have been identified as surplus and offered to other departments or otherwise disposed of).

In short, the consultant is concerned with the control techniques being used to ensure that the control objectives are being met. Although specific issues will vary from firm to firm, the charts in Exhibit 6.14 provide guideline lists of audit issues of effectiveness, efficiency, economic acquisition, and management of office systems.

NOTE

1. Gerard E. MacLean, "Furnishing the Automated Office," *Words* (Feb.-March 1985): 30–32.

REFERENCES

Brilliantine, Lance R. "Design and Selection Guide to Local Area Networks." *Administrative Management* (Oct. 1985): 34–37.
Butler Cox Foundation. "Implementing Office Systems" (May 1982).
Rourke, Richard. "Less Noise Means More Productivity." *Administrative Management* (Nov. 1985): 42–49.
Williamson, Arthur R. "OA Ergonomics . . . Changing the Workplace to Fit the Worker." *Words* (Feb.-March 1985): 19–22.

7

Future Office Systems

7.1 OVERALL TECHNOLOGICAL TRENDS AND THEIR IMPLICATIONS

The technology of office systems is advancing rapidly along with other computer-based technologies, and it does not appear that there will be any slowdown in the foreseeable future. These advances lead to new ways of doing things, as well as to continuing improvements in the cost-performance of existing systems. Many users perhaps feel that the continuing streams of new announcements by vendors merely add to the confusion about office systems and that most of the improvements are marginal to real user benefits. However, some of the potential advances could be significant indeed for the integrated system user and thus cannot be ignored in planning for the future. In fact, others may well provide unique opportunities for enhancing business operations.

On one point, all computer suppliers are in accord: The future of information technology lies with the distribution of computer power and of data. This trend does not necessarily herald the demise of the central computer. By 1990, Butler Cox has predicted that the cost of the processor and memory in the personal computer will be less than the cost of the keyboard and the power supply five years earlier. Large-scale memory of 100 megabytes will also be commonplace.

The ability of office systems to intercommunicate will undoubtedly improve in the future, especially as standards are established and agreed upon. New versions of the MS-DOS operating system will let end users handle 25 times the amount of information as is currently possible. In addition, the new software system will allow personal computer users to switch from one program to another rapidly and cleanly. The larger the PC memory and switching ability, the easier it will be to link into networks and into larger computer systems. In addition, new chip technology will allow the execution of programs two to four times faster than on the fastest existing personal computer. Easier-to-use programs with icons, overlapping screens, using artificial intelligence for imprecise commands, will be a major benefit.

The planner will want to take advantage of these capabilities, but as they will tend to cross organizational lines, he or she must be concerned with gaining agreement from and assessing the impact of the different organizational interests involved. Similarly, the planner will want to take existing investments in office systems into account and incorporate the new developments, or at least plan for a transition from one to the other.

The main demand among users of distributed systems will be improved control over the system development, in order to facilitate the long-delayed task of basic system conversion and the need to increase responsibility for system operation, to offset the risk inherent in remote data processing.

In a genuine distributed system, users are unaware of and indifferent to the physical location of data. The route to this ideal situation is still far from clear. Successful implementations of such networks are few in number and sometimes too specialized in purpose to provide general guidance. Data integrity versus cost remains the central problem.

Telecommunications costs are falling at a much slower rate than computer costs, partly because the electronics component of telecommunications systems is much less than in most computers and partly because of the high intrinsic costs of cabling offices. At the same time, the unit costs of transmitting data has dropped because of the improved performance of newer, more advanced telecommunications systems.

Some software costs have actually risen over time, and the ongoing costs of program maintenance are well known to experienced users.

Software design and programming remains a labor-intensive activity. Nevertheless, IBM has estimated that the worldwide software industry is growing at a compound rate of over 30 percent a year, with 1994 revenues expected to reach more than $150 billion.[1] Improvements in software development methods (together with better programming environments and standards) have had some impact on software costs but do not compare with hardware cost reductions.

A second, more important factor has been the spread of software packages. Software packages do not necessarily involve lower develop-

Exhibit 7.1
Software Cost Trends

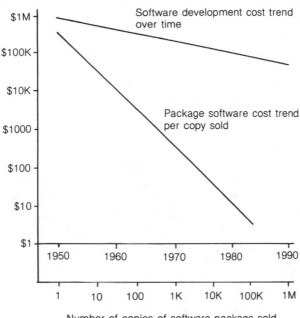

Number of copies of software package sold

ment cost. In most cases, the cost increases because of the higher standard of testing and documentation required. Also, while software packages cost the software supplier virtually nothing to copy, the costs of marketing and distribution can still be significant.

Many personal computer software packages for businesses sell for $500 or so, because of the large number of sales over which the development costs are spread (Exhibit 7.1). However, software for office systems is likely to become more and more specialized, which will result in higher costs. There are two reasons for this: First, because custom software must meet a specialized need, fewer copies of a package will normally be sold. Second, there is additional custom work associated with installing the package.

The heavy reliance of printers and on-line disk storage on electromechanical contact reduces the extent to which prices can fall for items such as storage devices and printers. On-line disk storage comes in several forms. Traditionally, the single-spindle, multi-layer 14-inch unit has been used in data-processing systems. Current state-of-the-art disks can hold 1,266 Megabytes or more. For PC-based office systems, this may remain common, but the standard for office systems is likely to be the

Winchester disk with a potential for 300M + of storage. Improvements in recording techniques will allow denser storage, perhaps resulting in a dramatic change in the early 1990s. The reason is the likely widespread use of vertical recording techniques in the future (referring to the way in which the magnetic domains are oriented on the disk).

High-density floppy disks are expected to reach the market soon. Initially these are expected to store around 10M per side. A switch from horizontal magnetic recording to vertical recording could increase this capacity by a factor of ten. Personal computers then would be able to store 100M on a single side of a disk.

Likewise, optical disk storage will come into widespread use. Its main disadvantage is that it is currently nonerasable, which limits its applications to archival storage or reference files with limited rates of change. Eventually, however, optical disks may become so cheap that the lack of erasability will not matter. But for the next decade, it does appear that magnetic disks will remain the dominant storage media.

The more complex integrated office systems packages, combining word processing, spreadsheet and data management, are already straining the capabilities of the standard personal computer. Adding communications facilities demands some level of multi-tasking to enable communications to proceed simultaneously with other work on the system. This means that the typical workstation of the future will need to be a much faster unit, with more storage capacity, than today's standard. This will offset to some extent the performance improvements arising from the technological advances just discussed.

A related complication is the implicit demand placed on data-processing systems by attached devices. The need to access corporate data will increase rapidly, and it is a well-established fact that every terminal device accessing the central computer facilities adds to the overall work load and requires the installation of additional processing capacity.

Convergence is a moving target and depends on the point of view taken (Exhibit 7.2). Clearly the modern supplier sees convergence as a marketing tool—a framework within which new products can be developed and sold. For the user, it represents a struggle to superimpose a structure on a group of diverging organizational interests. This whole issue is further complicated by the role of IBM, whose mainframe systems, together with the family of communications products collectively known as Systems Network Architecture (SNA), are almost certain to set the standard for commercial data processing for at least another decade.

The overall business market was forecast by Butler Cox in 1984 to reach annual expenditures of over $336.5 billion by 1991, with the most dramatic changes in the markets for software and for information storage and retrieval. The biggest growth is forecast to occur at the local corporate level, where annual expenditure is forecast by Butler Cox to be over 5.5

Exhibit 7.2

Evolution Paths for Multifunction Terminals

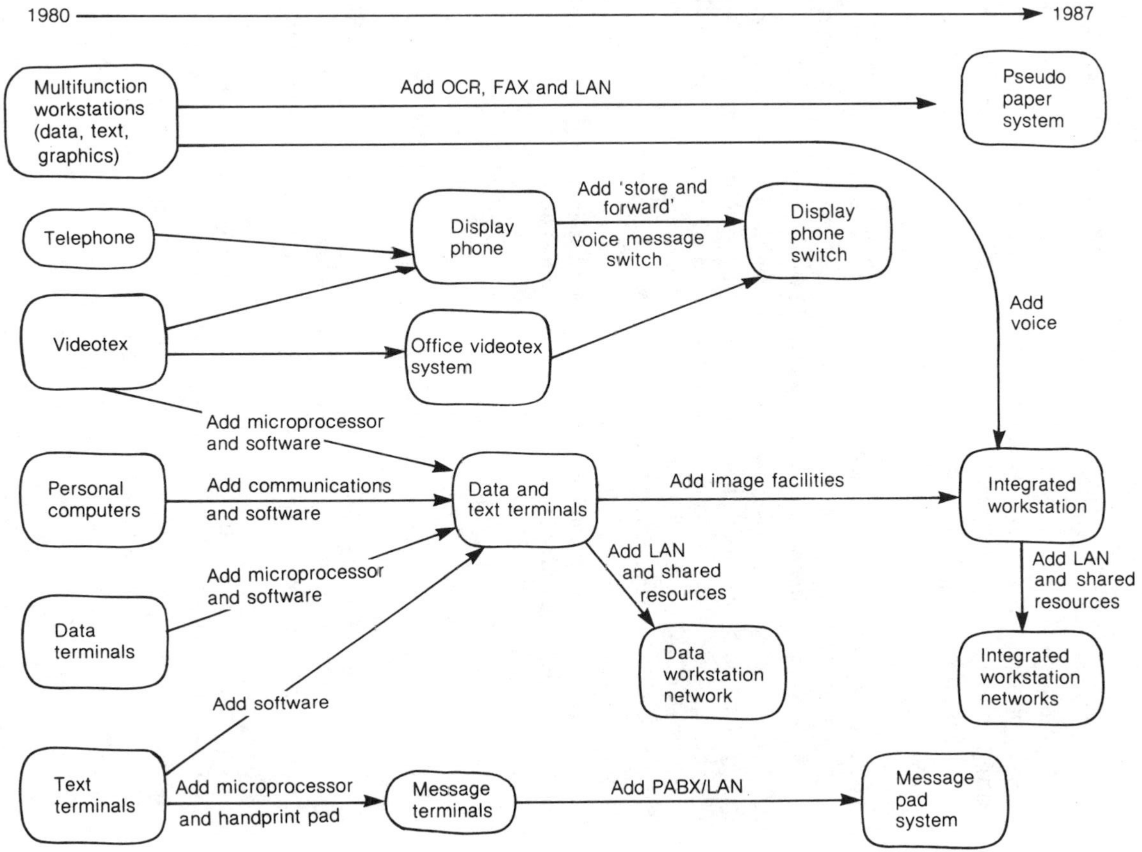

times its size in 1982. Expenditure at the corporate shared and public shared levels is projected to increase only marginally (Exhibit 7.3). Communication expenditures, though growing substantially in absolute terms, were seen as declining in terms of overall share in the market.

7.2 THE OBSOLESCENCE ISSUE

Technological advances also have a negative side: They can lead to earlier obsolescence of expensive hardware and software. How does this problem arise, and what can the potential purchaser do about it?

It should be emphasized that "early" obsolescence can arise in three ways:

1. Technological advances. In the early stages of a new technology, new designs and new methods are introduced in rapid succession. This results in early obsolescence of installed equipment and software.
2. Market forces. When a supplier loses out in the marketplace, the supplier's products become obsolete faster. Most commonly this happens when another supplier becomes dominant, and the other supplier's products become the de facto standard (IBM is the classic example). The emergence of industrywide standards have similar consequences for installed systems.
3. Supplier strategies. Suppliers' new products can render their installed base obsolete by offering improved price and performance. Suppliers may not provide technical support for earlier product lines beyond a cutoff date.

Therefore, technological advances are only one of the ways in which the effective economic life of an office system can be shortened, although it should also be recognized that the three factors are strongly interrelated.

The danger for the user is that he or she becomes paralyzed into inaction through fear of obsolescence or, as more frequently happens, chooses the dominant supplier as a form of insurance against premature obsolescence.

The user has a means of dealing with the obsolescence issue: the payback period used in assessing the original system investment. The higher the risk of early obsolescence, the shorter this payback should be. Unfortunately, the peculiarities of current office systems practice make this difficult because most investment in office systems is not assessed against tangible benefits. And estimates of rate of obsolescence are subjective and difficult to confirm.

Nevertheless, preparing a formal analysis of every investment in office systems is highly desirable, as it lays out for the benefit of the decision-maker all the relevant factors—at least the decision is not made in the dark.

Exhibit 7.3

Comparative Growth in Expenditure 1982/1991

By product function — business market

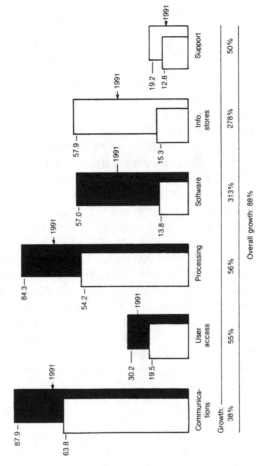

	Communica- tions	User access	Processing	Software	Info. stores	Support
Growth:	38%	55%	56%	313%	278%	50%

Overall growth: 88%

A further factor is the role of a particular investment in the overall system framework of the user organization. For isolated systems intended to support one office of the organization, an assessment of obsolescence can be made on a case-by-case basis. For the organization's communications links, early obsolescence has many more wide-ranging implications. In this instance, varying the payback period is an inadequate means of coping with potential obsolescence, on its own. The key, instead, is to ensure that the overall architecture is right, so that obsolescence can be coped with as it happens. In other words, it is assumed right from the start that obsolescence will happen.

One of the risks of total reliance on one supplier's standards is that the strategy for dealing with obsolescence is a "Big Blue" (made by IBM) strategy. The smaller user may not have much choice in these matters, but the medium-sized and larger user does have a choice.

When considering replacement of obsolete equipment, the issue of customer service becomes even more important. Many vendors are now unbundling their customer support, offering help in such areas as planning, cost justification, and training, separately and frequently at a cost to the user. Vendors are also now offering new types of support, such as software support, training needs analysis, and other consulting services. Large vendors such as IBM offer assistance in helping firms implement large distributed systems for multi-branch firms. Also, vendors are finally beginning to offer a more integrated support for the customer, which can simplify contacts for coordinating hardware and software services. This can be a single contact or a client-specific team.

Yet, in the long run, it is the user who will be taking on the tasks of in-house support, training, and maintenance. Many vendors are encouraging this by training staff and providing key personnel with special instructions for implementations, with little vendor involvement. Repair is increasingly mail-in or carry-in service, and remote diagnostics are starting to replace some on-site service visits by vendor staff.

7.3 INTELLIGENT BUILDINGS

CityPlace, in Hartford, Connecticut, is a 38-story office tower with a difference. When it was constructed, a "data highway" was installed by United Technologies Building Systems. This backbone network combined communications and an intelligent control system over a microprocessor/fiber optic cable and PABX system. Services provided include energy management, lighting management, fire safety, security, and personnel movement, in addition to shared tenant services for office automation equipment. Tenants reap the economic advantages of an already-installed telephone system, communication system, and advanced facilities.

The sharing of multi-tenant systems is aimed at the small to medium-sized business which is unlikely to have its own telecommunications expert on staff. The advantages of the shared services are several:

• The costs of access to telecommunications services are reduced because bulk discounts can be negotiated with long-distance carriers.

• Most advanced facilities are available to all tenants. Because costs are shared, sophisticated facilities which would not be affordable to any of the tenants alone can be acquired.

• There is a reduced risk of obsolescence because equipment is leased, and tenants have access to expert advice.

• It is basically "one-stop shopping."

There are now over 200 intelligent buildings in the United States. By 1990, the figure is expected to be thousands. Services range from mainly PABX support to time-sharing a mainframe computer, networking PCs, and using fax machines, copiers, and all varieties of office automation equipment. More sophisticated features include automated light switching, designed to switch lights on and off as people enter and leave the room; automatic air and temperature control on each floor, with automatic heating/air conditioning turn on/off during and outside of normal work hours; automatic fire detection that helps to inhibit the spread of the fire and can automatically call for help; a parking garage with the ability to record time and date of arrival through a special card; and a voice-activated elevator with special information displays.

A computer, such as Honeywell's DP6 minicomputer, is at the heart of the system. The building uses the smoke detectors, access-control card readers, and telephone as "senses." These will, in the event of a fire, send signals to distributed processors which call the fire department, adjust the ventilation system, open fire doors, and send elevators to the ground floor. They can even tell you by voice messaging that something is wrong. Supervisory processors oversee all the separate "brains" in the buildings, and the wiring acts as its nervous system. Honeywell, for one, claims that intelligent buildings are less expensive to construct, operate, and maintain. The temptations to business tenants are savings that are gained by single-sourcing the computing, communications, and control needs of the office building.

Earlier versions of the smart buildings were so automated that human habits were confounded by the automated systems. For example, automatic light switching was a problem for a group trying to darken the room for a slide presentation. The building knew there were people in the room so would not turn off the lights. After trying to sit very still as a group for ten minutes, one member of the group finally unscrewed the light bulbs!

While the industry is new and growing, there is some disenchantment brewing. The former need for economies of scale are becoming less obvious as newer systems are developed at rapidly decreasing costs to the user firms. In addition, smaller tenants, for whom such shared services were supposed to be attractive, may not need all of the advanced systems available to them in intelligent buildings. Tenants frequently find cost-justifying the occupancy of an intelligent building difficult. And the very integrated nature of the building—combining information processing, telecommunications, facilities management, and so on—makes it difficult for corporate management to find the exact cause of problems that may appear.

It is even difficult to decide which corporate department will be in charge of the integrated facility: should it be the data-processing group already knowledgeable about computers, the facilities group which understands running the building, or the telecommunications group which understands the communications system?

Very large developers, such as Olympia & York of Toronto, have plans to connect two dozen of their buildings in nine cities. Yet even for large developers, there are considerable expenses in intelligent buildings, including large real estate investments, the need to get at least 40 percent of the tenants to use the services, and the planning for future expandability to meet changing tenant needs. Some states make it legally difficult to provide shared tenant services because of local laws regarding the resale of long-distance telephone services, as in Florida and Arkansas, or prohibitive tariffs on such services.

Nevertheless, experts expect the trend to intelligent buildings to continue slowly over the next few years. Some experts have forecast a $10 billion market by 1990, up from less than $100 million in 1984.[2] These experts obviously expect tenant indifference to shift. While Dallas may declare itself the "shared tenant services capital of the world" with 25 percent of its buildings providing shared tenant services, it also has one of the country's highest office building vacancy rates.[3]

7.4 ARTIFICIAL INTELLIGENCE

Artificial intelligence is concerned with enabling computers to mimic the characteristics that make people seem intelligent. That statement raises the question of what is meant by human intelligence—a difficult concept to define. Intelligence appears to be an amalgam of many different information processing and information representing capabilities. Intelligence includes many abilities—to reason, to infer, to theorize, to prove, to acquire knowledge, to apply knowledge, to pursue, to communicate ideas, to learn, and finally to teach. Expert systems are programs that "can advise, analyze, categorize, communicate, consult, design, diagnose, explain, explore, forecast, form concepts, identify, interpret, justify, learn, manage, monitor, plan, present, retrieve, schedule, test and tutor."[4]

The central goals of research into artificial intelligence are to make computers more intelligent, and thus more useful, and to understand the principles which make intelligence possible.

Artificial intelligence began to become an active field of research within computer science in about 1955. Since that time, the study of artificial intelligence has embraced a wide range of topics, including problem solving, theorem proving, game playing, pattern recognition, search methods, linguistics, learning, and teaching.

Early on, researchers in artificial intelligence concluded that traditional mathematical techniques would not be suitable for their work. Symbol systems, which manipulate collections of symbolic structures, were considered to be more suitable for encoding intelligence-exhibiting processes.

One direct result of this was the development in the early 1960s by John McCarthy of Massachusetts Institute of Technology of the LISP language. LISP (logical inferences per second) is a computer language designed for manipulating symbolic expressions in a recursive way. It enables researchers to encode and to explore intelligence-exhibiting processes. Since the 1960s, LISP has gone on to become the prime language of artificial intelligence in the United States and is used in the implementation of many expert systems (defined later).

Artificial intelligence research was almost totally exploratory in the early years. Researchers tried to explore possibilities rather than produce results. Because of the open-ended work on seemingly intangible problems, artificial intelligence became isolated and unpopular within the computer science fraternity. But as years went by, researchers came under increasing pressure to deliver practical results. The pressure came both from within the academic world and from outside sponsors, particularly the federal government.

In the mid–1960s, a new school of thought arose within artificial intelligence, led by Edward Feigenbaum. He suggested several reasons why artificial intelligence was not making reasonable progress. The problems being addressed were too large and too vague, and they involved too many unknowns and too many interactions. Feigenbaum believed that a more useful application of artificial intelligence techniques would be to explore specific problems. His view was that a specific problem, carefully chosen, would provide sufficient complexity to make research meaningful and interesting. Furthermore, the development of new ideas or techniques would be applicable to other specific problems. In time, the specific solutions and techniques could find applicability to more general problems.

Feigenbaum's approach—to reduce problems to a manageable

size—did not immediately generate enthusiasm within the artificial intelligence community. His work was regarded as uninteresting by many researchers, but the Stanford Heuristic Programming Project (HPP) led by Feigenbaum was responsible for the development of a significant number of expert systems and has probably contributed more than any other single project to the credibility of artificial intelligence.

While most of the work by HPP was carried out in narrow, well-defined areas of medicine and chemistry, at Carnegie-Mellon University, development work was more commercially oriented. With collaboration and financial support from Digital Equipment Corporation, a pragmatic approach was used to avoid some of the more difficult problems associated with expert systems.

According to Butler Cox (and definitions vary in complexity elsewhere), an expert system is a computing system embodying organized knowledge about some fields of human expertise in both heuristic (informal, judgmental knowledge of an application area) and factual forms, and capable from that knowledge of producing useful inferences. Expert systems differ from conventional computer programs in a variety of ways. A conventional program is an integral unit. The whole is determined analytically in advance. In contrast, the knowledge base of an expert system normally contains pieces of knowledge that are independent of each other. Each piece can be altered separately. This is an important, if somewhat imprecise, characteristic of expert systems.

Many people involved with expert systems agree that the most significant distinguishing characteristic of an expert system is its explanation facility, sometimes known as its "human window." Most expert systems designed can explain their own line of reasoning and can answer questions posed by the user, either during or at the end of a question-and-answer session. The form of user query can be "why" (are you asking me for this information) or "how" (was some particular conclusion reached).

The performance level of an expert system is primarily a function of the size and quality of the knowledge base that it possesses. The knowledge represented in the knowledge base consists of both facts and heuristics about the application area ("domain"). An important distinguishing feature of an expert system is the inclusion of heuristics. They are rules of good judgment—the common sense, informal, judgmental knowledge of actions to take when a situation arises.

The knowledge base of an expert system can be easily extended or modified. Knowledge is represented in the knowledge base as a collection of individual and independent pieces of fact and heuristics. Any one of these pieces can be changed, or pieces removed or added, with no great impact on the remainder of the knowledge base. This contrasts with the traditional procedural program, where a small change to the logic can have serious effects on the system.

In most expert systems, the processing logic is an integral part of the knowledge base. The facts and the rules are sufficiently comprehensive normally to contain all the information that is logically required to make any decision. All the reasoning mechanism does is to ensure that relevant facts and rules are retrieved at the right time. In a traditional computer system, the processing rules are embodied in the program, and the data are held in a separate store.

The reasoning mechanism of an expert system, which is known as the inference engine, is separate from the knowledge base. The inference engine interprets the knowledge base and so is sometimes also known as the "rule interpreter." This inference engine tests the individual rules or pieces of knowledge by pattern matching—activating them when there is a match. The rule interpreter uses a predetermined control strategy for searching through the rules and deciding which rules to apply ("enabling" the rules).

The search is normally carried out through a question-and-answer session. The system can ask the user for guidance or for further information when it is unable to deduce the next step. Moreover, the expert system is able to explain its own line of reasoning. This is why the user interface is so important, and why so much effort—up to 80 percent of development time in some cases—goes into the design of the user interface.

Most of the serious applications of expert systems to date are designed to be used by, and to benefit, people who are experts in the field. This is because the consultation session relies on the user having a highly developed understanding of the subject matter. The reason for this is that many of the questions call for a judgmental answer. Only a person knowledgeable in the field ("domain expert") and familiar with the domain's assumptions and ambiguities, is able to place in context the final suggested solution, or the advice or answer offered by the system.

A typical expert system provides the user at the end of a consultation session with a possible or plausible solution to the problem posed at the outset. Rather than being presented in the form of a definite answer, the solution takes the form of advice to the user. The solution may not be right, but it is more likely to be right than other plausible solutions. It is the outcome of deduction involving both the facts and the heuristics stored in the knowledge base.

Expert systems have had a number of limitations that have kept them from being commercially successful, especially in the business marketplace. Their domain has to be sharply focused, and the problem to be resolved by the expert system has to be constrained, neither involving an indefinite number of commonsense concepts and facts about the work nor involving a very large number of objects and relations in the problem area itself. In addition, tremendous time is needed to develop expert systems. Most have been constructed laboriously by a team of specialists over several years. To help reduce the problem, some research groups have explored ways of automating the construction of knowledge bases, while others have tried to write routines that conduct a dialogue with an expert, for the purpose of extracting knowledge without the help of a knowledge engineer.

Most successful expert systems have a knowledge base containing several hundred rules that has taken a team of systems builders and domain experts years to construct and organize. As a result, most expert systems have cost more than a million dollars to build, excluding the cost of the very considerable effort needed to maintain and refine the developed system. Because of the expense and the associated risk involved in developing an expert system, the domains that have been explored so far have tended to be related either to the industry sections, such as oil and chemicals, that are able to justify the investment in terms of the value of results, or to government-sponsored sectors, such as medicine and mineral exploration. Finances have influenced the selection of domains more than applicability.

Most of the best-known expert systems have attempted to capture expertise in domains where human experts themselves are both expensive and scarce and where training takes many years. At the same time, the knowledge of these domains has been widely available, having been published over the years in textbooks and reference books.

Another limitation of expert systems is the "human window." Despite the acclaim that has sometimes surrounded it, the explanation facility actually offers little insight into an expert system's way of reasoning. Neither the utility programs for constructing knowledge bases, nor the reasoning programs themselves, contain much knowledge about their own assumptions and limitations. This explains why most present-day expert systems can be used only by experts who already have gained sufficient appreciation of the system's knowledge and limitations to enable them to interpret its conclusions sensibly.

Disadvantages aside, the market for artificial intelligence is just beginning in the office environment. Knowledge-based systems have an obvious contribution to make to computer-aided training, particularly in areas where the knowledge is highly specialized and difficult to acquire. In addition, providing advice is a very broad field. Tax advice is a field where the expert system would be helpful, as in the area of general advice in counseling about benefits or tax rebates, for example. Decision support systems will probably grow in stature and usefulness following the application of expert system techniques.

Large vocabulary speech recognition systems that can recognize up to

20,000 words are becoming available. Indeed, some predict that these machines will become the professional's office typewriter of the next decade. Through a microphone, users can dictate memos, letters, even lengthy reports, without touching a computer keyboard. The spoken word then becomes written text, even while using a popular software package. Several vendors, including Kurzweil Applied Intelligence of Waltham, Mass., Dragon Systems Inc. of Newton, Mass., and Speech Systems Inc. of Tarzana, Calif., as well as IBM (which licenses a package from Dragon Systems), have introduced products. Prices are currently in the $2,000 range for the Dragon System Voicescribe–2000 which runs on a high-end personal computer.

Using complex software is a knowledge-intensive activity. Manuals are complex, filled with detail, and easily (and usually) forgotten. Manuals are often poorly written, containing merely the facts about the system and not the rules of thumb necessary for using the system. Expert systems that are knowledgeable about particularly complex software could radically improve matters. With their extensive knowledge base, they would be able to interpret and fulfill user requests. The knowledge base would be provided by the system developers and augmented by the user community itself. In this situation, the manuals of the past would become active and influential in the service of user needs. The market for expert systems of this sort would be as broad as the market for software.

Voice recognition and natural language processing are other areas where expert system software techniques will be used to try to solve problems for which traditional techniques have proven inadequate. And computer games will become more challenging and complex with the use of expert system applications.

Artificial intelligence is already moving to workstations. Many established companies are translating their complex products into more standard programming languages and adapting their LISP programs to particular workstations. The agreement on using Common LISP as a standard version of the language has allowed workstation makers to enter the artificial intelligence market sooner than expected.

Xerox, IBM, DEC, Apollo, Prime, Sun, and Symbolics all have workstations on the market today using some type of expert system. Most are used for technical applications, but applications such as corporate database access will soon see the use of expert systems in the office environment. Prices are dropping substantially, and in 1986 some workstations were available for as little as $8,900 with a charge for software around $3,500. The most potentially lucrative market is commercial data processing, which will soon expand the use of even trivial forms of artificial intelligence to the user of the standard personal computer.

7.5 IMPLICATIONS OF NEW ELECTRONIC PAYMENT AND CASH MANAGEMENT SYSTEMS

As with any technologically based change, the truly crucial question concerning the revolution in cash is whether it will actually happen. The short history of information technology is already littered with the wreckage of overconfident forecasts based on an overestimate of the appeal of technology and an underestimate of the powers of social, economic, and attitudinal inertia. These errors are particularly common, and the margins vary widely, when the proposed change depends on the creation of a mass market. It is relatively much easier to persuade a thousand companies to use a new software package than to persuade a million people to subscribe to a new service.

In spite of these precautions, it appears that significant changes in the field of information technology and cash will occur. In a sense, the hard part of the task of creating a new market has already been achieved, since much of personal and corporate credit management has already been computerized.

The reader might examine his or her own personal finances. How much of the total inflow and outflow of funds is already being handled electronically? Tax and social security contributions are deducted, often electronically, at the source. Major and regular payments such as mortgage payments, insurance premiums, and subscriptions are made by standing order or direct debit. Other major transactions are aggregated electronically by credit card. Cash payments are already becoming a relatively minor source of outflow, at least in value terms. Many people, especially those in the professional and administrative classes, never receive cash at all—except when withdrawing from their own accounts. (And where do they get the cash? Probably an automated teller machine!)

Therefore, the introduction of electronic funds transfer at the point of sale (EFTPOS), although rightly regarded in some ways as a major change, really amounts to the setting up of a network of data capture points for data processing and communications systems that already largely exist and that already handle the bulk of our money transactions.

The impact of the new payment and cash management systems will be felt by nations, by individuals, and by organizations of most types, sizes, and in most sectors. They will affect not only current payment and funds transfer methods but will lead to whole new business practices, different organizational structures, and changed industry relationships.

For large companies, the developments in electronic funds transfer and cash management services will have some far-reaching consequences:

- Companies will increasingly regard effective cash management as an additional source of profit. The increased speed and precision brought by EFT to payment systems is likely to encourage this trend.

- EFT is likely to favor multinational operations. Companies will be able to exercise better financial control over foreign subsidiaries and their financial affairs, and they may be better placed to take advantage of business opportunities at remote locations. Therefore, financial control is likely to become more centralized.

- Credit and payment terms are likely to become even more specific than at present and play an even more important role in the negotiation of deals, with precision in payment timing a significant element. Many firms now rely on the credit game: deferring payment to their suppliers for goods received on credit, while receiving payment for the same goods from their customers. The new payment systems will provide an opportunity to question the continuation of such practices.

- The relationship between companies and their banks will continue to change. As the importance of cash management increases, companies will become more sophisticated. They will undertake more financial activities themselves, be more specific in their demands, and shop around more for individual services. Banks, too, are likely to contribute to the decline in the total banking relationship, responding to both internal pressures and market demand by unbundling services and by bringing charges for individual services more in line with costs. At the same time, organizations other than banks will be better placed than they are to fulfill and exploit some market needs, especially those that do not require a network of branches.

For banks in particular, two key issues arise. Will they achieve the anticipated benefits from EFT services? And what will be the impact of EFT on the structure of banking markets?

Banks see an opportunity with EFT services to reduce costs, in particular staff costs and costs associated with operating branch networks, and to gain a market advantage. The new banking services vary in the nature and extent of the benefits they are likely to deliver.

Automated teller machines have the potential to reduce branch costs by replacing small branches and staff, or freeing them for new tasks, and favoring a strategy of concentrating the provision of more complex services in larger branches. These savings have not been universally achieved to date, partly because of the high cost of ATMs and their installation. Just as retailers move into the management of cash resources, it is possible that banks will seek to exploit their expensive street locations by offering new financial services and perhaps even other kinds of services and products.

EFTPOS and bulk payment services offer banks the prime opportunities for reducing the costs of handling paper payments. Bulk payment services have undoubtedly been successful in achieving this objective, although they have not replaced as much paper as had been hoped. EFTPOS, once it is introduced on a wider scale, will help relieve the pressure from increasing volumes of paper arising from credit card transactions. However, volumes of check payments to retailers are likely to continue to rise because more people with bank accounts will write checks than initially use debit EFTPOS services.

Corporate cash management services offer the banks some scope for staff savings—for example, in the handling of telephone balance inquiries and manually processed funds transfer or dealing with other instructions. The main motivation for providing them, however, is to win new or retain existing corporate accounts which might otherwise go elsewhere.

EFT removes some of the barriers that prevent organizations other than banks from operating payment-related services by reducing the need for a network of central city branches and a labor-intensive payments-processing operation. But developing and providing EFT services requires not only high initial costs and expertise but also credibility in the marketplace, which the banks already have but which others will need to build.

Electronic payment and cash management services present some significant opportunities to software and systems houses, computer service bureaus, network suppliers, and value-added network service providers. They may adopt a number of different roles such as service retailer; service provider as agent for a bank or other financial institution; or system, software, or network service supplier.

In addition, there are related opportunities for user support training, maintenance, and so forth, and also opportunities to act as a broker between banks in circumstances where banks will not deal directly with other banks—for example, in the exchange of account information.

However, in most of these markets, suppliers will face competition from the banks themselves. Banks which lead in the technology can market their systems and services to other banks and set up arm's-length subsidiaries to compete with service bureaus in markets where the banks themselves are at a disadvantage. The activities of technology services suppliers may also be restricted by lack of banking expertise and by regulation.

Electronic funds transfer services are only viable if an appropriate telecommunications infrastructure is available. All on-line funds transfer systems—be they EFTPOS, home banking, or cash management—will increase traffic volumes over telecommunications systems. Although in principle the telecommunications services providers stand to gain from such increases in traffic volumes, current systems will need to be upgraded to provide the quality, reliability, and security required.

By far the most significant market for terminal equipment arising out of the various electronic funds transfer services is that for EFTPOS terminals. In terms of product life cycles, this market is still emerging in the United States. At present, product specifications vary considerably.

Standai   ay occur earlier than usual in the product life cycle, because   ation between banks. Therefore, vendors' wisest course of a   e to adopt product strategies which expose them to least risk in   f the current uncertainty. The most successful suppliers wil   e those who respond well to emergent demand rather than thc   k to preempt demand.

Treasury syst   ndardizing on common brands of personal computers, in pa   IBM. This reflects the dominance of this supplier in financi   ns, and it will be extremely difficult for other suppliers to m   inroads into this market.

Home banking and   payment-related applications for the home will increase the usefulness of home computers or videotex terminals. In most cases, they are unlikely to trigger the acquisition of terminals by the end customer. Such terminals may, however, be acquired by the banks offering home banking services for subsequent distribution to their customers. Therefore, a strategy for home equipment suppliers to sell such terminals to banks instead of to their ultimate customers makes sense.

Once the market takes off for all these systems and enters the growth phase, market conditions will be better suited to, and are likely to encourage the participation of, large information technology vendors and especially those with particular interests in the banking and retailing sectors. The ability to deliver high volumes of equipment at low cost and to provide national and international support and maintenance facilities are likely to militate against some of the small suppliers currently active in the market. To survive, they will need to identify and exploit specialized niches and exploit their ability to react faster to changing market requirements than larger suppliers.

NOTES

1. Christy Snyder, "The Looming Shadow of a Software Goliath," *ICP Business Software Review* (UK edition, Oct. 1985): 10–17.

2. Leopold Froehlich, "Are Smart Buildings a Dumb Idea?" *Datamation* (Oct. 1, 1985): 101–104.

3. Peter Meade, "Shared Tenant Services: The Hype Is Over. Now Comes the Work," *Communications Week* (March 10, 1986).

4. Robert H. Michaelson, Donald Michie, and Albert Boulanger, "The Technology of Expert Systems," *Byte* (April 1985): 303. This entire issue is devoted to detailed discussions of artificial intelligence.

REFERENCES

Bulkeley, William M., and Brenton R. Schlender. "New Disk System for Personal Computers Holds Promise of Big Changes in Software." *Wall Street Journal*

(June 17, 1986): 31.

Butler Cox Foundation. "Expert System" (Sept. 1983).

Butler Cox Foundation. "Trends in Information Technology" (Jan. 1984).

Butler Cox & Partners Ltd. "The Information Technology Market 1984 Overview."

"Developing Brain-Box Office Blocks." *Computing, The Magazine* (Aug. 1, 1985): 12–13.

"Find the Key to the Intelligent Office Building." *Computing* (June 12, 1986).

Fisher, Edward M. "Building AI behind Closed Doors." *Datamation* (Aug. 1, 1986): 46–49.

"Get Smart and Integrate." *Informatics* (June 1986): 18, 19.

Ives, Stephen R. "Future Directions in Local Area Networks: The Evolution of the Corporate Information Network." Paper presented at NETWORKS '86, Online Publications, Pinner, UK (1986).

Pippeteau, Jane. "The Intelligent Office Building Is Born." *Financial Times* (April 9, 1986).

Purton, Peter. "How Intelligent Are Buildings?" *Communications Europe* (Jan. 1986).

Verity, John W. "The LISP Race Heats Up." *Datamation* (Aug. 1, 1986): 55–58.

Glossary

Access time. (1) The time in which a machine is operating and available for use. (2) The time required to call up a certain piece of information on a computer.

Acoustics. An ergonomic consideration relating to the level of noise within an office and workstation. Noise can be controlled through the engineering and the architecture of the space.

Active files. Files that contain records that are used frequently.

Active records. Those records consulted in the performance of current administrative work, or records in working files.

Actuating. (1) Implementing or starting a process. (2) Putting a process into action.

Administrative support. The job function of assisting management in performing tasks of a nontyping nature.

Analog. Operating by directly measurable quantities from a continuum of possible alternatives (as opposed to digital).

Analytical staff. Personnel who collect information and data and analyze and define what is revealed by both statistical data and subjective collection of feelings and thoughts.

Anthropometry. The study of human body measurements for the scaling of sizes, heights, and shapes of furniture and equipment to the dimensions of workers.

Applications software. Sets of instructions used to tell the computer how to do a specific job. Applications are designed to perform specific tasks for the end user. Applications include word processing, spreadsheet analysis, payroll, electronic mail, graphics, statistical analysis, and even games.

Architecture. The schematic or functional design of a piece of hardware or software.

ASCII (American Standard Code for Information Interchange). A character coding system used for data storage and transmission.

Asynchronous transmission. The mode of transmission between equipment with different protocols, in which a "start" signal precedes and a "stop" signal follows each character to check synchronization. Thus, characters move one at a time along the communications line.

Authoring system. A software package that allows an individual to design a computer-based training course on the computer. The package "authors" the CBT course.

Back-office processing. Functions associated traditionally with the data-processing group in a firm that concerns the internal functions of a firm. Payroll and large transaction processing applications are typical back-office activities.

Bar graph. A chart that presents information through the use of horizontal or vertical bars.

BASIC (Beginner's All-Purpose Symbolic Instruction Code). A computer programming language that was developed in the mid–1960s at Dartmouth College as a simple interactive language for students learning how to program.

Batch mode. A method by which a computer deals with doing a number of tasks. The computer maintains a queue of tasks. The computer takes on one task at a time, finishes it, and moves on to the next.

Baud rate. In telecommunications, the rate of signaling speed. The rate of speed expressed in bauds is equal to the number of signaling elements per second.

Behavioralism. A task-oriented approach to learning which stresses repetition and permits the measurement of results.

Benchmark. A point of reference used in determining a plus or minus accomplishment.

Benchmark position. A job which has been measured; performance criteria have been established that provide a determination as to the worth and value of the position.

Beta site. A site, usually a department within a company, that is used as a test case for an office automation feasibility study.

Bit. A binary digit. The smallest element of binary machine language represented by a magnetized or optical spot on a recording surface. Six to eight bits are required to form a character or byte.

Bits per second (BPS). A measure of the speed of data transmission in information systems.

Black box. An intermediate interpretation device or program used to allow information to be transmitted between pieces of equipment that use different protocols; often called a translator.

Boilerplate. Prewritten and presorted documents that are used repeatedly, such as letters or contracts, to which variable information may be filled in at the keyboard.

Bus network. A network that consists of a length of co-axial cable (called a bus) along which individual devices tap into the communications cable. There is no centralized hub. Signals from one station move along the bus in both directions to all other stations connected to the cable.

Byte. A sequence of adjacent binary digits (bits) that represent a character.

Centralization. The concept of locating one or more functions at a single site with a central support staff.

COBOL (Common Business Oriented Language). A computer programming language developed in the late 1950s and intended for use in the solutions of problems in business data processing.

Cognitive approach to learning. An approach that stresses overall conceptual understanding of an entire system as opposed to the rote understanding of individual components. Trainees learn through comprehension not repetition.

Communicating word processor. A text-editing system equipped with electronic circuitry which enables it to transmit data to, or receive data from, a computer, another word processor, or, in some cases, a telex or other machine.

Communication processing. The control of digital communication switches with a computer. An operator can control the flow of information through a network from a video display terminal.

Computer-assisted instruction (CAI). See *computer-based training.*

Computer-based instruction (CBI). See *computer-based training.*

Computer-based message system (CBMS). The overall concept of communicating electronically and bypassing the standard paper medium. A system that allows the transmission of text messages to and from the users who are connected to the computer on which the system is based. Electronic mail is one application.

Computer-based training (CBT). A training course in which the trainee sits before a computer with a video display terminal and receives instruction directly from the computer. The computer presents information, elicits responses, and tests the trainee to find out how much he or she has learned.

Computer graphics. Graphic representations of information produced on a computer.

Computerized branch exchange (CBX). A digitally controlled communication switching device.

Computer management instruction (CMI). A form of computer-based training where the results of the training sessions are collected, tabulated, and sent to management for review automatically by the computer.

Computer output mailing system. A mailing system that allows computer-printed continuous forms to be fed into equipment that automatically bursts the forms, inserts them into envelopes, designates zip code breaks, and meter-stamps for mailing.

Computer teleconferencing. A telecommunications process in which text, data, facsimile images, and voice are transmitted from one geographical location to another.

Conference method. A training session in which trainees are encouraged to express themselves orally and to exchange and compare ideas.

Cost avoidance. The elimination or reduction of costs in a budget through elimination of the necessity for temporary help, overtime, or additional budgeted personnel.

Cost-benefit analysis. A detailed analysis of the costs and benefits, both quantifiable and intangible, of implementing a particular system or program.

Counting-documents method. A method used to determine the amount of typing produced. Any completed task (letter, report) is counted as one document, and the total number of documents produced in a given time period (a day, a week) is determined.

Counting-lines method. A method of determining the amount of typing by counting the lines produced within a given period of time.

Courseware. The software that composes a computer-based training session.

Central processing unit (CPU). The information storage area shared by multiple data- or word-processing terminals.

Cathode ray tube (CRT). An electronic vacuum tube, similar to a television picture tube, that displays text as it is entered from the keyboard. See *video display terminal.*

Data base. The compilation and storage of information consisting of data and text for the purposes of access, retrieval, and printout.

Database management. The management of data structures with a computer rather than with paper files.

Database management system (DBMS). A computer software package that handles the storage and retrieval of information stored in direct-access computer data bases.

Data processing. The manipulation of information through various digital computations by means of a computer.

Data storage. The preservation of information on any one of a number of available kinds of electromagnetic media such as magnetic disks, tapes, optical disks, or semiconductor chips.

Decentralization. The concept of locating computers and terminals, as well as word processors with standalone intelligence, in many different departments of an organization.

Decision support system. Special software that provides significant aids for financial planning, portfolio analysis, tax planning, and market analysis, and for projecting business situations that require mathematical formula calculations.

Desk manual. A guidebook to particular duties and tasks that remains with the job and the workstation for which it was written.

Digital. Data transmission in the form of discrete units; a process that transmits data by translating sound waves into on/off digital pulses.

Disk drive. The device into which a disk is inserted that reads information, writes information, and physically spins the disk to find information.

Disk pack. A stack of hard disks that share a spindle, have a standard specification, and a large storage capacity.

Display-oriented text-editing system. A world-processing or text-editing system which uses a video display terminal and a keyboard for the input of text. Information entered at the keyboard is displayed on the screen and subsequently can be printed or recorded on various media.

Distributed system. A computer system that provides decentralized processing, memory, and storage capacity. System components are linked through a network of digital communication lines.

Documentary information. Information that is recorded in some kind of permanent form, such as in written or printed materials.

Documentation. (1) A memo that describes an incident clearly and fairly and thus permits a problem to be confronted supportively and with just cause. (2) Observation of a machine in operation, to determine its usefulness to an office.

Dot matrix. An array of points in ink, light, or similar image-forming elements that are used to form alphanumeric characters.

Downtime. Time when equipment cannot be used because of malfunction.

Dvorak simplified keyboard (DSK). Developed in 1932, this typewriter keyboard makes it possible for 70 percent of the work to be done on the home row of keys and a majority of the keystroking to be done by the right hand.

EBCDIC (extended binary coded decimal information code). An eight-bit alphanumeric code used on all IBM computers.

Editing. The correction, refinement, or revision of written material.

Electronic blackboard. A blackboard, developed by Bell Laboratories, that transmits graphics and handwritten communications over telephone lines for viewing on video monitors in distant locations.

Electronic data processing. The manipulation of data through the use of electronic computers.

Electronic file. A logical grouping of information, data, or text that is stored and accessed on a computer as a discrete whole.

Electronic mail. A system of communicating messages electronically to a recipient who receives either a hard copy or a visually displayed message on a CRT screen. The message may be transmitted electronically by facsimile, communicating word processors, computer-based message systems, public-carrier-based systems, public postal services, or private and public teletypes.

Electronic mailbox. A computer-based message system on which messages can be left until the user makes an inquiry.

Electronic proof. Database storage from which information can be recalled and reconstructed by electronic means. Proofing is accomplished by viewing the copy and editing it right at the visual display terminal.

End user. An individual who uses a computer for a business task directly related to his or her job.

Ergonomic concerns. Workstation features designed to promote optimum employee performance.

Ergonomics. Facilities planning focused on the aesthetics of the workstation and its surrounding space, for example, the needs for privacy, a smooth flow or paperwork and communication, balanced territorial and social concerns, adequate access to electrical and communications circuits, and proper lighting, climate, acoustics, and color/decor.

Event schedule. A written timetable of steps to be taken to accomplish a goal, such as a step-by-step to implement office automation.

External information. Data that originate outside an organization, such as information concerning the products and services of competitors.

Facsimile (also called *fax*). A process that involves the transmission of an exact copy over communications lines. Facsimile combines replication and distribution functions; it duplicates exact copies of graphs, pictures, and other materials and transmits them to other locations.

Feasibility study. A study of the possible consequences and costs or benefits of following a particular plan of action.

Fiber optics. The technique of converting digital communication signals to light pulses that are sent over strands of hair-thin glass fibers.

File. An organized, named collection of data records treated as a unit and stored on some external storage device.

File classification system. A logical and systematic arrangement of files into subject groups or categories based on some definite scheme of relationship using numbers or letters for identification.

Filing. The activity and manner of keeping, organizing, and maintaining information in an orderly and retrievable form.

Financial lease. A lease arrangement whereby the lessor recovers the full cost of the equipment plus expenses and a profit. The lessee may receive title to the equipment at the end of the lease period.

First-line supervision. Management of ongoing operations at the department level.

Fixed information. Hard copy, microfilm, and other image storage that is unalterable in time and format.

Floppy disks. A small flexible disk, five and ¼ inches in diameter, that has become the primary storage medium for personal computers.

Flowchart. A diagram that uses symbols to illustrate the flow of work and paper through the office, from origin to completion.

Formatting. The process of composing the basic form or style of text.

FORTRAN. The first widely used procedure-oriented, computer programming language. Commands are expressed in a language that combines English and mathematics. Developed in the 1950s, FORTRAN is an acronym for "formula translation."

Front-office processing. Processing functions that are performed by end users who deal with the firm's clientele directly or with the firm's nontechnical personnel. Word processing, database management, spreadsheet analysis are typical front-office activities.

Guideline method. A technique for interpreting and reflecting the value of jobs in the marketplace.

Hard disks. A disk resembling a phonograph record that is used to store large quantities of information that can be updated. Hard disks are used in personal microcomputers but are known primarily as the storage medium for mini-computers and larger mainframes.

Hard dollars. Expenditures of money that can be measured and controlled such as the salaries of employees and cost of equipment.

Hard-dollar savings. Those salary and fringe benefit costs that can be saved through reduction of staff.

Hardware. A basic piece of equipment.

Historical data approach. An approach to studying an office that involves gathering information from past records about the time and amount of work associated with a certain job.

Horizontal software. Generic applications software designed to perform a general application in any business.

Icon. A picture or symbol on a video display that depicts or symbolizes a computer function. When a user points to the icon with a "mouse" (a pointer displayed on the screen), the computer performs the function depicted.

Impact printer. An output unit that prints characters on paper by physical contact.

Incremental budget. A budget in which expenses for the coming year are based on the preceding year or on some average of preceding years.

Information management. Supervision and control over a system that creates, gathers, processes, replicates, distributes, stores, or destroys the information utilized by an organization.

Information processing. A concept that embodies both data processing and word processing. An information processing system manipulates and handles all forms of business information (date, text, image, and voice).

Input. The entering of source data or text into a system for processing.

Instruction. A coded sequence of binary numbers that is interpreted by the computer processor and causes the computer to perform a primary function.

Integrated circuit. An electronic circuit made up of a large number of components, semiconductors, or transistors fabricated onto a computer chip. ICs are the building blocks of computer processors.

Integrated software. A type of software which is becoming increasingly dominant and which features programs that combine the functions of word processing, spreadsheets, graphics, communications, and sometimes accounting, often by using "windows" to promote ease of use and entry from one function to another.

Integrated systems. Systems that permit multiple functions to occur simultaneously and permit the user to combine text and data in a single application with little or no difficulty.

Intelligent copiers. Copiers that can electronically store materials such as often-used forms and thereby eliminate the need for hard-copy storage facilities.

Intelligent typewriter. An enhanced typewriter that has the ability to perform certain difficult typing tasks automatically, such as centering of characters and decimal alignment.

Interface. This term applies to an information exchange capability either between two machines, two people, or a machine and a person.

Internal information. Information generated within the organization (examples are production schedules, payrolls, policy manuals, organizational directives).

Job classification. The analysis and rating of jobs according to predetermined classes (the same or similar task groupings).

Job description. A written, organized presentation of the duties involved in a specific job.

Job enlargement. See *job enrichment*.

Job enrichment. The process of heightening both task efficiency and human satisfaction by providing greater scope for personal achievement and recognition in jobs, more challenging and responsible work, and more opportunity for individual advancement and growth.

Job evaluation. Any formal procedure for appraising, classifying, and weighing a set of functions.

Job redesign. The rethinking of a job and what it contains, with a view toward expanding the job by including in it more horizontal and vertical activities.

Job specifications. The minimum requirements of a job.

Keyboarding. The process of entering data into a computer system with a keyboard.

Keystroke counters. Electronic counting devices that count the number of keystrokes produced on input devices.

Knowledge worker. Any management, professional, or clerical worker who processes information for use in decision-making.

Large-scale integration (LSI). A manufacturing technique in which large numbers of highly miniaturized electronic circuits are combined or integrated on a single chip of silicon or other semiconductor material. LSI has permitted very significant reductions in the cost of microprocessor and memory circuits.

Laser. (light amplification by stimulated emission of radiation). A device that uses the natural oscillations of atoms to generate coherent, focused electromagnetic radiation. Lasers are used to cut optical disks and to read them.

Laser printing. A printing process similar to image printing, except that it operates by laser control rather than direct impact.

Learning curve. A measure of the rate of learning in relation to the length of training.

Life cycle. The length of time for which a system meets the objectives of the organization.

Line counting. The electronic or manual process of counting typed lines.

Line graph. A chart that uses various types of lines to show fluctuations in a value or quantity over a period of time.

Local area network (LAN). A network that is designed for a particular installation to connect various elements of its office systems. A LAN could connect large computers, personal computers, remote terminals, or telephone lines.

LSI (large-scale integration) circuits. A mass-produced electronic circuit that contains up to 10,000 transistors on one silicon chip.

Machine dictation. The act of speaking into a microphone and recording ideas on magnetic tape for later transcription onto paper by a secretary or word-processing operator.

Magnetic bubble memory. A magnetic memory that must be accessed serially but has a higher storage density than many other storage media.

Magnetic media. Any type of magnetically charged belt, card, disk, or tape used to store, make corrections, erase, or rewrite documents.

Main memory. The data storage capacity built into the computer itself.

Mainframe. The central processing unit (CPU) that houses the hardware, software, and operating controls of a computer.

Management by objective (MBO). A management strategy that focuses on goals.

Managerial workstation. A work area designed for the professional knowledge worker. It usually contains a computer terminal with time management controls, text-editing features, electronic mail capabilities, files processing capability, and other features.

Memory. The capacity of a computer to store information electronically. Information in main memory may be accessed at any time to allow the computer processor to complete its functions.

Menu. A list on a display screen that gives the extent of available choices in response to a prompt.

Microcomputer. A small standalone computer that is operated from only one console and can perform only one task at a time. Personal computers are microcomputers.

Microprocessor. A minuscule logic circuit on a microchip of silicon that can perform over 1 million calculations per second.

Minicomputer. A minicomputer comprises a central processor, a console, and also a number of peripheral devices such as disk drives and operating terminals. More than one user can perform tasks at the same time in either a real-time or time-sharing operating environment. The minicomputer is distinguished from larger mainframes by not being suitable for massive number-crunching tasks.

MIS. An acronym which stands for management information systems.

Modem. A device that converts analog signals to digital signals or vice versa for transmission over telephone lines or other communication facilities.

Mouse. The electronic pointer that comes with a video display terminal. With a mouse, a user may designate the function he or she wants the computer to perform.

MTM (measure time and motion). The measurement of time by applying time measurement units (tmu) to each singular function or task to determine time and motion standards.

Multifunction terminals. Systems based on mainframe computers or minicomputers equipped with special software that provide specific services on computer terminals; such terminals generally are used for many functions.

Multi-tasking software. System software that gives a computer the capability to simultaneously perform two or more tasks.

Needs assessment study. A study aimed at providing an overall perspective on an organization's needs as a basis for future planning.

Network. A system that interconnects a wide assortment of information processing devices through a communications link.

Networking. The linking of various information processing devices, such as word processors and data-entry units, storage devices, printers, processors, and other peripherals, to send, receive, exchange, store, or reproduce information.

Node. A terminus in any sort of network. In a computer it could be a terminal, a disk drive, or a communications interface. For instance, in a PBX it would be any telephone.

Nondocumentary information. Information that is not recorded and only obtained through word of mouth or personal observation.

Nonimpact printer. A printing device in which the paper is not struck but imaged by other means such as an ink jet, an electrostatic process, or a laser.

OEM. An acronym standing for "original equipment manufacturers."

Off-the-shelf applications package. Software packages sold by computer vendors or by separate software outlets. Such packages provide freedom and flexibility to experiment, as they can be obtained and used or discarded quickly and easily.

Office automation (OA). The introduction to the office systems that offer word processing as part of a bundle of office functions that include electronic mail and message distribution, electronic filing, data access, data processing, and administrative functions such as calendaring, scheduling, and tickler systems.

Offset printing, A printing process in which copies are made from an original copy produced on either a paper or a metal plate.

Online. (1) Pertaining to equipment or devices under control of the central processing unit. (2) Pertaining to a user's ability to interact with a computer.

Online data base. An integrated accumulation of machine-readable data maintained on one or more direct access storage devices.

Online terminal. A device that permits the interactive transmission of data to, or the reception of data from, a computer or other information processing device via electronic digital pulses transmitted over some medium.

Open-office planning. Designing office space with minimal enclosed areas, using movable wall panels.

Operating lease. A lease arrangement whereby equipment is leased for a fixed sum each month. The lessor does not normally recover the full cost of the equipment over the period of the lease.

Operating system. A set of digitally coded instructions that enables the computer processor to function and to control its own operations.

Optical disk (OD). A plastic and metal composite circular medium on which data may be stored and retrieved by means of directed laser beams.

Organization chart. A graphic presentation of the organizational structure that points out responsibility relationships.

Organizational culture. A company's values, attitudes, and degree of competitiveness and commitment, which reflect top management's approach to decision-making.

Organizational objectives. Company goals.

Organizational structure. The hierarchy of authority, span of control, and areas of responsibility within an organization.

Orientation or induction training. Training that acquaints new employees with the company's history, philosophy, policy, practices, and procedures (such as office rules and regulations or employee benefits).

Original input. Information put into a system for the first time.

Originators. Individuals who create information or text.

Overhead transparency. A clear plastic sheet that, when placed on a lighted glass surface, projects the image on the sheet in magnified form onto a screen.

PBX (private branch exchange). An electromechanical communications device—usually a staffed switchboard.

Peripheral device. A device not central to the operation of a computer but which is connected to it and supports it functionally.

Personal computer. A computer designed for use by managers and professionals rather than by computer specialists.

Phase-in process. An area-by-area approach to office automation.

Pie chart. A circular diagram divided into sections ("slices") that normally is used to present information in percentages.

Pilot. A prototype installation.

Point method. A method of evaluation in which a range of points is assigned to a set of common factors such as education or skill.

Presorted mail. Mail that is sorted according to zip codes, carrier routes, and so on before mailing.

Processing. The manipulation of information of any sort by a computer system.

Processor. The central device within a computer that executes the instructions provided by the user.

Productivity. Measurement of the ratio of work done to time spent doing it.

Productivity gains. Improvements in employee work output.

Programmed instruction. A self-instruction method in which information is systematically presented to the trainee.

Protocol. The language in which a message sent from one machine to another is packaged and handled.

Prototype. A test situation involving installations or equipment being considered for wider use in the company.

Qualitative data. Employee perceptions of how and why things are done within the system.

Quality circles (QC). A group or circle of employees that meets to discuss how to improve the quantity and quality of work.

Quality of work life (QWL). A factor of work life that can be enriched when employees are involved in decisions affecting their work environment.

Quantitative data. Measurable work being accomplished, the type of information required by management, and the time it takes to produce such information.

Random access memory (RAM). A computer memory device from which information may be accessed by pointing directly to its location.

Real labor costs. All labor costs, including payroll costs.

Real-time processing. A mode of computer processing in which information about a transaction or other event is processed at the time the event occurs, as opposed to batch processing in which there is an interval of time between the occurrence of an event and the processing of information about that event.

Record. (1) Official document that furnishes information that is stored for future reference. (2) A discrete unit of information stored in an electronic file.

Recording density. A measure of how tightly data bits may be stored; a measure of the store capacity of a medium for a given space occupied.

Replication. The duplication of information in another form.

Reprographics. The various techniques of replicating information with the ultimate objective of distributing it in some form. Replication techniques include printing, phototypesetting, duplicating, and COM (computer output microfilm).

Request for proposal (RFP). A document prepared by a potential user addressed to a vendor which delineates the user's needs and requirements.

Resource sharing. The facility that enables a number of users to operate the same piece of hardware or software.

Satellite communications. Electronic telecommunications via worldwide satellite transmission.

Self-paced instruction. Instruction through individual learning packets that consists of a planned program through which an individual moves at his or her own pace.

Semiconductor. A material that is neither a good conductor of electricity or a good insulator of the flow of electricity. It is used in transistors to permit the flow of electricity in one direction, but not in the other direction. Semiconductors allow the bifurcation of electrical current and are therefore essential to computer processors.

Sequential access. See *serial access.*

Serial access. A method of finding a piece of stored data by reading through the medium from the beginning until the desired piece is found.

Shared-logic system. A system in which multiple video display screens and output devices simultaneously use the memory and processing powers of one computer.

Shared resource system. In word processing, a text-editing system that combines standalone input stations capable of local operation and text storage with other components, such as printers or large capacity disk storage or computer-assisted retrieval systems, which are shared by the various input stations. The purpose of shared resource systems is to maximize the utilization of infrequently used and expensive equipment components.

Silicon chip. See *microprocessor.*

Smart terminal. A microprocessor-controlled terminal that offers display and printing features not found on conventional "dumb" terminals. Unlike intelligent terminals, however, smart terminals are not programmable and have no integral information processing capabilities.

Soft dollars. Expenditures of money that can be estimated but not controlled (for example, improved productivity through conversion from longhand to machine dictation).

Soft-dollar savings. Reductions in expenditures that come about when management delegates work and uses time management techniques.

Software. Instructions to a computer that tell it what operations to perform.

Standalone display system. A self-contained word-processing unit that uses its own memory and processing powers for keyboarding, storage, text editing, and printing.

Statistical approach. An approach to studying an office that uses one or all of the following methods: historical data, work sampling, and time studies.

Storage. The systematic preservation of information within the system in some form.

Study team. A group of people responsible for conducting a study. The team is usually made up of representatives from key office areas.

Support-systems feasibility study. A study conducted to determine the volume and kind of work done in an office by both management and support employees.

System. A collection of office machines unified in their function and connected in some way to enable designated tasks to be accomplished and applications to be performed.

System software. A set of instructions that enables a computer to function and control its own operation, as opposed to application programs which accomplish some user-specified task. The most common example of system software is the group of programs described as the computer's operating system.

Tape unit. A peripheral device that reads and writes digital data to a magnetic tape.

Task-oriented responsibility. Responsibility without much opportunity for creativity or personal initiative.

Telecommunications. (1) The electronic transfer of data or information from one point in an information system to another through a unit that performs data format conversion and controls the rate of transmissions, including transmission from one computer system or station to remotely located devices. (2) The ability to relay messages from one place to another without paper.

Teleconferencing. Simultaneous processing of data messages and visual connections for the purpose of sending pictures and voices through telephone wires to screens and speakers in other locations.

Telex. A network of telegraph-grade lines and terminals designed for the interchange of domestic and international messages.

Text-editing systems. In word processing, systems designed to capture keystrokes on magnetic media for subsequent printing, correction, revision, or other manipulation.

Text input. The keyboarding of text into an information system.

Theory X and Theory Y. Two theories of management. Theory X assumes that successful management of people requires total control. Theory Y assumes that employee self-control and self-direction, with minimal managerial involvement, will result in successful management. A combination of both theories usually is required to perform daily supervisory functions.

Theory Z. William Ouchi's theory based on the belief that a company's management philosophy should be less rigidly structured than theories X or Y. Formal reporting relationships, job assignments, and divisions between departments remain purposely imprecise and unclear.

Third-party service. Service obtained from a company other than the equipment manufacturer.

Throughput. The volume of typing, including dictation, transcription, and revision.

Time ladder. A list of tasks performed by employees together with the time periods indicating when employees performed each task.

Time standards. The amount of work that should be done under specified conditions and methods.

Time studies approach. An approach to studying an office in which an individual job is analyzed or reduced to individual tasks, which are then timed to determine the average time per task.

Topology. (1) The physical and logical configuration of a network. (2) The way in which devices are connected to one another and to a traffic processing system.

Total support system. A planned structure for integrating all services formerly considered separate functions into a support staff under centralized supervision and control.

Total system solution. A comprehensive, integrated support system in which priority consideration is given to compatibility with a mainframe.

Transaction documents. Documents that record the individual day-to-day transactions of an organization.

Transaction processing. The processing of a specific business action such as a sale, a paycheck, or a change in inventory.

Transcribing. The keyboarding of information into a system for future access.

Transitional office. The conversion of a traditional office into an electronic office through a series of logical steps and an overall strategic plan.

Turnkey. The total preparation of a facility by a contractor which includes the acquisition and setup of all necessary premises, equipment, supplies, software, and personnel so that the user only needs to "turn the key" to begin full operation.

Typewriter-based text-editing system. A text-editing system that uses a modified typewriter as a combined input/output device.

Typing production. Typing volume measured in lines, pages, documents, or other criteria for a specific period of time.

Unbundled services. Services not included in the original purchase of equipment and provided by vendors for a separate charge.

Understaffing. The hiring of too few people to meet the demands of the work load.

Upgrades. Additions to or replacement of software or hardware that updates existing software or hardware.

User friendly. The description of a computer-based system that is easy to use.

User manual. A guidebook for computer users describing the operation of the system.

Value added. Additional benefits that accrue to the user of a particular product or service that are not paid for directly.

Vendor. A company that sells hardware, software, or any other supplies or services to meet the needs of the automated office.

Verbal input. The dictation of information into an electronic dictation system or the voice input of information into a voice recognition system.

Vertical software. Software programs created for a specific industry, industry segment, or professional vocation. Such programs usually have only one specific application.

Videoconferencing. The use of television monitors, cameras, and specially designed studios to conduct a conference among groups of persons in geographically separate locations.

Videodisk. See *optical disk.*

Video display terminal (VDT). A terminal that displays information on a video screen like that of a television. The screen may be color or black-and-white. It may display graphics or text. The VDT comes with a keyboard attached.

Videotex. Television-based information services that allow users to access publicly available data banks through modified television sets in the home or office.

Virtual memory. The storage capacity that the user of the computer can employ to accomplish a task. Virtual memory is larger than main memory when the architecture of the computer permits mapping onto storage media other than main memory.

Visual display. The process of displaying information on a video display terminal (VDT).

Vital records. Information needed to establish or continue an organization in the event of a disaster.

VLSI (very-large-scale integration). Circuits that incorporate vast quantities of logic. More than 10,000 transistors are compressed on a single chip.

Voice activation. A feature on dictation equipment that activates the tape when a person speaks and deactivates it when there is a pause.

Voice mail. The storing of messages in digital form for transmission to a receiving point at a later time.

Voice recognition. The process by which systems "recognize" spoken words and convert them to digital signals sent to an attached system or display device.

Voice response. The process by which systems "respond" to an inquiry by converting the answer stored digitally in computer memory.

Voice synthesis devices. Machines that enable visually impaired workers to interact with computers or word processors.

Winchester-type disk. In microcomputer systems, a disk with a hard, rigid surface used as a high-capacity alternative to floppy disks.

Word processing. The transcribing of an idea into a document by means of automated computer equipment.

Work-count unit. A standardized, predefined specific quantity of work. For instance, a character, a line, a page, or a document may be considered a work-count unit for work processing.

Work measurement. A method for determining work-load volumes and improvements in work or in work groups by comparing what has been accomplished against a standard.

Work sample. A collection of sample materials for quantitative measurement by size, nature of the materials, and required format.

Work-sampling approach. An approach to studying an office in which a manager observes work at random periods or gathers copies of work to determine the amount of work accomplished in sample periods.

Work standard. A standard amount of work, either described subjectively or measured statistically, used in work measurement.

Workstation. An office space equipped with automated technology that is designed either for a particular individual or a particular task. Typically, the central component is a personal computer.

Index

About the Author

BARBARA S. FISCHER is an office systems consultant in New York City.